Scott Tappan
Christmas of '96

Wooden Boat Renovation

Wooden Boat Renovation

New Life for Old Boats Using Modern Methods

Jim Trefethen

Illustrated by Clint Trefethen

**International Marine
Camden, Maine**

to Susan

─────────────

10   9   8   7   6   5   4

Copyright © 1993 International Marine, a division of The McGraw-Hill Companies.

Library of Congress Cataloging-in-Publication Data
Trefethen, Jim 1942
    Wooden boat renovation: new life for old boats using modern methods/Jim Trefethen; illustrated by Clint Trefethen.
    ISBN 0-87742-366-0
    1. Wooden boats—maintenance and repair. I. Trefethen, Clint. II. Title.
VM322.T74 1993
623.8'207—dc20   92-40572
                                CIP

Questions regarding the content of this book should be addressed to:
International Marine
P.O. Box 220
Camden, ME 04843
207-236-4837

Questions regarding the ordering of this book should be addressed to:
The McGraw-Hill Companies
Customer Service Department
P.O. Box 547
Blacklick, OH 43004
Retail customers: 1-800-822-8158
Bookstores: 1-800-722-4726

♲ *Wooden Boat Renovation* is printed on 60-pound Renew Opaque Vellum, which contains 50 percent waste paper (preconsumer) and 10 percent postconsumer waste paper.

Printed by Arcata/Fairfield.
Production and Design by Faith Hague.
Edited by Jim Babb, Don Casey, and Pamela Benner.

Contents

Acknowledgments

Writing an illustrated technical book is far more complicated and involves many more people than the layman reader can ever imagine. I, as author, get my name on the cover, my likeness goes on the back flap, and I'm given credit for the entire effort. Such is the nature of book publishing, and I have neither the power nor the inclination to change it. But the process is inherently unfair to those who names and photographs do not grace dust jackets.

Thus, special thanks go to: my family, without whose support this couldn't have been written; my friends Dick and Kathleen, without whose encouragement this wouldn't have been written; my editors, Jim Babb, Don Casey, and Pamela Benner and the staff at International Marine, without whom what was written would be unintelligible; and my readers who understand wooden boats, without whom what was written would seem the babblings of a fool.

And of course there were many people in the boating industry, people like Dick Welch at *National Fisherman*, Jim Derck at Gougeon Brothers, and Ken Bassett at Onion River Boatworks, to name just a few, who were always ready to answer my calls no matter how busy their schedules or how silly the questions.

All these people and many more labored long and hard to make this book a useful tool to guide you, the reader, in fixing up your old wooden boat. Despite the best efforts of everyone involved, there are bound to be typographical errors, confusing statements, omissions, and plain old mistakes that sneak in and surprise us once the book is printed and on the shelves. If you discover any of the above, drop us a line, addressed to me in care of the publisher, and let us know what you've found. Then, if fortune smiles on our efforts and this book is revised and reprinted, we can make appropriate corrections . . . and you'll have become part of a terrific team.

Introduction

This book is for doers and dreamers and world cruisers and armchair navigators. It is dedicated to those of us who habitually search for an excuse to drive by marinas, piers, docks, or boatyards and, failing to find one, drive by anyway; to those for whom the crash of the surf and the scream of the gull is as essential to life as the rhythmic thump of our own hearts; to those who have experienced the solitude of a midnight passage in the dark of the moon—or would like to; to those for whom a firm hand on the tiller and a steady eye on the compass is an allegory for day-to-day life; to those of us who thrill to the crack of the mainsail and the gurgle of the wake as our tiny craft heels to a favorable breeze and heads off across the oceans of our mind to somewhere we've always wanted to go. It is written for those who can look a nor'easter straight in the eye from a cockpit filled with saltwater spume and gale-force wind or from an easy chair filled with Melville and Conrad. In general, it is a book written for those who love boats. In specific, it's written for those who love wooden boats, believe that you need not spend a fortune to own one, and are willing to do a little work to prove it.

This book was difficult to write, as how-to books about boats tend to be. Some who read these words are likely to be highly accomplished boatwrights with skills that could easily handle the wormshoe-to-masthead renovation of a 60-foot schooner. Indeed, some of you may have done just that. If a writer presumes to tell this experienced segment of his audience that a ¼-inch, four-TPI skip-tooth ATB blade is the best bet for his bandsaw, not only will these readers know just what the writer is talking about, but some will feel compelled to compose lengthy letters to the writer's editor, extolling the virtues of the six-TPI chisel-tooth blade and calling into question the intelligence, integrity, and genetic origins of the misguided and misinformed writer.

Other readers of this book may be new to boating but are intrigued by the idea of skippering a fine-looking craft that they themselves salvaged from an untimely demise in the local landfill. Many of these novices will not, in all due respect, know the difference between a cedar plank and a blueberry pancake. For these readers, the printed word is gospel, but they require and deserve information and instruction of a more basic nature.

Any author attempting to write a book of advice for this diverse readership faces a dilemma. Trying to appeal to everyone, he risks boring the more knowledgeable reader with basic information this reader neither needs nor wants while at the same time confusing the less experienced reader with overly complicated details and difficult procedures beyond his or her level of competency. I have attempted to avoid the pitfalls of such generality by directing my writing to the vast middle ground of readership that lies between these extremes.

The ideal reader of this book is an aspiring boat rebuilder who has read several other books on the subject and has perhaps even owned one or two boats. He or she does not need a picture showing the bow and the stern or the port and starboard quarters of a boat, nor does he need to be shown how to tie a bowline or a clove hitch. Most already know the difference between a ketch and a yawl, but a detailed explanation of the difference between strip planking and carvel planking might serve a useful purpose, if only to refresh the memory.

In writing for this middle-ground reader, I've tried to keep the technical material free of jargon and clear enough for anyone to understand. At the same time, in an attempt not to lose the advanced reader, I've interjected opinions and observations from my own experiences, some of which may be considered iconoclastic by the Wooden Boat Establishment. Risking the ire of the tradition-bound, I hope this slight element of controversy engages the attention and interest of the more knowledgeable boatbuilder.

Although a broad range of boats is covered—everything from heavy commercial boats to wood-and-canvas canoes and mahogany runabouts—this book is not intended to stand alone as a step-by-step guidebook for renovating old wooden boats, and such heavy-duty projects as stem, transom, and other backbone repairs are noticeably absent. The topics that must be covered are far too vast and the assortment of wooden boats available too diverse to do the subject of major repairs justice in a single volume. The serious boat renovator will need a library of books by current authors such as Steward, Calder, and Spurr as well as the classics by such giants of marine literature as Chapelle and Herreshoff (see Appendix A).

Before we move on to the nitty-gritty of wooden boats, a brief word on semantics may help to keep our bow headed into the rhetorical wind. Out of respect for (and admiration of) the skill and dedication of the wooden-boat traditionalists who "restore" old boats, the word "renovation" is used to describe the process outlined in this book. The restoration of a classic yacht or workboat involves returning that boat to the condition that it was in and with the equipment that it carried when it was first launched. This is a tedious process requiring a commitment to detail and research that is way beyond the scope of this book. Restoration may also mean ignoring, in the interest of authenticity, recent advances in technology, materials, and equipment, advances that make boating safer and more enjoyable.

The renovation process detailed here involves making an old wooden boat strong and safe and getting her bottom wet as quickly and as economically as we can. And while maintaining the period look of an old boat is important (a radar arch on an Elco Cruisette would look pretty silly), tradition must be secondary to safety and economics if you're going to enjoy your boat as a boat and not as a museum-quality monument to a bygone era.

Another term that may need some clarification is "wooden boat." A few years ago, it was obvious that a wooden boat was a boat made out of wood. But with the application of space-age glues, goos, and glops to the boatbuilding process, the line is no longer as clear as it once was. I mean, really—is a boat with a hull made from constant-camber plywood panels that are saturated with epoxy, then vacuum bagged into the shape of a boat, a wooden boat or a plastic boat? Conversely, is a boat made entirely from the finest woods with expert joinery throughout, but which just happens to have a fiberglass hull, rightly called a plastic boat? Borrowing a line from Johnny "if-it-sounds-like-country-music-it-is-country-music" Cash, if it looks and feels like a wooden boat, it *is* a wooden boat. Is this a cop-out? You bet. Now let's get to work.

Start with a casual walk through any boatyard or with a leisurely drive through any neighborhood close to a navigable piece of water and you'll find lots of faded old wooden boats. You'll see them in backyards and beside driveways, surrounded with weeds and hidden under blue plastic covers sagging under a load of last year's leaves. A hand-lettered "For Sale" sign may hang halfheartedly from the lifelines. "Probably asking too much," you may think, with a passing glance. In fact, chances are very good that no one knows the asking price because no one has ever stopped to inquire.

A great many of these old veterans were well conceived, well built, and well cared for over the years, but now are deteriorated, worn out, and nearing the end of their useful lives. Possibly you already own such a boat. You may have even tried to find her a new home, thinking that once she was gone you would find one of those younger models to run around with. But several months of very expensive advertising failed to produce a single serious call. If you tried to list her with a brokerage, you likely met with an overwhelming lack of enthusiasm. Another listing of an old wooden boat is not what most brokers need right now. The sad fact is that most boatowners prefer plastic boats because—well, because wooden boats are so much work and fiberglass, as they say, lasts forever. Anyway, it seems you're stuck with her for awhile, and since she has upheld her end of the bargain for so many years without complaint, perhaps you should fix her up and keep her a few more years. After all, they really don't make 'em like that any more.

Perhaps you don't even own a boat—yet. You may have spent the past few years crawling over the megayachts at the boat shows, pouring over shiny brochures, wandering through marinas and prowling waterfronts, calculating and scheming and dreaming. One more raise in pay and a little more equity in the old homestead could mean summers cruising Cape Cod with the whole family, or even a trip down the Intracoastal Waterway and a cruise to the Bahamas when the kids are grown. But of course, the harsh reality is that the next raise will have to go toward fixing Suzie's teeth, and refinancing the house to buy a boat with the kids facing college and the family car on its last legs would not exactly make you a paragon of fiscal responsibility.

A boat, it seems, is out of the question—or is it? There are literally thousands of worn-out old wooden boats for sale in a market that even the most extravagant optimist would have to call deader than a scraped-off barnacle. Why not buy one and fix it up? Granted, many used wooden boats are still nice enough to command respectable or even premium prices. And others that may seem nice from a casual inspection have actually deteriorated past the point of no return. But if you look at enough boats and really work at it, your persistence will pay off. Eventually you will find just what you're looking for: a friendly old classic with blistering paint, peeling varnish, tattered canvas, out-dated electronics, and a take-her-as-she-is price that wouldn't cover the luxury tax on a new boat.

My wife and I recently bought such a boat, a venerable 38-foot power cruiser typical of the boats available to the do-it-yourself rebuilder. She was built by the Henry R. Hinckley yard in Southwest Harbor, Maine, for the U.S. Coast Guard just before the start of World War II—one of 538 cabin picket boats built for coastal patrol duty against the threat of German submarines. She was assigned to the Point Judith Coast Guard Station in Rhode Island and served through the war years with distinction. The highlight of her military career came when she rescued 22 survivors from the *Black Point*, sunk just a few miles off the Rhode Island coast by torpedoes from the German submarine U283.

Her patrol duties continued after the war until the early 1950s when she was sold into civilian service and converted into a pleasure cruiser. Her first non-military owner christened her the *Duchess*, and she has carried the name with grace, dignity, and pride ever since. Subsequent owners recognized her for the lady she was and treated her accordingly. As a consequence of this special care, she survived for nearly half a century. We can only speculate on the fate of her 537 sisterships.

Figure I-1. The *Duchess* as she appeared when first launched in 1937.

When I first met the *Duchess*, she was tied stern-to in a slip at a Boston Harbor yacht club. A cold October drizzle was falling, and a 20-knot easterly was kicking up a chop in the harbor. It was not love at first sight. She was old and dirty. Someone had grown tired of varnishing her brightwork, and everything was painted either a dull white or dark brown. The decks were covered with crudely applied fiberglass, and polyester resin was slathered everywhere. A cheap sliding-glass door, more appropriate for a backyard patio than for a boat, opened to a dark and musty interior. The cabin sole was covered with dirty beige carpeting that stank of diesel fumes and stale cigarettes and stuck to your feet when you walked on it. The dingy gray topsides and superstructure were streaked with black soot from the city. And the rear third of the cockpit was unpainted, construction-grade plywood where someone had ripped up the deck to get at the fuel tanks. A huge, slab-sided, plywood flying bridge on the cabin roof was topped off by a stained Bimini top, which made the whole thing look even more out of proportion than it was. "Full canvas on the upper station," the owner proclaimed proudly. The overall effect was one of gloom and age and neglect.

She did appear structurally sound, however, and something about her—other than the ridiculously low price the owner was asking—caught my eye and kept me from walking away. She had been designed originally by the well-known naval architectural firm of Eldredge-McInnis; even under the top hat of a flybridge the original McInnis lines were unmistakably evident. The boat also seemed to have a spirit that belied her advanced age. Big-money boats of all descriptions lined the yacht-club floats. The Hatterases and Pearsons were content to lie at berth, safe from the waves and wind, while lesser boats appeared even to cower in the face of the modest tempest. The old *Duchess*, however, bobbed happily in the fall chop, her bow pointing to the open channel. She tugged playfully on her spring lines as if to say, "Come on. What are you waiting for? Let's go have some fun." I stood in the cold rain with my wife and watched for awhile, slowly realizing that for all her dowdiness and her old-lady-in-a-funny-hat looks, the *Duchess* had the potential for as much class and style as any boat in the marina. We gave the owner a deposit on his asking price and went home boatowners.

Our first season on our new old boat was short and glorious. Except for removing the Bimini top to reduce windage and fitting her with decent ground tackle and a good alternator (her previous owner had relied on shore power to keep the batteries charged), we sailed her the way she was, and she performed nearly flawlessly. Our vacation that year was a 20-day trip up the coast of Maine with stops at such places as Pott's Harbor, Linekin Bay, Matinicus Island, and Blue Hill. Mostly we gunkholed, and only in Rockport were we forced to pay for a mooring. At other times we rode at anchor, sipping cocktails in the sunset while our two children swam off the stern or practiced rowing in the dinghy.

It was a storybook trip we will always remember, but it was not without its problems. The old *Duchess* was showing her age, and she found countless little ways to remind us that she wasn't a new boat. Her bilge pumps ran constantly as seawater seeped through a thousand tiny cracks in her old cedar planking; a solid week of caulking seams had not been able to stop all the leaks. Little things broke

Figure I-2.
The *Duchess*
as she
appears
today.

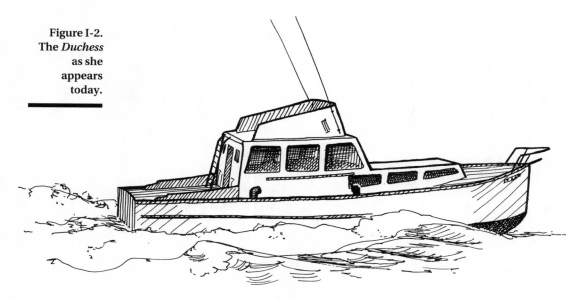

without warning. The handle to the raw-water intake seacock snapped in half because it was corroded clear through. One of the knobs on a galley drawer pulled out, and when I fixed it, the entire drawer fell apart. At a fuel dock in North Haven, one of the big bronze deck cleats ripped out by the roots. None of these problems were serious, but they gave solid testament to the fact that the old girl was just plain tired.

All during that trip and the months that followed we talked about how we would fix her up. New bottom planking would stop the leaks. New teak decks and a mahogany cabin would give her a real yacht look. And a complete new interior with a teak and holly cabin sole would make her much more comfortable. Of course the flybridge would have to be redesigned. Her entire electrical system had deteriorated to the point of being hazardous. All her electronics would be replaced, and radar would be added to help cope with the notorious New England fog banks. And even though the old Detroit diesel ran like new, a replacement engine would be a lot smaller and quieter.

When we were finally finished planning, the estimated cost of the proposed changes and repairs amounted to something just in excess of the value of a brand-new boat of the same size. Even if we stopped the kids' music lessons and took part-time jobs after work, we still couldn't afford to fix up the *Duchess* the way we wanted to. What eventually evolved after we returned to Earth from our flight to fantasy land was a workable, practical, and affordable plan that would revitalize the *Duchess* and allow her to continue to serve her owners with style and distinction for another 50 years.

This book is only partly the story of how I fixed up the old *Duchess* and converted her from an outdated artifact to an up-to-date, safe, and comfortable cruiser loaded with character and style. More important, it's a handbook for you to use in your quest for an affordable watercraft. It will show you how you can have the satisfaction of saving one of these proud old vessels from the scrap heap and get yourself a safe and seaworthy boat in the bargain.

Boat ownership is never inexpensive, regardless of whether you have an 18-foot canoe or a 60-foot yawl, but in the market conditions of the past few years, used wooden boats are available at a fraction of the cost of new ones. Desperate sellers are everywhere, and they're ready to bargain. Don't worry that these old vessels may not look as glitzy as the new boat-show stars; many of them were better built than most production boats are today, and they can be made to look just as good as new and to function even better. All you need is the boat, a place to work, a few good tools, a little free time, the desire and persistence to get the job done, and some basic instruction and guidance. You provide the first items, and I'll provide the last: That's what this book is all about.

CHAPTER ONE

Why Wood?

W hy would anyone in their right mind even consider buying a wooden boat when boats made from fiberglass bound into a matrix of polyester resin have clearly demonstrated their superiority over every other material commonly used for pleasure boats? In the past 20 years, steel, aluminum, ferrocement, wood, and tied-together bulrushes have all taken a back seat to fiberglass as the material of choice for pleasure-boat construction.

The reasons for this profound change in how we make our boats are well known to all of us who are interested, since we hear them repeated endlessly anytime the subject of hull construction and materials comes up. The argument that fiberglass boats are much easier and less expensive to maintain is undoubtedly the most frequently heard argument espoused by plastic-boat advocates, but the advantages of durability and low initial cost are usually a close second. Less frequently touted are increased flexibility in hull design and the interior layout fiberglass affords, and the additional interior volume for a given displacement and waterline length.

So what are the advantages of a wooden hull? Unless you're talking to a real wooden-boat aficionado with sunken cheeks and granola in his beard, you aren't likely to hear many. Mention at any gathering of modern boating people that you're the owner of a wooden boat or thinking of buying one and you can expect eyes to roll heavenward in disbelief. Cries of dismay will come from those who profess sympathy for your plight and furtive glances from those who see this as reason to doubt your sanity. Wooden boats are perceived as the toys of the rich who can afford to have them professionally maintained, or the lot of the nautically disadvantaged who lack the judgment or the resources to find a "modern" boat.

Well, let's just spend a little time to take a closer look at each of the supposed advantages fiberglass enjoys over wood—up close and personal, as my daughter likes to say. And, while we're at it, we'll try to justify our decision to purchase an old wooden boat.

IS FIBERGLASS REALLY EASIER TO MAINTAIN?

When people are asked why they prefer fiberglass over other construction materials, particularly wood, the most popular answer is "low maintenance." Wooden-boat owners are frequently depicted as slaves to the scraper and paint brush, endlessly chipping, sanding, caulking, recaulking, filling, and brushing in a never-ending battle to stay ahead of peeling, cracking, and fading paint and varnish. Plastic boats, on the other hand, supposedly need only a touch of auto polish, a dash of teak oil, and an occasional blast from the garden hose. Their lucky owners spend their time blissfully trimming sails instead of masking tape, and stirring martinis instead of paint buckets.

As a self-proclaimed champion of the wooden hull, I'd like to report that there is absolutely no validity to these arguments. But, of course, I can't. Like most bits of folklore, these contentions are based, somewhat flimsily, on facts. Boats *do* require a lot of work to keep them in good repair. The brightwork on wooden boats may require more effort than on a plastic boat simply because there often is more of it. But the next time you see a really nice-looking fiberglass boat, you can bet your buttons that someone works their buns off keeping it that way.

On the other hand, every harbor is full of plastic boats whose owners have bought into the fiberglass-needs-no-maintenance argument. Their boats look like hell because no one spends any time working on them. A fiberglass boat not assiduously maintained will become shabby and drab-looking just as quickly as a wooden boat.

A few years ago *WoodenBoat* magazine printed an interesting article comparing the maintenance costs of a wood boat with a similar one made of plastic. Not surprisingly (the article *may* have been a bit slanted), their survey showed it's actually more expensive to own and maintain a plastic boat than a wood boat. Charges of marginal objectivity aside, the article indicates quite clearly that the perceived savings in maintenance of plastic boats is illusory. If you keep your boat in reasonably good condition, the amount of maintenance required usually will be about the same for similar boats, regardless of the hull material.

The real difference in periodic maintenance between plastic and wood is not in degree—both require a lot of maintenance to be kept Bristol fashion—but in the consequences of neglect. A neglected wood boat will suffer serious structural degradation much more quickly than will a comparable fiberglass boat, which brings us very nicely to our next subject—durability.

FIBERGLASS BOATS LAST FOREVER

Fiberglass is forever. So says the guy at the boat show. And he's partly right. *Fiberglass* might last forever, but fiberglass *boats* don't. Consider the following exercise in hyperbole and theoretical extremes.

If you were to take (hypothetically, of course) two similar boat hulls—one made of wood and the other made of plastic—place them side by side in a field, and just leave them alone for, say, 1,000 years, what would be the hypothetical result? Wood was once a living tree, and like all living things, when a tree dies it immediately begins to revert to that from whence it came, i.e., humus. After 10 centuries, all that's left of our wooden boat is some dust intermingled with bits of assorted metallic oxides—residues barely detectable, much less identifiable, as a boat.

Where we left the plastic boat, on the other hand, we would have . . . well, we don't really know what we would have—no one's ever had one that long. So resorting to conjecture (and hypothetical conjecture is the very best kind), I strongly suspect what we would find is a pile of fiberglass junk intermingled with bits of assorted metallic oxides—a mess hardly identifiable as a boat, but highly detectable.

Sure fiberglass lasts forever. So do Clorox bottles. The landfills are full of them.

WOOD ROTS AND FIBERGLASS DELAMINATES

Enough of this philosophical silliness; let's get on to the facts. And the first fact is that wood rots and fiberglass doesn't. But if fiberglass boats don't rot, they will delaminate, and that can, in many cases, easily make up the difference.

Fiberglass delaminates when the bonding matrix—the petrochemical glop that sticks the various laminations together—fails, and delamination can take several forms. In production boats, fiberglass cloth or mat frequently is bonded to a wood core using polyester resin. The wood used is often construction-grade plywood (plain old lumberyard stuff) or end-grain balsa. Wood cores are used in areas such as in transoms and under decks where extra thickness and stiffness are required. Some of the more expensive custom and semi-custom boats and a lot of multihulls will have their entire hulls cored with balsa in this way. If this core becomes saturated with water, particularly fresh water from above through improperly bedded deck fittings, the bond between the wood and fiberglass will fail. In extreme cases, the wood core can rot away, leaving a hollow plastic shell. A recent example of this core rotting came to my attention when a distressed individual called to tell me his outboard motor had fallen off the transom of his trailered powerboat. Two layers of ¾-inch plywood had rotted away inside a fiberglass casing, allowing the mounting bolts to pull out. His only consolation was that it happened in his driveway and not on the interstate—or several miles out to sea.

Another form of fiberglass delamination is the dreaded osmotic blister, or boat pox. Small, water-filled bulges appear in the hull below the waterline. When they first started popping up on older boats, these blisters were thought to affect only the gelcoat. Now we know the entire thickness of the hull can be involved, and blisters can lead to serious structural problems. Leading chemical and petroleum companies—notably Mobil Oil—have made great strides in determining what causes blisters, and new boats are not likely to develop this problem. The older boats, however, will continue to deteriorate, and the all-too-frequent repair procedure of grinding the blisters off and filling the voids with Bondo is a short-term, cosmetic solution that neither corrects the problem nor prevents its recurrence.

Other forms of delamination are beginning to show up as more and more plastic boats enter middle age. Many of these problems are related to poor production standards and lax quality control procedures at the boat factory. Hulls were constructed too slowly or too quickly, preventing the resin from curing properly. Others were laid up improperly with pockets of uncured resin or air trapped in the laminate, causing trouble for unsuspecting owners 15 or 20 years later.

There are a lot of fine boats made from fiberglass, and the stuff has proven beyond argument to be a superior material for hulls. But we're learning the hard way that many manufacturers' claims and buyers' expectations of durability were overly optimistic. For our purposes, suffice it to say that delamination problems do occur in plastic boats, and when they do, they're every bit as serious and as expensive to repair as deteriorated fasteners or a rotted keel in a wooden hull.

WOODEN BOATS COST A LOT TO BUILD

Initial cost is the next area of discussion in our informal (but passionately objective) comparison of plastic and wood hull construction, and this is where the plastic boats really shine. It's much cheaper to build a standard fiberglass boat than a wood boat.

In the heyday of wood pleasure-boat construction, boatyards with names like Hinckley, Dickerson, Williams, and Herreshoff employed thousands of skilled tradesmen. Machinists, mechanics, riggers, and woodworkers all held prestigious jobs that required years of experience and training to master, and they were compensated accordingly. Framing and planking a hull was (and remains) a painstaking process that took weeks or months to complete. Even in the production shops of Chris-Craft and Elco, where all the wood parts were precut and the hulls constructed assembly-line fashion, an enormous amount of skilled labor went into the final product.

In today's plastic-boat factory, a chopper gun can be mastered by an unskilled worker in an hour or two of practice, and a hull for a 40-footer can be laid up in a day or so. The savings in time and labor over wood construction are enormous.

When a boatyard builds wooden boats one at a time, it can make substantial changes to each one as it is built to accommodate the whims of the customer, the discretion of the designer, or to take advantage of improved efficiency. As each boat is completed, the builders can tally up the numbers and see if they made or lost money on the deal. Once a mold is completed at a boat factory, however, each boat will be exactly the same as the one before it, and typically several hundred must be made and sold before the company will turn a profit. It's a textbook perfect comparison of a labor-intensive system vis-à-vis a capital-intensive one. Anyone trying to make an honest buck by building wooden boats today is playing against a stacked deck. The advantage is with the plastic-boat factory.

A striking example of the direction boatbuilding technology is headed appeared in *Professional Boatbuilder*, a boating industry trade magazine. Thermoplastics, according to the author of the article, is the predicted wave of the future—destined to have an impact on production boatbuilding equal to or greater than the wholesale switch from wood to fiberglass in the 1960s. Forming boat hulls from thermoplastics can be accomplished in several ways, but the most promising seems to be an evacuation molding process whereby a large sheet of specially formulated plastic is heated until pliable and then sucked into a mold by a vacuum. In another technique, powdered plastic is injected into a heated mold spinning about in a huge centrifuge. Both of these methods are now being used to profitably manufacture boats that range in size from kayaks and dinghies to small daysailers, and the application of thermoplastic to larger boats is simply a matter of scale and time.

PLASTIC BOATS HAVE MORE SPACE

In the next areas of comparison, design flexibility and interior volume, there is no contest; plastic boats win every time. Properly constructed, a molded fiberglass hull needs no internal support from frames, ribs, clamps, shelves, deck beams, floors, knees, headers, and the myriad other parts that work together to give a wooden hull its shape and strength. A fiberglass hull can be much thinner than wood because fiberglass is much stronger than wood—any way you twist it, bend it, stomp it, or stretch it.

A 40-footer's hull-and-deck assembly can be constructed without any internal encumbrances, giving the designer the freedom to place galleys, heads, sleeping areas, tanks, ports, and just about anything else anywhere he wishes. And while this design flexibility has resulted in some funny-looking boats—especially to a lubber like me with an eye toward the traditional—it must be admitted that the designer of wooden boats is severely limited by the requirement that all those critical parts be accommodated. You just can't leave out the deck beams to increase headroom in a wooden boat without facing some fairly serious consequences. (Cold-molded and constant-camber hulls, which we will examine briefly in Chapter Six, are the notable exceptions to this argument.)

Let's take a look at where we stand in our comparison of wood and plastic hulls. In maintenance and durability, wood and plastic boats are about even. (Yes, I expect plenty of arguments on both points.) In original construction cost, the plastic boat clearly has the edge. And for flexibility in design, there is no contest; the plastic boat wins again.

The argument for wood seems to be lagging behind here. But two subjects we haven't discussed yet may help make up lost ground: relative cost and intangibles.

USED WOODEN BOATS COST LESS

In our earlier discussion of cost, we found it's clearly cheaper to make new plastic boats than new wooden boats. But this is a book about *used* boats. Given the prevailing economy, any boat, new or used, is difficult to sell, and used wooden boats especially are a drug on the market.

When boats (or anything else for that matter) are hard to sell, the quickest way to make them easier to sell is to lower the price, and that's just what a lot of people have done. In many cases the owners of good wooden boats who would like to sell them have given up advertising altogether and are just letting the boat sit there in the yard with a sign stuck on the bow. The lack of advertising makes them hard to locate, but if you can find them, the owners are often receptive to nearly any offer.

If you like sailboats, there are plenty on the market, a lot of them proven boats from proven designers and built by famous yards like Dickerson or Hinckley. A new Hinckley these days would set you back the better part of a million bucks. A 1950s-vintage Hinckley Islander built of the finest oak and mahogany can be had in structurally sound condition for under $10,000—less than 10 percent of what you would expect to pay for a fiberglass Bermuda 40 in really rough shape: snob appeal at a rock-bottom price.

Figure 1-1. Hinckley Islander under full sail.

If trawlers are your cup of tea, you may find a wooden Grand Banks (affectionately called "woodies" by their fans) for much less than half what an equivalent fiberglass version of the same boat would cost. And if it's a power cruiser or sport-fisherman you want, then you have your pick of just about anything imaginable; powerboats in every size and shape from nice old Lyman outboards to 50-foot-long Chris-Craft Constellations—floating motels with all the amenities of the local Holiday Inn—are available for less than the salvage value of their engines.

Why, you may ask, are so many owners of these old wooden boats so desperate to get rid of them? And why are they so hard to sell? There are a lot of answers to these questions. As I write this, the national economy is in a shambles, but a more important answer, I believe, lies in the human penchant to be fashionable. By the time this book is published, the economic conditions will have changed dramatically, for better or worse. But one thing that will not change is man's desire to curry favor with his fellows. It's just not fashionable to own a rundown old boat, and rundown old wooden boats are least fashionable of all.

Interestingly, the reverse is true of wooden boats that have been maintained in or restored to tiptop shape. A true classic, such as an old

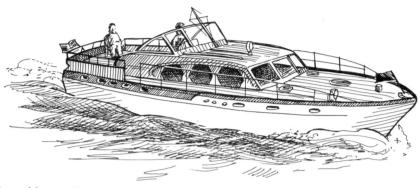

Figure 1-2.
Chris-Craft
Constellation.

Rosenblatt cruiser or an Alden schooner, in showroom condition is the epitome of snob appeal at many yacht clubs and marinas, and that appeal is reflected in the price you would pay for one.

Trefethen's First Law of Economics: Everyone else's problems are our opportunities. That old Matthews cruiser the guy down the street has been trying to get rid of for the past two years could be the star of the fleet with a little varnish and a lot of elbow grease. Buy that sucker and fix her up, and not only will you have a boat that skipper and crew will be proud to sail, but you won't break the bank doing it.

Do it right and you will have one of the most distinctive boats around, and (this is the good part) one of the least expensive. Then when that guy at the club starts to tell you about his brand-new StubaStuba 44, you can pull out pictures of your old Matthews, pat him on the back, and tell him, kindly of course, that if he works hard and saves his pennies, someday he might be able to afford a real classic, just like yours.

So now that we all agree it's cheaper, sometimes much cheaper, to buy a good used wooden boat than a good used plastic boat, we've recovered quite a bit of lost ground. And we still have one more area to cover: intangibles. Although this is the most difficult to explain, it's where the good proponents of wooden-boat construction can carry the ball downfield against the evil advocates of plastic and, with the crowd on their feet and seconds remaining on the clock, score the touchdown that wins the game and ends the controversy forever.

WOODEN BOATS ARE REAL BOATS

A long time ago, when I was much younger and much less wise, I went to work for a large utility company in a large office building in a large city. My job was to write

Figure 1-3.
Matthews Cruiser.

and edit huge volumes of material few people cared about and even fewer read. In return for my efforts, the company periodically deposited large sums of money in my bank account and on a regular basis told me what a fine job I was doing. I received health insurance, life insurance, stock options, practically unlimited sick leave, expense accounts, and several weeks of vacation every year. In short, it was a job a lot of people would kill to get.

Every weekday I walked to work down alleys and through urban canyons where sunlight seldom penetrated. This was the mid-sixties, so I wore the obligatory textured polyester suit and knitted polyester shirt. My socks were made of nylon and my shoes of Corfam. Even my underwear and necktie were made from stuff that bore trade names registered by companies like DuPont and Dow Chemical. The building I worked in was made of concrete and steel with a marble lobby and neat rows of polished-aluminum elevators. In my fluorescent-lighted office with its asphalt-tile floor, I worked at a metal desk that had a plastic-laminate top, and I sat in a steel chair upholstered with Naugahyde. The office contained about 100 people just like me, doing numerous other little things no one really cared about either.

In the four years or so I worked in this office, four of my fellow workers met untimely ends. One died when he stopped suddenly on the pavement 20 stories below the balcony from which he jumped. Another inhaled an excessive quantity of carbon monoxide in his garage. A third, the man who worked at the desk next to mine, and a close friend, died of heart failure while I was on one of my 20 or 30 daily trips to the water cooler. The fourth died of a mysterious illness no one could understand but everyone knew was related to stress. She was barely 50 years old, and the others were all under 40.

Outwardly, I was content in my job, which, except for the frequent funerals, was not the least bit demanding. I lived like many of us live, in a world of plastic and glass and cement, a world where the very air I breathed was adjusted to just the right temperature and filtered of any organic impurities. I had everything a young executive could want, yet internally I was uncomfortable and unhappy. There was something terribly wrong with life in an artificial environment with its artificial security and artificial functions. Some critical part of the whole was missing—something that can't be defined, but when it's not there we miss it and long to get it back.

Things have changed a lot since The Sixties. Today, all my shirts and slacks are cotton or wool, reinforced perhaps with a bit of synthetics. In fact every piece of clothing I own is made of natural fibers, and my shoes are made of top-grain cowhide. I don't think they even make Corfam shoes anymore, and polyester clothes are only for the aggressively unfashionable.

It can't be denied that clothing made from synthetics is more practical than the same things made from natural fibers—they're easier to maintain, and they last longer (sound familiar?). But the fashion industry has learned the hard way that people don't want plastic clothing. So what do natural products have that is missing from artificial ones? No one really knows, but it's there, and whatever it is, people like it and are willing to put up with a degree of inconvenience to get it.

In today's corporate environment, wood is used as a reward for achievement and as a sign of status. As executives climb the corporate ladder, they eventually will reach a level where they are given a wooden desk. As they progress upward, more and more of their external accouterments will be made of wood. When they finally reach the very top of their profession, they will, likely as not, be ensconced in a wood-paneled office with a wooden desk and a wooden door. On the oak floor will be a wool carpet, and their mahogany chair will be upholstered with real leather. They have arrived, and in doing so, they have earned the right to have real things.

Some time ago, Harold Kushner, author of *When Bad Things Happen to Good People* and several other books of an inspirational nature, wrote a delightful little book entitled *Who Needs God* (no question mark). Now I like to go to church more or less regularly, especially in the off season when it doesn't interfere with cruising, but I'm not an overly religious person. I do, however, strongly recommend everyone read this book simply because it helps to keep life in a hectic modern society in perspective.

One of Kushner's tenets that is interesting to us in our arguments on the relative merits of wooden-boat construction is that mankind has demonstrated a real need for real things. We cannot completely substitute plastic things for real things; if we try to, we suffer.

Real things possess something that plastic does not, something the human spirit finds comforting and relaxing, something that is connected with the needs of our soul and makes possible an emotional attachment. My wife and I have owned many boats, both plastic and wood. We have never been able to develop any affection for the plastic ones, but the wooden ones we've owned and sold are like members of the family that have moved away.

Now that we've established the metaphysical and spiritually therapeutic nature of boats and other things made from wood, we need to throw in a disclaimer and back up a little. This is not a fanatical call for a return to The Good Old Days. One of the first boats I can remember sailing was a relic from the 1920s—a genuine artifact with cotton sails and hemp lines. Today only the most rabid traditionalist would give up braided nylon for sisal, and Dacron sails are so far superior to cotton as to make not using them unthinkable except for museum replicas. Even there, if you look closely, you'll see that a lot of museums sneak in Dacron when they think we won't notice. The pressures of population and the demands of a modern society make plastics an absolute necessity in day-to-day living; even in our wooden boats we can't escape from them entirely.

The society we live in tends to be shallow and superficial, but as a way of keeping warm and well fed, it's hard to beat. Traffic lights and parking lots, pollution and shopping malls, and long lines at the checkout counter are part of the price we pay for comfort and convenience. Most of us have decided it's worth it.

Within this artificial world our wooden boats become little islands of reality that help us live successfully in society—not get away from it. Can you do the same thing in a plastic boat? Of course you can—it's just better in a wooden one.

OK gang, first down and inches to go. The wooden-boat steamroller is moving, and it looks like the forces of truth and justice may prevail after all.

WOODEN BOATS ARE TRADITIONAL BOATS

The next intangible we want to cover, and our last topic before we move on to the previously promised nitty-gritty, is tradition. Wooden boats have been with us for a long time. The scenario of a caveman pushing a log into a river and thereby inventing the first boat is a bit of silly speculation and has become a cliché from which I'll spare you. But by the time of the Phoenicians, more than 3,000 years ago, the construction of wooden boats had evolved into the type of plank-on-frame structure we are familiar with today. By the early Dark Ages the Scandinavian tribes of the North Sea and the Baltic were building lapstrake hulls capable of traversing the North Atlantic and possessing a grace and beauty of form that has never been surpassed. Four or five hundred years later, when construction was underway on the boats that eventually would bring Columbus to the New World, shipwrights were fashioning knees and beams and clamps that worked the same as those made today by boatbuilders in Maine working on new lobster boats for the local fishermen. The scantlings, proportions, and types of wood used may have been quite different, but the function of each part remained the same.

A traditionally built wooden boat may be the most highly evolved form of construction built by modern man. The buildings we live and work in, our manufactories, and our means of transportation have all evolved through the process of new technology replacing the old, so that each new procedure is substantially different from the one being replaced. Most of these things important to modern life have progressed in leaps and spurts, with little or no continuity. A historian discussing land transportation might end up comparing freight trains with Conestoga wagons, and stage coaches with camels. However, the technology of the wooden boat has progressed with painstaking slowness as each generation of boatbuilders made practically imperceptible changes that, if successful, were passed on to the next. It is doubtful if a camel driver from the time of Hammurabi would have found much in common with a nineteenth-century train engineer, but a boatbuilder from ancient Greece magically transported to a boatyard in turn-of-the-century Essex, Massachusetts, would instantly realize what was going on and, within a day or two, would feel right at home building Gloucester fishing schooners instead of Athenian war galleys.

The fact that we can trace the art of building wooden boats back through the centuries to the dim beginnings of recorded history is fascinating, you say, but of little tangible value. Correct, I answer; there is little there to take to the bank. However, the more we know about traditional wooden boats and how they're constructed, the more we have to marvel at how wonderfully each part works with the whole, and how the whole suffers with the failure of a single tiny part. A well-built wooden boat is a symphony of thousands of pieces of wood and iron and copper and bronze, each perfectly in tune with its neighbors and singing a song we can hear and see and feel and sense right down to the soles of our feet. You're right, it's not *worth* anything, but it would be a shame to loose it.

Touchdown!

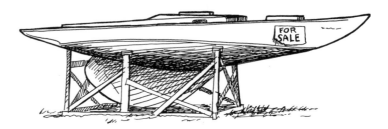

CHAPTER TWO

Selecting the Perfect Project Boat

Mankind is a species of desires—strong, insatiable cravings that originate in the depths of our psyche and propel us headlong through life, compelling us at times to do things pure reason would dictate we not attempt. And as we are a species of individuals, we desire different things and pursue the things we desire with different intensities and with different degrees of success. Some long for love and affection while others want power and money. Some want to belong to groups and organizations while others long for solitude. Many lust after material possessions and the social prestige they bring. To some of us, awards and recognition from our peers are so important, be they Pulitzer prizes or bowling-league trophies, that we will go to incredible lengths to get them.

When our desires become obsessions, they can destroy us. But as long as they remain under control, our desires are the positive forces that guide us through life and dictate where we go, who we marry, what we do, and to a large extent, who we are and what we will become.

When our desires are fulfilled, we become self-confident and successful. To the degree that they're not, we become reclusive and depressed. The urge to create things with our hands is strong in many of us, and fulfilling that urge through working on an old wooden boat can be one of the most truly satisfying experiences in our lives—or one of the most frustrating.

That you bought this book suggests you would like to fix up an old boat, and the cleverly convoluted arguments of Chapter One have convinced you the old boat should be made of wood. You've determined through Gestalt theory (also known as the Woody Allen School of Armchair Psychology) that you have the temperament to do the job and that *why* you want to do it doesn't matter; that you want to is reason enough. Now it's time to understand just what you're letting yourself in for.

ATTEMPTUS FUTILITUS

Many people possessed by strong creative impulses attempt to satisfy them by building their own boats. Some do very well at it. Others do not. The failures are most often classic cases of *attemptus futilitus*, better known as biting off more than you can chew.

Boatbuilding is hard work. And building even a small boat from the ground up takes an assortment of skills that must be slowly and patiently acquired through study and practice. Just as a boat is the sum of thousands of parts working together to make the whole, successful boatbuilders are adept at thousands of small procedures—most of which aren't particularly difficult to master in and of themselves—which, when taken together, result in a boat. A boatbuilder is a draftsman, an engineer, a metallurgist, a chemist, a machinist, a welder, and a consummate woodworker—in addition to being a diplomat and a hopeless optimist.

This isn't an argument against people building their own boats. To the contrary, I believe do-it-yourself boatbuilding is one of the most rewarding pastimes you can have. The problem is that, to the layman, the process looks much easier than it is, and beginners tend to become romantically involved with their projects and to get in over their heads. Among fledgling builders, *attemptus futilitus* is a raging epidemic.

In my short but eventful life I've met many ambitious builders who started something they couldn't finish, or finished eventually at a far greater expense than they originally expected. Recently I met a man building a rather large (20 tons) Roberts ketch in his backyard. By his estimation, after about 10 years of part-time work, he was 80 percent done. He was trying to sell the boat for $45,000—just enough to recoup his accumulated cash expenses but none of his substantial labor. By my estimation he wasn't yet half done, and if he should find someone foolish enough to offer $10,000 for the whole works, he would be equally foolish not to grab it.

In another case, I was aboard a 37-foot Jim Brown Searunner trimaran (the Searunner, one of my favorite designs, is actually a collaboration between Brown and John Marples, both pioneers in multihull design and construction) that was 15 years old, on its third owner/builder, and still not complete.

In yet another example, a friend of mine purchased a nearly complete, full-size replica of Joshua Slocum's *Spray* from an amateur builder who just got too old to work on her any more. My friend doesn't say what he paid, but it wasn't much.

Examples like this abound—undoubtedly you know of several yourself—so the lesson should be clear: If you want to build your own Colin Archer world cruiser, and you've never built a large boat before, fine—go for it; but before you lay the keel on a 35-footer, build a Nutshell Pram or even one of those neat little Phil Bolger dinghies constructed from one sheet of plywood and some bailing wire. You'll be amazed at how long it takes to complete even a relatively simple project and at what you'll learn by doing it. Besides, you'll need the dinghy when you get to Tahiti.

Everything that has been said so far about the dangers of first-time boat-builders overestimating their abilities and getting in over their heads is true in spades for inexperienced hobbyists contemplating a renovation project. But a renovation project has some significant advantages that make the process easier than building a new boat. If your objective is boat*ing* instead of boat*build*ing, you can buy a shabby but seaworthy boat, launch immediately, enjoy the season, then start work this winter and be back in the water in the spring. If you're a handy sort of person but not skilled in woodworking, you can select a boat that needs minor repairs and a coat of paint. If, on the other hand, you're an accomplished wood-wright who thrills to the chink of the adz, and the zing of the jack plane is balm to your troubled soul, then maybe you want to look for a basket case needing total renovation, or find a nice old classic for a complete and authentic restoration.

Fixing up an old boat is easier than building a new one because the parts, even broken or rotted ones, are usually there. When a naval architect lays down the plans for a new boat, he or she will presuppose a certain amount of knowledge on the part of the builder. Anyone starting a new boat must not only understand these plans but also must know how each part represented on the drawing works, why it's needed, and how it's built. (For example, architects use a simple and fast notation for offsets. A dimension given as 12 6 3+ translates to 12 feet 6$\frac{7}{16}$ inches, but if you aren't used to this type of notation, the numbers are meaningless. [Hint: the fractions of an inch are expressed in eighths with the + indicating an additional sixteenth, i.e., $\frac{3}{8}$ + $\frac{1}{16}$, or $\frac{7}{16}$.]) In renovating an old boat, since each part can be studied carefully before it's removed, its function will be easier to understand. Then, when it is removed, the old part becomes a pattern for the new one.

Don't make the mistake of a man I met recently who bought an old Thompson inboard cruiser in considerable disrepair and proceeded to strip it of everything that could be removed. He put the things he wanted to save into a large box and threw out everything that needed replacing. After spending all his spare time for several months removing every trace of paint and varnish from the hull, it was time to start reassembly. Unfortunately he hadn't the slightest clue how to proceed. The last time I saw the boat, it was sitting behind his house slowly filling with leaves and reverting to you know what. In a few years he'll at least have something to put around his tomatoes.

Attemptus futilitus is a terrible affliction. What starts out as a head full of dreams ends up as a yard full of junk and a wallet full of overdue bills. So the first thing we want to do in the selection of our project boat is to analyze carefully and objectively our own abilities and potential. We also need to determine the time and resources we're willing to devote to a rebuilding project. Only then are we equipped to make an appropriate choice.

WHAT KIND OF BOAT DO WE WANT?

The next thing we want to consider in our quest for the perfect rebuilding project is the function we want our renovated craft to fulfill when we're done. Bill McGrath, assistant harbormaster of Beverly, Massachusetts, loves old powerboats. His latest restoration project, a 50-foot cruiser he plans to live aboard, would be a bit of a handful for most of us. But Bill has done it before and knows just what he's doing. For him, it's the perfect boat.

My first restoration project was a canoe my dad and I found in an old barn while quail hunting and mooched off the farmer who owned it. After applying fiberglass cloth and polyester resin to the outside and some varnish to the inside, we had just the boat we needed for exploring the reaches and rapids of the Potomac River and the backwaters of the Chesapeake Bay near where I was raised.

If you're a fisherman who likes to troll for stripers, you should be working on a fishing boat. It would be silly to spend your time restoring an old Lightning Class one-design. And if your idea of boating is cruising with your family to faraway places with funny-sounding names, then don't waste your time fixing up a boat you can't use for that. This sounds obvious, but there are a lot of people who spend a lot of time and money fixing up boats they never use. One of the best boatbuilders I ever met gets chronically seasick and can't even work on a boat that's tied to a dock; everything he does must be on dry land. The enjoyment he gets from working on boats obviously comes from the work itself, not from boating. Not that there's anything wrong with working on boats for the pure joy of it, but if this is your inclination, you may be better off spending your time and money on a restoration rather than a renovation.

How about buying just any old boat, fixing it up, selling it, and buying the boat you really want with the profits? It sounds great, but except in rare cases, it doesn't work. A few professionals manage to make money restoring and reselling certain classics that have a high nostalgia value, such as the Chris-Craft runabouts from the 1950s (see Chapter Ten), but as a general rule don't expect to make money selling your renovation project. You may be able to recoup your out-of-pocket expenses, but you'll rarely receive enough to cover your time—especially for your first project. If it happens, great, but don't count on it: Ours is a labor of love. Besides, when you get done with your new old boat, you'll be so proud you won't even think of selling her.

WHERE CAN WE WORK?

Now that we have resolved to select a boat that fits our needs and that we can actually repair, the next thing we want to consider is where to do the work. While it might seem more logical to get the boat first, then find a place to work on it, I know from sad personal experience how frustrating it is to buy a boat only to discover, after the fact, that it won't fit in the space where you intended to work on it. To most of us this question may seem to have a fairly obvious answer, but even so, it deserves considerable thought. Perhaps you have a workspace you think is just right for your project, but before you drag home the wreck of the *Mary Deare* and start banging away on her hull, make sure she'll fit through the basement door, under the wires on your street, or into the backyard without your having to back an 18-wheeler through your neighbor's prize petunias.

Speaking of neighbors, let's take a moment to consider what those who live with you and around you will think of your project. If you live alone on a farm, an island, or out in the woods, no problem. Otherwise, your spouse, your kids, and the guy next door are all going to take a keen interest in what you're up to. Routers, sanders, Skilsaws, grinders, hammers, and other assorted tools of the trade all produce two common by-products—noise and sawdust—both of which can have undesirable effects on family harmony and neighborly relations. Most suburban communities have laws protecting the peace and quiet of their neighborhoods. You may want to check with your local planning board for zoning restrictions and permit requirements, especially if you intend to construct a temporary shelter over your project.

If your yard is the domain of small children, either your own or your neighbor's, you'll want to consider their propensity for being punctured or bashed by things commonly found lying around a boat project. Almost all boat renovations require ladders, and almost all children are born with an undeniable urge to climb them. If your project will require large amounts of solvents, and most do, the local fire chief may be very interested. And nothing makes insurance people apoplectic quicker than finding a barrel of acetone in the insured's basement.

Despite all this, your home is undoubtedly the best place to work on your project as long as you can do it without encouraging divorce, bureaucratic intervention, or the wrath of neighbors. After all, even though Noah had the support of his family and the approval of authorities of the highest order, history's first and most famous home boatbuilder still had to suffer ridicule from the neighbors.

What if, after careful consideration, you decide it just isn't practical to renovate your boat at home? Don't despair; a lot of options are available if you look around a bit. There may be unused commercial space nearby that can be rented or subleased for a reasonable fee, especially if you agree to move out on short notice if the landlord finds a permanent tenant. Renting outdoor space or space at a boatyard are other possibilities to consider. In all cases of using someone else's property, make sure they understand what you intend to do and how you intend to do it; landlords face the same problems with neighbors and local authorities that homeowners do.

In my case, working on the *Duchess* at home wasn't an option. The boat was far too big, my yard was far too small, and my neighbors were far too grouchy. The first year of my project was spent in a rented loading dock at a down-at-the-heels local factory. The owner was delighted to have even a small income from what was otherwise wasted space. The second year I moved the *Duchess* to the Green's Point boatyard in Ipswich, Massachusetts. This turned out to be a particularly agreeable place to work on a wooden boat. The owners, Fred Ebinger and Mike Lord, understand wooden boats and were very accommodating when I explained what I needed and what I wanted to do.

If you do plan to work at a boatyard, check first with other boatowners who use the yard. Most yard owners are great people, but some tend toward the mercenary, and a few are outright greedy. Some yards won't let owners do anything but minor repairs; others will even bill you for work you do yourself. At one boatyard I used a few years ago the owner was extremely helpful, always showing me how he thought something should be done. It was always "let me help you with that" or "give me a holler if you want me to move those barrels." At the end of the season when the bill came, every minute was itemized and billed at $35 an hour. I think he charged me for a morning hello. There is nothing wrong with a yard charging for what they do; that's how they make their living. But make sure everyone understands who is paying how much for what. Read the fine print before you sign the contract.

LET'S STOP PLANNING AND START LOOKING

Now that we've decided how big a renovation job we want to get involved in, determined the type of craft we want when we're finished, and found a place to work, we can start looking for a boat—and looking is going to take some time and patience. Our first objective isn't to find a boat right away but to look at as many boats as possible.

There are several good reasons for looking at a lot of boats. First, the more boats you look at, the more you'll learn about the type of boat you want. You're very likely to make many small adjustments in your requirements as you go along. It's not uncommon for someone making a careful selection from the available stock of used boats to end up with something completely different from what he first started looking for. I know one couple with two children who were looking for a liveaboard sailboat to take to the Caribbean. Originally they thought a 35-footer would do. Now, a year later, they're considering a 55-footer and still looking.

Another reason for looking at as many boats as you can is that as you look, you'll learn a lot about wooden boats and how they're made. As each prospective purchase is carefully studied, you'll want to find out all you can about the designer and the builder. You'll want to find out how many of this particular boat were made and why. If a lot were made, why did people like them so much? If only one or two were made, why weren't they more popular? Perhaps they didn't live up to the designer's expectations. Or maybe they were unusually expensive to build, and the builder made no money on them.

You will also learn, as you stick your head into one oily bilge and smelly forepeak after another, what a broken rib or a sprung plank or a rotted stem looks like and when these things are repairable and when they aren't. And, most important, you'll learn to look past the dirt and dust and beyond the superficial and cosmetic into the very soul of the boat—where things really matter.

WHERE DO WE LOOK?

The first places to start looking for your project boat are the obvious ones: the classified ads in your local paper, listings in the "Boats For Sale" sections of

WoodenBoat and other national magazines, and broker's listings. Unless you're really lucky, you won't find much in these sources. First of all, you're looking for a bargain, and a lot of the ads you'll see are placed by owners who have just recently decided to sell their boats. A high percentage of owners of boats new to the market have inflated expectations of what their boats are worth. After a wooden boat has been on the market for a year or so with only a few phone calls in response to expensive ads, her owner usually becomes much more realistic and willing to listen to offers. Unfortunately, about this same time most sellers also stop advertising.

My personal experience with yacht brokers hasn't been all that great. Most of the ones I've called looking for boats were arrogant and lazy. They all seemed to be looking for the big sale and didn't have a lot of time for anyone looking for anything under $100,000. To be fair, it's a tough racket, and boat brokers don't get paid unless they sell boats. Yet frequently a broker will knock himself out finding just the right boat for a client only to have the client buy essentially the same boat somewhere else, or worse, wait until the broker's contract with the seller expires and buy the boat directly from the seller. It's no wonder many brokers have an attitude problem.

Two notable exceptions are Jaye Ann Tullai of Southern Trades in the U.S. Virgin Islands and Hope Swift of Lawson Yachts in Quincy, Massachusetts. Both are very knowledgeable about wooden boats, and once they know what your budget is and what you're looking for, they will scour the Earth looking for appropriate listings. And they won't quit until you find your boat.

If you can hook up with a decent broker, you'll only need to talk to that one. They all share in computer links that give them access to each other's listings, so one broker can tell you what all the others on their network have available. The good ones, like Hope and Jaye Ann, will make appointments for you to see the boats, make travel arrangements, go with you to show the boat when that's practical, and handle delicate negotiations with the seller and the closing.

One area where brokers might help you find bargains is the frequent case of the boatowner who wants to move up. A broker may have a customer who's anxious to buy one of the broker's other listings but can't move until he sells his current boat. Such sellers will be receptive to offers, and you can bet the broker will be on your side urging them to accept.

OK, so we've tried the ads with no luck and the brokers haven't been any help. What next? Well, hop in the family car and take a ride to every boatyard in your area and look at what they have in the back lot. Boatyards get commissions on boats they sell, so you'll always find someone willing to show you anything that's for sale. You'll also find that most boatyard proprietors are up-to-date and candid about the current boatyard scuttlebutt and gossip. They know which of their customers are having financial trouble, who is getting divorced or separated from whom, and who's just plain anxious to sell.

Boatyards are occasionally forced to seize boats from owners who haven't paid their yard bills. After certain legal procedures, depending on the state you live in, the ownership of the boat reverts to the boatyard. As you can imagine, these boats are frequently in a sad state of disrepair, and the boatyard is usually glad to get rid of them.

As you're driving from boatyard to boatyard, be on the lookout for boats wearing a For-Sale sign—particularly ones that look like they've been sitting there for a season or two. An unwanted boat sitting in someone's yard quickly becomes a major source of annoyance, and the owner may be particularly eager to sell at a reasonable price. Most owners of wooden boats also realize there's a limit to how long a boat can sit out of the water without suffering irreversible damage from the elements. They know that the longer they go without finding a buyer, the harder the boat will be to sell and the less it'll be worth.

If you find just the boat you're looking for early on in your search, well . . . just keep looking. You want to find out just what's on the market before you make a commitment. The boat you like will probably be there for a while, and if it does sell to someone else while you're looking at other boats, don't worry about it. The chances are very good you'll find something you like even better. After all, you're more knowledgeable than you were at the start. Keep looking.

WHAT TO LOOK FOR

Learn to be particularly suspicious of boats that look like real bargains. Many old boats, particularly wooden ones, have simply lived out their lives and are, in reality, worthless. While almost any boat can be repaired, no matter how badly it's damaged or deteriorated, a lot of boats on the market are so far gone that repairs aren't practical. They have simply deteriorated beyond the point of no return, and their owners either don't realize this or they want to get rid of them just to save the expense of taking them to the dump. Some worthless boats can look quite nice at first glance, particularly if the owner has a devious inclination and is good with Bondo and a paintbrush.

The useful life of a wooden boat is determined by a lot of different things; among them are the original design, the way the boat was built, the quality of materials used in critical parts, how hard the boat was used, and how well it was maintained. But regardless of the circumstances of a wooden boat's demise, ultimately it will be done in one or more of four ways: It will break, it will rot, it will fall apart, or it will be eaten.

Boats Break

Breakage usually occurs as the result of an accident. When a boat is run onto the rocks, something's going to give, and unless it's an unusually strong boat, it won't be the rocks. Bumps at the fuel dock, encounters with floating debris, and unintentional groundings can all lead to cracked and broken ribs, planks, and hulls.

Poor handling in a boatyard is another major cause of breakage not fully appreciated by many owners of wooden boats. Those new trucks with the hydraulic arms the yards use to transport boats over the highway and around their yards weren't designed with wooden hulls in mind. It's easy for a boat to suffer broken ribs and cracked planks at the hands of an inexperienced operator of one of these rigs.

Improperly placed jack stands are another threat. If too few stands are used or if they are improperly positioned, cracked ribs will surely result. Most wooden hulls stored out of the water benefit from a cradle that supports the boat at several places.

Boats Rot

Rot, one of the biggest destroyers of wooden boats, is almost always the result of owner neglect. What we call dry rot is actually a fungus that grows inside the wood and feeds on the fibers that give wood its strength. If not detected, dry rot will progress quite rapidly, eventually destroying the wood.

Mold and mildew are similar to dry rot in that they are also caused by fungi; however, they grow on the surface of anything that is dark and damp. They particularly like fabrics, but they aren't fussy; any surface, even plastic, will do fine.

Ironically, dry rot requires moisture to thrive, and it much prefers fresh water to salt. All three forms of fungi dislike fresh air, and they despise sunlight. The ideal environment for the dry-rot fungus is a piece of wood that is alternately soaked with fresh water then allowed to dry in an unventilated dark space. An improperly bedded deck fitting or a leak around a portlight provide perfect opportunities for rot to get a foothold. Don't worry about a little seawater in the bilge, though. Wood that's always soaked won't support rot any more than wood that's always dry. In fact, seawater contains trace amounts of iodine, zinc, and other natural fungicides that inhibit rot; so don't ever wash down your boat with the hose at the dock—get a washdown pump and use seawater instead.

In my neighborhood in eastern Massachusetts it's becoming increasingly popular to shrink-wrap boats for winter storage. The process involves encasing the boat in thermal-reactive plastic that, when heated, shrinks and forms a tight seal. Ventilation and sunlight are effectively shut out while moisture is trapped inside, encouraging condensation. Meanwhile the greenhouse effect of the plastic assures high temperatures inside the boat whenever the sun shines—even on the coldest days. A team of PhD horticulturists couldn't devise a more favorable environment for rot, mold, and mildew. Even people with all-plastic boats who shrink-wrap them wonder why their interiors smell so bad in the spring.

The best way to fight rot and molds is to stop them before they start. A boat that's dry and well ventilated, with an owner who's alert for the first sign of leaks and responds quickly with paint brush and caulking gun, seldom has a problem.

Because the most interesting renovation candidates are boats that have been neglected and are therefore likely to have problems with fungus, you'll need to learn to recognize it when you encounter it. Fortunately, detection isn't difficult: You can usually smell it before you see it. When you first inspect a boat, be alert for any wood weeping moisture or showing brown discoloration, and be very suspicious of any area that recently has been touched up with paint. Gently tap the suspected area with a small mallet or the handle of a screwdriver, listening for a flat or hollow sound. It's surprising how easy it is to identify the sound of rotted wood.

Figure 2-1. Places to look for rot. The forepeak rope locker is always suspect because it's almost impossible to keep dry; the fittings leak fresh water, and the anchor rode always comes aboard soaked. The area under fuel and water tanks is prone to fungus growth. Check the inside surface of the transom in back of the rudderpost on boats with inboard rudders. The floors and keelson in the bilge are usually easy to check. Look at the sheerstrake. The shelf, clamp, butt blocks, and all backing blocks on deck hardware should be checked from the inside where possible.

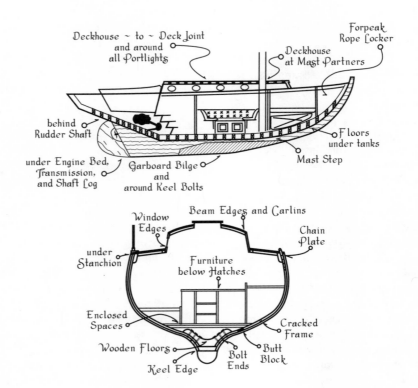

Resist the temptation to probe the suspect wood with an ice pick or knife blade even though you may have heard that this is standard procedure among surveyors. The owner will appreciate your not defacing his paint job, and it really isn't necessary.

Another form of rot to look out for isn't rot at all but galvanic electrolysis of the wood around metal fittings and fasteners in the hull below the waterline. It looks like rot and has the same effect as rot, but instead of being caused by a fungus, it's caused by an anode/cathode electrical current between the fitting or fastener and the protective zincs—or any other underwater metal, such as an iron keel. The wider the spread on the galvanic scale between the elements below the waterline, the more likely this problem will exist. (Interestingly, dry rot and fungus feed on the cellulose in the wood, leaving the lignin; electrolysis causes a caustic reaction in the wood that doesn't harm the cellulose but destroys the lignin.)

Most boatowners are aware that fresh zincs and a good bonding system are necessary to prevent deterioration of the metal parts; however, many are not aware that too much zinc will destroy the wood that is in contact with the metal parts they're trying to protect.

More and more, boatowners are loading their boats to the bulwarks with fancy electronic gear such as radar, Loran, and fancy gadgets that digitally display everything from water temperature to fuel consumption. I must confess to being a bit of an electronics nut myself, and although I am the first to admit that most aren't necessary, I get a big kick out of all these little doodads and gilhickies. We pay the piper for this electrical gadgetry in much higher levels of electrolysis, especially if our boat is tied into a leaky shore-power system.

Many owners, aware of this problem, load up on zincs, thinking more zinc means more protection from electrolysis. But on a wooden boat the added cathodic reaction can be entirely counterproductive; it helps save the metal, but it raises hell with the wood.

Most electrolytic deterioration is easy to find because we know right where to look for it. Simply tapping the wood around the through-hull fittings and around other underwater metal such as the rudderstock and the grounding plate is usually enough to indicate a problem.

The wood around underwater fasteners is harder to check because it usually involves pulling a bung. Of course this should only be done with the owner's express permission, and it is probably better left to the surveyor. But if you do pull a bung and the fastener is loose but looks to be in good shape, it may indicate a serious electrolysis problem.

Boats Fall Apart

It has already been observed that a wooden boat is little more than "a bundle of sticks" held together with various types of fasteners. As the boat absorbs stresses encountered in normal use, each individual part works by shouldering its share of the load and supporting its neighbor. And in doing so, each part moves ever so slightly in relationship to the part next to it. This movement is imperceptible between any two parts, but when it's taken together, it gives a well-built wooden hull a degree of flexibility that helps to give wooden boats their amazing strength. But as the boat ages, fasteners deteriorate and the wood changes dimensions with the seasons and the moisture content, allowing increasing movement between the parts. The flexibility of the hull increases over the years, and eventually, if it isn't corrected, the boat will become so flexible that it will simply fall apart.

**Figure 2-2.
To check for hogging, sight along the sheerline for a droop or sag in the stern or bow. Check for cracked seams by inspecting the paint over the seams at the stem and stern. Any excessive gaps at the ends of the deck beams where they rest on the shelves or clamps indicate spreading.**

Wooden boats are about the closest thing man has ever built to The Wonderful One-Horse Shay of Oliver Wendell Holmes. This, you will recall, was the Deacon's Masterpiece, the horse cart "that was built in such a logical way it ran for a hundred years and a day" and then disintegrated all at once. Wooden boats are like that. They appear to just fall apart all at once, but the process really starts when the boat is launched. All this will be covered in more detail in later chapters, but as you look at boats, you should be particularly alert for signs of excessive looseness, notably hogging, spreading, and loose seams.

Boats Are Eaten

Samuel Eliot Morison, in his engaging biography of Christopher Columbus, *Admiral of the Ocean Sea*, gives a fascinating account of how on Columbus' fourth and final voyage he had his last two caravels (he started with four) literally eaten out from under him by teredo worms. The ships began leaking so badly from worm holes that the pumps were unable to keep up with the incoming water. With their decks awash and under full sail, the boats were grounded on the coast of Jamaica, where the Admiral spent a year on the beach before finally being rescued.

Teredo worms aren't worms at all but mollusks, more closely related to snails than to worms—even though they can grow more than six feet long. They're found just about everywhere but are most common in southern waters. Their modus operandi is to attach themselves to a piece of bare wood as spat, then spend their lives munching away protected by a small shell that covers the entrance hole.

Boatbuilders over the centuries have tried a fascinating assortment of tactics to dissuade hungry worms from chomping away at keels and hulls. Felt soaked in tar was popular in Columbus' time. Tallow mixed with lime, called white bottom, was used on the Gloucester fishing schooners. Eventually, for those who could afford its considerable expense, copper sheathing nailed to the hull with all the seams soldered became the most popular defense against worm infestation. Eric Hiscock's first around-the-world boat, *Wanderer III*, had her hull protected by copper, and by his accounts it performed quite well. Today a good, fresh coat of bottom paint, which contains mostly powdered copper or cuprous oxide, is considered adequate protection against worms, but care must be exercised to ensure every bit of wood below the waterline is covered, including the inside of the shaft log and rudderport.

I must admit that, being a child of the frigid north where worm damage is relatively rare, I have little personal experience with these tiny varmints. I do, however, recall one memorable encounter with termites.

The boat was a nice old Chesapeake Bay crab boat a neighbor had purchased with the intention of restoring it to its original splendor. The project was delayed, as many such projects are, and the boat sat on blocks in my neighbor's backyard for several years while he talked of quitting his job at the post office and making his living as a waterman catching crabs and tonging oysters.

One morning, as I walked to school, I noticed my neighbor's boat looked a little low in the bows; when I returned home that afternoon, she had collapsed. She sat with her shattered bow flat on the ground and her stern pointing skyward—

much like the *Titanic* as she made her final plunge to the ocean floor. On closer inspection, it was obvious even to a young boy that it wasn't an iceberg that had done in my neighbor's boat. It was termites. They had eaten their way up through the supporting blocks and into the keel, devouring everything but the outside shell and leaving behind nothing but brown powder.

What was left of the crab boat made a grand bonfire. And as all the parents gathered around drinking beer and telling jokes while the kids roasted marshmallows on the dying embers, my neighbor announced that he had decided not to be a waterman after all.

NARROWING THE FIELD

After having looked at every wooden boat for sale within a 100-mile radius (more or less, depending on your requirements) that even vaguely resembled what you have in mind, you should have the serious prospects narrowed to two or three possibilities. Ideally all of them will be boats you could be equally content with. However, it's much more likely that there will be one boat you're crazy about, one that's a great boat but not as great as the first, and a third you could live with if you had to.

These options will be very important when you begin the bargaining process since without them you're much more likely to become overly enamored with your first choice. If that happens, you'll likely pay more than you want to, especially if the seller senses you really want his boat and don't have anything else on the back burner.

NEGOTIATIONS

Negotiating the purchase and sale of anything is an exchange between personalities that we all approach differently. To some it is adversarial, the opposite party viewed as an enemy to be vanquished. Negotiations proceed in the manner of a jousting tournament between medieval knights who batter each other with lance and sword until one or the other yields.

To others it's a contest of wits where every form of chicanery, half-truths, omissions, or exaggerations is considered fair play. Painted-over Silly Putty may hide dry rot; extra heavy crankcase oil might mask loose engine bearings; fuel consumption might be grossly understated; the age and condition of sails might be misrepresented; and the fact that the hull desperately needs to be refastened just might never be mentioned at all. All's fair in love and boat trading: *caveat emptor*.

Just as there are some people who are good at selling boats and others who are not, some people are good at dickering over prices and others aren't. I've never been very good at either, and I must approach the purchase or sale of a major item very carefully or I'll get burned every time.

My problem is having to contend with a strong aversion to offending anyone. If I were to find a boat I wanted, and I thought it might be worth $10,000, and the seller was asking $50,000 (and, believe me, in the used-boat market this isn't an extreme example), I would stutter and stammer and nod my head and tell the guy

I'd think it over. We might eventually reach an agreement, but it would take delicate and protracted negotiations—all because of my inability to look the guy in the eye and tell him his asking price is ridiculous.

A good friend of mine who buys most everything he needs secondhand doesn't have this kind of hang-up. He would approach the sale with two checks in his pocket already made out to the seller. The first check would be for about half what he planned as his top offer, and the second would be for three-fourths of his final offer. He would hand the hapless seller the first check, claiming it represented all the money he had in the world, and the seller could take it or leave it. If the seller showed the least bit of interest in this first offer, the second check would stay in my friend's pocket and the negotiations would proceed. If, on the other hand, the guy ripped up the check, threw it on the ground, and began to stomp on it like a deranged square dancer trying to kill a snake, then my friend would offer the second check. The third and final offer wouldn't come for several weeks or even months, during which time the seller would get several calls to see if he had reconsidered the second offer.

Although I might admire my friend's approach, I know I can't negotiate in this manner; I'm just not that kind of person. And since I've gotten accustomed to being the way I am, I probably wouldn't change if I could.

THE OFFER TO PURCHASE

Now that we've found two or three good solid prospects and have prepared ourselves psychologically for the negotiation process, we're ready to approach the seller of our first choice with an offer to purchase. This is a legally binding document that will be signed by both parties and to which both parties will be held accountable. If the purchase involves a substantial amount of money, more than $10,000 or so, the offer should be prepared by an attorney. Below that amount a handshake might be fine and is equally binding, but some sort of written document that spells out the proposed deal will certainly be useful if any controversy arises.

The important part of the offer to purchase will contain a description of the boat with hull numbers and engine serial numbers along with the agreed-on price. It will also include a list of all the equipment, electronics, spare parts, tools, fixtures, and anything else that is to be a part of the sale. Occasionally a phrase like "and all related equipment and supplies" will be substituted for a comprehensive list of external equipment, especially if the seller or the seller's lawyer is the one drawing up the agreement. Don't accept anything this vague but insist that every little item from the boat hook to the coffee cups in the galley be listed. This seemingly minor item can save you a world of aggravation when you finally close the deal and notice that stuff is missing or has been switched.

The offer to purchase must be accompanied with some form of deposit to be binding. Ten percent of the offered price should be more than adequate; deposit less if the seller will agree to it. When a large amount of money is involved, it's a good idea to insist the deposit be held by the seller's attorney, or by your own attorney if the seller doesn't have one. If the deal falls through, it can be a lot easier to

Purchase and Sale Agreement

Between

___(name of seller)___

and

___(name of buyer)___

This agreement between ___(name of seller)___ of ___(address)___ hereinafter called the SELLER, and ___(name of buyer)___ of ___(address)___ hereinafter called the BUYER, will transfer ownership of the yacht ___(name of yacht)___ described as ___(description of yacht)___ hereinafter called the YACHT, from the SELLER to the BUYER under the terms and conditions set forth below:

1: Price: The selling price shall be the sum of (selling price) dollars (U.S. $ _____) which the BUYER agrees to pay to the SELLER and the SELLER agrees to accept as full payment from the BUYER, to be paid as follows: the sum of _____ dollars (U.S. $ _____) is to be paid at the time this agreement is signed and will be held by the SELLER or his designee as a deposit. The balance of _____ dollars (U.S. $ _____) is to be paid at the time of closing as set forth below.

2: This agreement includes the YACHT and ancillary equipment in its entirety as described on the inventory which is attached to and made a part of this agreement.

3: The SELLER warrants that he is owner of the YACHT and inventory in its entirety and that he has full and legal authority to execute this agreement and that the YACHT is unencumbered by liens, attachments, or interest of third parties unnamed of any sort.

4: This agreement is conditioned upon a full and satisfactory survey of the YACHT and inventory of ancillary equipment to be conducted by a surveyor chosen by and paid for by the BUYER. Such a survey is to be completed by _____ 19 _____ at which time the BUYER will advise the SELLER of his acceptance or rejection of the YACHT.

5: This agreement is subject to the BUYER's ability to obtain suitable financing at a rate that is consistent with current rates on or before _____ 19 _____ and on the BUYER's ability to obtain suitable insurance on or before _____ 19 _____ .

6: The rejection of the YACHT by the BUYER under the provisions of P#4 and P#5 above shall constitute termination of this agreement, and the SELLER shall return the deposit to the BUYER in full.

7: The SELLER agrees to maintain the YACHT in its present condition, to maintain insurance presently in force, and to pay any and all fees and charges resulting from maintenance and storage of the YACHT up until the closing as specified below.

8: The closing on this agreement shall take place on or before _____ 19 _____ at _____

9: Other provisions: _____ .
_____ .
_____ .
_____ .
_____ .

Witness whereof this _____ day of _____ 19 _____

_____	_____
Witness	BUYER
_____	_____
Witness	SELLER

**Figure 2-3.
Sample purchase-
and-sale agreement.**

get your deposit back from the lawyers than from a disappointed seller who may think he has been wrongly treated.

The offer to purchase should also be worded to contain one or more escape clauses—contingencies that will allow you to cancel the contract and retrieve your deposit if specific things don't come out the way you want them to. For example, if your Uncle Harry has recently sailed off into his last sunset and you're planning to buy your boat with the substantial inheritance you expect once the estate is settled, it is important to say that in the offer to purchase. If the old codger ends up leaving everything to a go-go dancer named Mona he met on his last trip to Vegas, you get your deposit back—no questions asked.

The phrase, "This offer is subject to the buyer's ability to obtain adequate financing from an appropriate lending institution within 90 days of the signing of this document," or something to that effect, is one important escape clause your lawyer will insert in your offer to purchase even if you happen to have the cash to buy the boat. It's also very important to make the sale subject to the satisfactory inspection of a registered marine surveyor of the buyer's choice—even in the unlikely event you don't plan to use one. Another clause might make the sale conditional on your ability to sell an existing boat within a reasonable period of time. Yet another might burden the seller to document his ownership of the boat—this may not be easy with an old boat. Don't be afraid to add anything if there are other circumstances that might affect the outcome of the deal. Remember, though, that the seller must agree to all contingencies, so don't be too outrageous.

The contingencies should be enough to allow you to weasel your way out of the deal with your deposit intact should you need to, but remember that an obviously capricious effort to cancel a contract based on an escape clause can land you in court. The judge may agree with the seller that scratches on the rubrail pointed out by the surveyor don't constitute an unsatisfactory survey and award the seller the deposit plus costs.

GET A SURVEY

Well, we've finally found a boat, made an offer that has been accepted, and have a neatly signed offer to purchase secured with a deposit. What next? In most cases, before doing anything else, we'll need to enlist the services of a good surveyor. If the boat you're buying is small, if there's not a lot of money involved, or if you're very knowledgeable about boats, you might skip this step. If, however, the project boat will represent a substantial investment when you consider the total amount you plan to spend on the renovation, it would be foolish not to get a survey. By using the final amount of your investment instead of just the purchase price as the determining factor in your decision to get a survey, you'll avoid the possibility of spending a lot of money on a hull that's not worth fixing up. For the same reason, you should even consider getting a survey on a boat you already own, or on one that is given to you, if your planned renovations will involve a lot of money.

Many fine-looking old wooden boats will have loose or deteriorated keel bolts; a rotted stem, horntimber, or keel; broken or rotted strings; excessive spreading or hogging; or other major defects that are beyond the scope of this book. These problems, while repairable, may very well require the services of a professional boatyard, and work done by a boatyard can exceed the value your boat with astounding swiftness. In many cases, your surveyor will be the only one who can accurately assess the extent of the damage, and a good one will be able to help you judge your ability to do the repairs yourself or will help you estimate the cost of professional help.

A good survey is not inexpensive in dollars, but it can be cheap in the long run. My wife and I were recently considering replacing our present boat with a 30-year-old ketch that was for sale at the Billings yard in Stonington, Maine. The *Duchess* has been good to us, but we like to make fairly long passages for coastal cruisers, and when the barometer falls and the wind rises, we really miss not having the sails to take advantage of a favorable breeze. The whole family drove to Stonington to give the new old boat a once over, and everyone fell in love with her. Like the *Duchess*, *Sultana* was a warm and friendly boat, and the kids instantly started fighting over who would get which berth. Unlike the *Duchess*, she spread over 1,000 feet of canvas.

The boat was reasonably priced, so we quickly reached an agreement on the amount and conditions of the sale. For the survey I turned to Captain Paul C. Haley, a Marblehead surveyor with a solid reputation for his work with wooden boats. Paul drove to Stonington and spent a full day between bilges and bulwarks, going over every inch of the old ketch. Now, I was raised with boats and have owned and worked on boats most of my life, and I thought I had a pretty good idea of what that boat needed in the way of repairs, but Paul came back with a list of 53 items that needed attention. The cost of his survey, including meals, transporta-

**Figure 2-4.
Captain Haley
surveying a boat.**

tion, and an overnight at a motel, was less than $800. The total cost of the repairs easily could exceed $20,000. I'd call that a pretty good return on investment.

The point of this little anecdote is that no matter how much you think you know about boats, when you're buying one it's easy to be blinded by the excitement of finding just the right boat. A surveyor like Captain Haley doesn't care how much you love the boat any more than he cares about the crush you had on your third-grade teacher. All he cares about is the keel not falling off because the bolts are deteriorated, or the mast not going by the boards because the backstay turnbuckle was cracked.

There are reasons to get a survey other than finding out what condition a prospective purchase is in. If the boat you select is less than 10 years old, is in fairly good shape, and you plan to finance the purchase, the people from whom you borrow the money will almost certainly insist that the boat be surveyed before closing the deal. They'll also insist that the boat be insured, and the insurance company will also want a copy of a current survey before it agrees to grant coverage.

Speaking of insurance, most companies feel about as friendly toward wooden boats as chicken farmers toward foxes. An exception is Hagarty Marine Insurance of Traverse City, Michigan. They make a specialty of placing wooden boats with carriers that realize the age of a wooden boat doesn't matter. What does matter? A clean and recent survey.

FINANCING YOUR PURCHASE

If you're planning on using as collateral a wooden boat that is over 10 years old, is not a collectable antique, and is not in pristine condition, I have two words of advice: Forget it. Unless your mom happens to be president of the local savings and loan, the bankers won't even talk to you. The finance companies will be more willing to talk, and they might even agree to lend you some money, but only at a rate that will redefine the word usury.

It makes a lot of sense to pay cash for your project boat, but if you must borrow money, try to borrow it against another piece of real property. The banks will be more receptive, the rates will be lower, and if you use a second mortgage on your home, there may be substantial tax savings because the interest you pay will be deductible.

As of this writing, a boat with a galley and a head is considered a second home by the IRS, and as such, any money borrowed against it is deductible. Unfortunately the abuses of this ruling are so flagrant that it's only a matter of time before this particular loophole has a bung hammered into it.

By the way, subchapter "S" corporations registered in Delaware were once a popular and effective way of hiding larger boats from the tax man. But as one "sheltered" boatowner after another gets his butt kicked through the goal posts of reality by the federal golden toe, this is becoming an increasingly less popular option.

SO LET'S BUY IT ALREADY

If you've done everything so far, just as I've suggested, your life of happiness and bliss with your project boat is virtually assured. All that remains is for you to pay for the boat and it's yours. But wait—there is one more important thing that must be covered, and that's the final inspection.

Before you close the deal, go over the boat very carefully to ensure everything is as it should be. See that the boat hasn't been damaged in any way, nothing has been removed, and the boat is in the same condition as when you last inspected it. Carefully review the list of equipment that was made part of the offer to purchase to ensure that everything that's supposed to be there is there. Then, if it is at all practical, take her out for a test sail.

If something is wrong at this point—if a piece of equipment has been removed or switched, or the boat has been damaged in any substantial way, or if anything else has changed that affects the value of the boat or its utility to you—you have a perfect right to postpone the closing or even cancel the deal. However, unless the keel has fallen off or some other catastrophe has befallen your prize, the more appropriate response, and the one most people should use, is to go ahead and complete the deal with the buyer holding back a portion of the final payment until the seller can correct the problem.

When completing a deal in this manner, it's important that the buyer hold back enough money to assure the performance of the seller rather than just enough to cover the cost of the item involved. In one deal I was indirectly involved with, a depthfinder was discovered to have a broken mounting bracket. Replacing it involved a lot of nuisance work looking up part numbers and writing to the manufacturer for a replacement, so even though the bracket was only worth about $10, the buyer held back several hundred—enough to ensure that the seller would take the trouble to order the replacement part.

If there is an important piece of gear missing, a VHF say, and the seller promises to deliver it to you sometime after the closing, fine. But keep a couple of hundred bucks in your jeans just in case, and make sure it's more than the radio is actually worth.

Remember, you can walk away from a deal at any time up to the final closing, and no matter how badly you want to own the boat, you should be prepared to do just that. Once you hand over that last payment, you have very little recourse against the seller in a private sale. If you discover a problem after the fact, it is usually to late. What were the seller's problems are now your problems.

With that in mind, go ahead and buy it.

CHAPTER THREE

Work Schedule and Budget

Developing a comprehensive work schedule and a realistic budget is probably one of the most productive ways to spend our time in the early stages of our wooden-boat renovation project. Each hour we spend with a calculator and note paper now will save us many hours later on. Plus, once we have our plan and budget written down, we can keep track of each step we take toward our goal and chart our progress. We will know exactly what is going to happen next and have advance warning if things aren't working out the way they should. Then, when our project is complete, we'll have an accurate record of what we've done, how we did it, and how much money it cost us.

In spite of the obvious and demonstrable advantages of a well-thought-out work plan and budget, a lot of readers may be tempted to skip right over this section. Don't. Just keep reading. Many people, including me, have a well-developed resistance to planning of any sort. To many of us it's boring, time-consuming, not at all natural, and particularly tedious when our newly purchased old boat is waiting in the garage.

Wouldn't the time be better spent scraping paint and caulking seams? No, it wouldn't. Even a small boat project can get out of hand in an amazingly short period of time. You've taken great pains to buy a boat that won't tax your resources. Now you want to make sure your resources are distributed wisely so you can complete the job.

My old Grandpappy was fond of saying that there are people who plan to do things and there are people who do them. And while this might be stereotypical and a gross oversimplification, it does serve to point out the two behavioral extremes in the way we approach scheduling. In the first group are the Type Xs. They approach a task with little or no planning, charging through life full tilt without the slightest idea of where they're going or how they're going to get there. When they run into a wall, they just pick themselves up, dust themselves off, and charge off in another direction. In the second group are the Type Ys who tend to plan everything to death.

You probably know several people of each type; maybe you even recognize yourself. One fellow I knew a while ago was a chronic Type Y. He spent five years planning to sail his 35-foot sloop from Cape Cod to Halifax, Nova Scotia. He bought a sextant and diligently studied every navigation course offered by the local power squadron. He memorized every chart available for every harbor of refuge between the Chesapeake Bay and Glasgow, Scotland. He learned cold-water survival techniques and got himself into trouble with the Coast Guard test-firing his flare gun. He rigged his boat with a new man-overboard pole, the latest EPIRB, and the best radar reflector. He did everything he could possibly think of to prepare himself for the adventure of a lifetime. But to my knowledge he never made the trip.

Typical of a Type X, I didn't do a lot of planning when we first bought the *Duchess*. After the deal was closed, I called my favorite boat trucker, Clayton Crabtree, owner of Joselyn Trucking in Newburyport, Massachusetts. Also typical of a Type X, I first called Clayton several years ago not because he was highly recommended but because of his Dickensian name. I figured he was like Smucker's jelly: With a name like that, he had to be good. I was right. Anyway, I called Clayton this time to haul *Duchess* to the rented loading dock where I planned to do some major repairs. I had eyeballed the boat and I had eyeballed the door, but I had measured neither.

"Sure it'll fit," I said to Clayton as we neared our destination. "No problem."

And it would have, too. If the trailer hadn't added 2 feet to the overall height, she would've slid right in with about 1½ inches to spare.

"Oh well," I said, with aplomb typical of Type Xs faced with trying to get a two-pound mackerel into a one-pound sack. "That flybridge has to come off anyway. Might as well be now as later."

Somewhere between these two extremes lies a realistic compromise. Most of us aren't exactly like either, but almost all of us are closer to one end of the scale than to the other. If you are close to the X end of the scale, you might have to force yourself to sit down and work out a budget. On the other hand, if you're closer to Type Y and like to plan things *ad nauseam*, you might have to limit your planning time if you ever want to get that new old boat into the water.

The example above shows that I'm a lot closer to X than to Y, but I've encountered so many self-inflicted disasters that a little planning and forethought would have prevented—like trying to get a 12-foot-high boat through a 10-foot-high door—that I've learned the planning process really pays off. Before we go galloping off to rescue the princess, let's reign in the horses on a hilltop, take a long look at what lies on the road ahead, and figure out how we're going to handle that dragon sleeping on the bridge before we go and wake him up.

PLANNING WITH A COMPUTER

If yours is among the ever-growing number of American households with a personal computer and even a rudimentary spreadsheet program, the planning process can be greatly expedited and can even be a lot of fun. A spreadsheet is nothing more than a bunch of boxes arranged in columns and rows that can relate to each other in ways you, the operator, dictate. Box R34 can be added to box Z86, the result posted in box R43 and subtracted from the total of boxes A27 and N65. Half the remainder can be rounded to two decimals, converted to a percentile, and posted in the box entitled Coefficient of Collateral Contingency—which tells us how many arrows we have left to kill the dragon with.

You can arrange your boxes any way you like, and you can make them do anything to any other box you want them to. Every time you change or enter a number in a box, every other related box in the system changes with the speed of an electronic heartbeat. The process can instill in the operator feelings of omnipotence that can be quite seductive. And it's great fun thinking up intelligent-sounding names for the boxes, like Front End Capital Loading for the amount you spent on the boat, or Recurring Static Assemblage Expense for your monthly yard bill.

Although entertaining, spreadsheet programs also put you at risk of getting so carried away by the pure creative thrill that you end up spending all your time trying to think up new things for one box to do to other boxes. The Type Xs who like to make things happen fast can become so engrossed in spreadsheets that they're quickly converted to chronic Type Ys, forget all about their boats, and end up devoting the rest of their lives to manipulating their data.

That's all I'm going to say about computers and spreadsheets. If you already have one, it's unlikely you need any instruction from me on how to use it, and you should be able to adapt easily the planning and budget procedures that follow to whatever software you're using. If you don't have a computer and a spreadsheet program, I would never suggest that you buy either just for a boat project. Some graph paper, a pencil, and a pocket calculator will do fine.

THE WORK SCHEDULE

The work schedule I'm going to describe to you is a compilation of the best features of several job-planning systems used by project managers and construction supervisors in many unrelated industries across the land. You'll see similar systems in use at large boatyards where major repair projects are routine, and many custom boatbuilders use their own versions of this system.

The mechanics are simple enough that anyone, regardless of their aversion to paperwork, can easily master them. The schedule is easy to update and maintain, will not sap time from your actual project, and is flexible and easily adapted to your individual requirements. In fact, I'd be surprised if anyone using this system didn't refine it to make it better fit the needs of their project. But remember to keep any additions or modifications simple; the more complicated the system, the more work it will be to update, and the less useful it will be for planning.

To start our work schedule, we'll need a large pad of graph paper. I like 11 X 17-inch pads available in most well-equipped stationery stores; use larger or smaller paper to suit your project and temperament.

Across the top of the sheet from left to right (the X axis for those of you with a mathematical bent) we will form a calendar of work progression divided into equal time periods—days, weeks, or months—depending, again, on the magnitude of your project and the number of hours you can spend on it each day. For most projects a weekly schedule is best. Pretty easy so far, right?

The column on the far left (the Y axis) will become a list of the things we're going to do to our boat. Make it as complete as you can, listing everything that's either going to cost money or take significant time. Arrange the list in chronological order and leave a couple of blank lines between each entry. The first item might well be "find boat," because this most likely will take some time and you'll spend some money on gas and an occasional motel room. The second item might be "survey and purchase," the third "transport home," and so on down the page. Your schedule will now look something like the one in Figure 3-1.

Of course you may still be unsure about just what has to be done at this early stage, but the system can accommodate any changes you may want to make later

Figure 3-1.
Drafting a work plan such as this will be a big help.

	1	2	3	4	5	6	7
1			WORK PLAN FOR DUCHESS				
2	Week No:	Week 1	Week 2	Week 3	Week 4	Week 5	Week 6
3	Date/Week Ending:	7/6	7/13	7/20	7/27	8/3	8/10
4							
5	Make offer						
6							
7	Obtain survey						
8							
9	Purchase boat						
10							
11	Obtain insurance						
12							
13	Change documentation						
14							
15	Transport to workshop						
16							
17	Clean and inspect						
18							
19	Remove electronics						
20							
21	Remove all deck hardware						
22							
23	Remove all thruhull fittings						
24							
25	Strip paint from hull						
26							
27	Strip paint from deck						
28							

on. If there's something you think *may* have to be done, but you won't know until a further investigation, enter it anyway. For example, if the surveyor suggested that the floors under the water tank in the forepeak might need replacing, but he couldn't tell for sure without removing the tank, go ahead and make the entry. If it turns out you don't need to replace the floors, your schedule will simply reflect the change.

When you run off one page and onto another, you'll need to key each page to its neighbor by labeling each sheet with a row letter and column number. Thus, the sheets across the top of our schedule, the ones divided into weeks, will be labeled A-1, A-2, A-3, and so on, on the back of each sheet. The sheets in the left-hand column that contain our list of functions will be labeled A-1, B-1, C-1, and so on.

Next we'll need a large bulletin board or an empty wall space that won't suffer from pushpin perforations. This will be our planning board onto which we'll tack our sheets in alphanumerical order. Resist the temptation to tape the sheets together into one large sheet; you'll want to be able to remove the individual sheets to update them or to replace them when they get too messy.

Now that we have our column and row headings all neatly filled in, we can start estimating the time it will take to complete each function. Since we've already purchased the boat and have it safely squared away in our work area, we know what to put in the first three lines. Taking a green felt-tipped marker, fill in the blocks on the row entitled "find boat" in the columns representing the time period that you were looking for the boat. The green marker represents our *estimate* of how long each item should take. Now use a red marker to fill in the row immediately below the green row. The red marker represents the *actual* time it took us to complete each function. Since we've already bought the boat, our estimate (green) in this case will be the same as the actual (red).

Continuing down the list of tasks in the left-hand column, fill in your best estimate for each function with the green marker. You should estimate when you plan to start each item, how long each will take, and when each will be complete, filling in the blocks accordingly.

Obviously this process of estimating time requirements for different functions will involve a lot of guesswork, particularly if you've never done this sort of thing before. Don't worry about it. Just do the best you can with the information you have available, and try to err on the long side. It will always be easier to handle an overestimation than an underestimation.

Your surveyor might be willing to help you with the tough ones. If, for example, he thinks the planking needs to be refastened, ask him how long he thinks it should take. His guess will be more accurate than yours, but it's a guess just the same. If there are things you're at a complete loss to estimate, just leave them blank for now. You can fill them in later as you gain experience.

The reason we listed our functions in a rough chronology is now obvious. There are many things that can't be completed until something else is complete first. You can't paint the hull until the seams are caulked, and you can't do that until the planking is refastened, and so on. In fact, almost everything you do will depend on something else being done before it.

	1	2	3	4	5	6	7
1	WORK PLAN FOR DUCHESS--PHASE ONE						
2	Week No	Week 1	Week 2	Week 3	Week 4	Week 5	Week 6
3	Date/Week Ending	7/6	7/13	7/20	7/27	8/3	8/10
4							
5	Make offer	XXXXXXXXX					
6		O					
7	Obtain survey		XXXXXXXXX				
8			O				
9	Purchase boat			XXXXXXXXX			
10				OOOO	OO		
11	Obtain insurance			XXXXXXXXX			
12				OOOO	OOOOO		
13	Change documentation			XXXXXXXXX			
14				OO	OOOOOOOOOOOOOOOOOOOOOOOOOOO		
15	Transport to workshop			XXXXXXXXX			
16					O O		
17	Clean and inspect			XXXXXXXXX			
18					OOOO		
19	Remove electronics				XXXXXXXXX		
20						OOOOO	
21	Remove all deck hardware				XXXXXXXXX		
22							
23	Remove all thruhull fittings					XXXXXXXXX	
24							OOO
25	Strip paint from hull						XXXXXXXXX
26							OOO
27	Strip paint from deck						XXXXXXXXX
28							OOO

Figure 3-2. A section of the work plan for the *Duchess*. "X" (green) indicates when the item was scheduled, and "O" (red) indicates when it was started and when it was completed.

If your project is a really ambitious one that might take as long as several years, such as mine was when I started the *Duchess*, or if you plan to complete the job in stages, it may be advisable to divide your project into major phases. On the *Duchess*, Phase One involved replacing a 10-foot section of the keel, replacing all the wiring, installing engine-room blowers, installing a new alternator, updating the propane system, and installing an anchor winch and new ground tackle (Figure 3-2).

Dividing the work schedule up in this way makes the project much more manageable. And if you wish, and your wall is big enough, you can still view the entire project just by pinning the phases together on your planning board. Updating the list will be a simple matter of using the red marker to fill in the blocks between the time you start each function and the time you finish it.

Once you have all the functions listed, the time requirements estimated to the best of your ability, and the sheets pinned together, you should have a good feel for what lies ahead. If you've made reasonably accurate estimates of the work requirements and your ability to complete them, a mere glance at the board will tell you everything that needs to be done. It's starting to look a lot more involved than you thought, isn't it?

THE PROJECT BUDGET

One of the features of this system that makes it superior to all the others I've worked with over the years, besides its simplicity, is that the budget is actually an integral part of the work schedule. This linear integration (as job planners in big companies like to call it) makes the budget easily used and understood by the average person. At the same time, this integration makes it hard to make a mistake because each budget item is matched with a job function on the work schedule.

To start your budget, you could use the five or six columns at the far right of your work schedule, but I prefer to use a separate sheet of graph paper with the same spacing. The first step is simply to copy all the work functions from the work schedule onto the budget. (Yes, if you have a copy machine, just making a copy of the first column of work schedule sheets will save a case of writer's cramp.)

The next step is to fill in the column headings as follows: Column two is called "Boat Capital," column three is labeled "Non-Boat Capital," column four is labeled "Expense," and column five is labeled "Total." That's it—couldn't be simpler.

Now, in case you don't remember your Economics 101, boat capital will represent every physical thing you buy or do that adds value to the boat. The original purchase price, a new anchor, a box of screws to refasten planking, and a replacement bilge pump are all things that should be included under this heading.

Non-boat capital represents the money we spend for physical things that don't add value to the boat but will retain some use and value after we're finished with them. An electric drill, jack stands, a prefabricated storage shed, and ladders and scaffolding are all examples of non-boat capital.

The expense column represents the money we spend for products and services that retain no value after we use them. What you paid the guy with the trailer to haul your boat home, insurance, and yard fees are all obvious examples of this category. Supplies you'll be using up as you go—dust masks, masking tape, sandpaper—will also fit nicely into the expense column.

Frequently you'll encounter items where the distinction between categories isn't that clear. For example, the paint brushes you'll be buying for epoxy cost about 50¢ each and are used once and discarded. These should be included as an expense item. The fine badger-hair brushes that you'll want for varnishing, however, will cost around $35 each and should last you a lifetime. These should go in the non-boat-capital column. As with everything in boating, a little judgment and common sense here will serve you well.

There is another category of expenditure that, depending on your project and how you plan to proceed, you might want to consider. This is called "contract labor" by the experts and represents the money you pay others to work on your boat. If, for example, you have a sign painter put your boat's name and hail in gold leaf on your newly varnished transom, this would be a contract-labor expenditure. If you'll have a lot of this sort of thing—like hiring a professional boatbuilder to help replace the deadwood in a deteriorated keel—you might consider keeping this item in a separate column. Otherwise, just include it under boat capital.

After you've completed the columns and rows to your satisfaction, simply go down the list and enter your estimate of the cash expenditure you expect for each item. Make your entries in green pen directly opposite the green line that represents your time estimate on your work schedule. Here, as before, judgment and guesswork will come into play. Consult catalogs and call supply houses to obtain quotes on equipment and supplies. Don't forget to include shipping charges, service charges, taxes, and any installation expense in your estimate. You might want to keep track of separate items, such as taxes and shipping charges, on a separate sheet—I use a spiral notebook—but lump them all together for your budget. Keep it simple, remember?

OK, now simply add up all the green numbers and post the result in the total column with your green pen. If it's a large budget, it may help you to figure subtotals at logical intervals. However you do it, the last green number in the total column represents your budget.

Figure 3-3. A small section of the budget for the *Duchess*.

If the final figure is larger than you thought, join the club—it almost always is. There are two ways to handle this situation. The first and most obvious is to go get some more money. If that isn't practical (or perhaps it's not too popular with you-know-who), simply go back over the list and cut back on items that are expendable (do you really need side-scan sonar?) or can be deferred to a later date. This is a

	1	2	3	4	5	6	7
1			BUDGET FOR DUCHESS--PHASE ONE				
2	Week No		NON-BOAT		CONTRACT	PROJECTED	ACTUAL
3	Date/Week Ending	BOAT CAPITAL	CAPITAL	EXPENSE	LABOR	TOTAL	TOTAL
4							
5	Make offer	$2000.00				$2000.00	
6		$2500.00					$2500.00
7	Obtain survey			$500.00		$500.00	
8				$625.00			$625.00
9	Purchase boat	$18000.00				$18000.00	
10		$22500.00					$22500.00
11	Obtain insurance			$800.00		$800.00	
12				$1000.00			$1000.00
13	Change documentation			$250.00		$250.00	
14				$250.00			$250.00
15	Transport to workshop		$0.00	$800.00		$800.00	
16			$342.50	$1000.00			$1342.50
17	Clean and inspect		$250.00			$250.00	
18			$295.00				$295.00
19	Remove electronics				$75.00	$75.00	
20					$75.00		$75.00
21	Remove all deck hardware		$0.00			$0.00	
22			$27.50				$27.50
23	Remove all thruhull fittings					$0.00	
24							$0.00
25	Strip paint from hull		$0.00	$150.00		$150.00	
26			$229.35	$82.53			$311.88
27	TOTAL					$20825.00	$28926.88
28							

normal part of the budgeting process used by all professional planners—although many of them don't like to admit it—and is appropriately called "backing down" or "backing into the numbers."

At the odd chance that your total estimate is smaller than you thought it would be, double-check your figures. You must have made a massive error in calculation somewhere; the total is never smaller than you thought it would be.

At this point, our budget will look something like the one in Figure 3-3. Please note that the most important feature in this layout is that each budget item corresponds to and lines up with the identical item on the work schedule. Now all we have to do is post the total cost of each item in red as it's completed.

Stick the whole thing together on your planning board with pushpins and stand back and take a look. Isn't it great? You can tell at a glance just what's going on, what your progress is, how much money you've spent, and how much you have left to do. With just a few hours of work you have information that gives you an enormous advantage over all those foolish readers who skipped this chapter—and the 99 percent of do-it-yourself boatbuilders who get involved in renovation projects without any plan at all. Now aren't you glad you bought this book? Shouldn't you recommend it to your friends?

CHAPTER FOUR

Something About Tools

There is something about both tools and boats that instills a feeling of competency when we use them properly. Both are accessible to nearly everyone who would have them, and both are relatively easy to use initially.

Almost anyone can manage to worry a board in half with a handsaw. However, to contrast this with a skilled boatbuilder ripping a plank dead true to the line with full, sure strokes of a bowsaw is to contrast an amateur housepainter with Henri Matisse.

Similarly, most anyone who can afford a sailboat can get the sails up and make the thing go downwind or off on a reach of sorts. But on any late-summer Sunday off Marblehead Neck when a gale comes boiling in from the northeast, unannounced and mean, and the wind-speed doohickey jumps off 10 and pegs out at 30, a few good sailors sheet her in hard, get the rail under, and head for Gloucester at eight knots—sailing like banshees through fleets of wildly flogging genoas and red-faced, hysterical skippers screaming profanities at their undeserving and terrified crews.

Yes, once we find the key that unlocks the mystery of their proper use and once we master them, both tools and boats will work for us and do things for us that are the envy of those too lazy or too preoccupied to learn how to use them correctly. Perhaps this feeling of mastery comes from knowing that when we become competent with tools or boats, we become members of small and select clubs. Most people in our modern society don't use either to their potential. A few do not have the

God-given propensity or the manual dexterity, but most simply lack the desire—that inner spark that makes us want to do complex things the right way.

Not that membership in either of these select groups makes us better than our neighbors; quite the contrary, tools and boats are both humbling entities that will surely step on all those who begin to feel superior or smug about their abilities with them. Just when you feel that you can sail away from the fuel dock and thereby gain the admiration of the gang of weekend hang-arounders, a freak gust will back-wind your main, and the jibe will send you scudding sideways into incoming traffic. After the shouting and swearing dies down and the rigging is untangled, you may notice that the grins of the onlookers are something other than admiring. It's the same with tools; once your head swells with overconfidence, you become an accident patiently awaiting the most inappropriate time and inconvenient place to occur.

Both tools and boats are, by nature, vindictive; fail to show them proper respect and they will repay you with injury. Boats, for example, will surely throw you overboard when you become cocky about your skill on the foredeck and try to jibe the spinnaker singlehanded. And they're notorious for their ability to run you hard aground right after you announce to your passengers that you don't need the charts because "I know these waters like the back of my. . . ." Likewise, your tools wait unforgivingly for a chance to nip off a piece of a finger that gets too close to a super-sharpened blade, or to drive a piece of wooden shrapnel from an exploding knot into your face when you decide you don't need to wear safety glasses.

I know of no one who sails on the water who doesn't have several tales of embarrassment and castigation at the hands of his boat. And I know of very few craftsmen who work regularly shaping wood who don't wear the scars and abbreviated digits that attest to the uncanny ability of tools to call in your markers when you least expect it.

The proper use of both tools and boats can make us feel humble and confident and calm and relaxed. We don't feel superior to others, just luckier. And there's a personal sense of achievement that makes us feel good; that's why we do it.

BUY THE BEST—YOU DESERVE IT

Many aspiring boat renovators reading this book will already have a good selection of hand and power tools at their disposal. Others will have a good start on a good selection, and almost all will have some tools. But no matter how many you have, you'll never seem to have quite enough. The shop I operated for a while in Beverly, Massachusetts, had a tool inventory worth well over $30,000, and even then we were forever going off to rent this or borrow that. Granted, this was a professional shop with a lot of large, stationary power tools, so don't get discouraged thinking you'll have to mortgage the house to buy tools. However, if you're planning a project much larger than a ship in a bottle, you're going to need good tools, and you'll have to spend some money to get them.

The catch word here is "good." Before you do anything else, take a scrap of cedar or pine and a lumber crayon and inscribe these three words on the front:

"Buy The Best." On the back, inscribe these five words: "I Told You So, Dummy." Using two screw eyes and a scrap of rigging wire, mount the board over your workbench so that it can be flipped from one side to the other. From now on, every time your cheap router throws a bit because the collet was made from pot metal, or every time you mess up an expensive piece of hardwood because you tried to drill a hole in it with a spade bit, go to the sign, turn it over, and read the back. You'll be flipping it a lot during the first part of your project, less frequently in the middle part, and hardly ever toward the end. Us boat renovators may learn slow, but we learn good.

Frequently the only difference between a truly professional job and a hack amateur disaster is in the quality of the tools used. You'll find very few professional or accomplished amateur boatbuilders buying tools from the Kmart bargain table. They've flipped the sign too many times and know better.

This is not to say that the best tools are the most expensive either, or that new tools are better than used tools. Buying the best means getting the best value for each dollar spent, and to do this effectively, you must learn to consider many variables, such as how often the tool will be used and what the tool is going to be used for. You must learn to fit the tool to the job, not vice versa.

Electric drills are a good example of good value in an inexpensive tool. If you use a drill just to drill small-diameter holes, you don't need a variable-speed, reversible, electronically governed monstrosity with a ½-inch chuck and a 12-inch price tag. A simple, single-speed, nonreversible, ¼-inch drill will do just fine. These simple drills retail for between $20 and $60. If you're tempted to buy the $20 model, you can save yourself a step by dropping your $20 straight into the trash can; spend $40 or $50 and you'll have the drill for the rest of your life.

There has been a flood of dangerously inadequate tools on the market in recent years. Modern tool manufacturers are facing the same ruinous increases in costs that other manufacturers are facing, and they're constantly being hammered (bad pun, good analogy) by competition and expensive liability suits. Companies who cater to professionals and knowledgeable amateurs have responded by raising their prices dramatically simply because they know this market won't buy poorly made tools regardless of the price. The companies that cater to the homeowner and inexperienced amateur market, however, have responded to the prevailing economy by dramatically reducing the quality of their products.

One clear example of this drop in quality is the bandsaw sold by Sears/Craftsman and made by Wen Manufacturing. For decades this little 12-inch bandsaw dominated the low end of the market. It was never a great saw, but for the money it was quite adequate. Thousands were sold to home craftsmen, and a surprisingly large number found their way into professional shops all around the world. I used one regularly for years without a single breakdown or even a legitimate complaint. The current replacement for this saw is a plastic and sheet-metal monstrosity so bad that to call it a cheap piece of junk would be to shower praise on it. And don't jump to the conclusion that I have an ax to grind with Sears either. I don't. Their industrial-rated tools are uniformly excellent, they make good on their warranties, and their prices are quite competitive. What they've done with their bandsaw is no different from other large tool companies putting low-priced tools on the market that are largely unusable.

USED TOOLS ARE GOOD TOOLS

I'm a firm believer in buying used tools whenever I can. For one thing, used tools can save you a lot of money, and for another, many old tools are of a higher quality than their new counterparts. Also, many tools useful to a boatbuilder simply aren't made any more. Those neat little 24-inch folding rulers with the brass hinges that were made in England by Stanley are one example. And although a limited selection of caulking irons is still available, no one to my knowledge makes caulking mallets anymore. I found a good one for 50¢ in a box of junk in the back of a shop in Kittery, Maine, and between the proprietor and me, only one of us knew what it was.

Another reason I like to buy used tools is that I get a big kick out of hanging around flea markets, junk shops, and antique stores. Even when I just stop to look around, I almost always find something I really need or have always wanted, or at least it seems that way at the time. And funny things happen in these stores that don't happen anywhere else. On one occasion, I stopped by one of those roadside flea markets where dealers set up little tables outdoors. One of the dealers had about 20 sets of machinist's calipers of different shapes, sizes, and types all arranged in neat rows on his table. Now it just so happened that I perceived a need for a pair of 6-inch, outside calipers.

"How much'er tha calipers?" I asked, trying not to appear too interested and thereby jack the price up on myself.

"Three bucks," the proprietor answered without even looking up.

At the time, $3 was about half the price of a new pair—not a great deal as flea markets go, but what the heck.

"Sounds good ta me," I said, reaching for my wallet. And as I paused a moment to consider which pair I wanted, the dealer scooped all 20 sets into a paper bag and handed it to me. Ten years later, I still have calipers scattered all over my shop.

The biggest problem I have with buying used tools isn't that I can't find the right things to do the job. In fact, I have a tendency to find so many irresistible treasures at bargain prices that I risk ending up with boxes full of junk I really don't need. I've discovered, however, that I can fight this tendency to buy unnecessary tools with simple expediency: I always take my wife, Susan, along on these trips, and I show her everything before I decide whether to buy it. Susan doesn't know the first thing about tools, but she has the uncanny ability to know what I want. When I show her a prospective purchase, she'll look first at the object, then at me. If at this point she rolls her eyes skyward and heaves a mighty sigh of resignation, I know it's something I must have. If on the other hand she knits her brows and glares at me as though I'd just tracked fresh dog mess into the house, I realize I must already have one, or at least I can get along without it. The amazing thing about this whole process is that she is always right. Someday I'm going to try her out on the stock market.

Unless you can find someone with Susan's incredible perception, you'll need to develop your own method of resisting the temptation to buy useless tools. First, make it a hard-and-fast rule never to buy anything you really don't need, regardless how big a bargain you think it is. Second, don't buy any tool that has a part missing or needs a lot of work to repair. Many people buy incomplete tools thinking they will make or buy the missing part, but they seldom do it, and the tool ends up in the junk box. Besides, our business is fixing up boats, not tools.

One notable exception to this rule is planes with missing plane irons. Good irons are available in most hardware stores, and the missing iron often means a bargain price. Also, a good, healthy coat of red rust seldom hurts well-made tools. If the rust has scaled or pitted excessively, though, the tool may be worthless.

Third, never ever buy a tool for its collector value. Tool collectors are the scourge of the Earth. They should be outlawed, banished, horsewhipped, hog-tied, and dipped headfirst into vats of unpleasant liquids. Why do I feel so strong about collectors? Because they buy up all the good old tools before decent, honest folks like you and me can get to them, that's why. They also run the prices out of sight. And besides, the guy who made my 50¢ caulking mallet made it to caulk seams, not to hang on the wall of some yuppie lubber who thinks it's a sawed-off croquet mallet. I feel so strongly about this that every time I see a choice tool I think might appeal to collectors, I buy it and put it in a big glass case in my office. I know it sounds like a lot, but to me no sacrifice is too great if I can manage to keep some of these nice old tools out of the hands of collectors.

BORROW IF YOU CAN, RENT IF YOU MUST

Let's face it, sometimes it just isn't practical to buy every tool you need. If you want to bore a hole for a replacement keel bolt through several feet of oak deadwood, you're going to need something more than your average electric drill. The old-timers would burn holes like this with iron rods heated white hot, or they bored them with huge T-handled augers that are simply no longer available (damned collectors). If you're built like Arnold Schweatzenberger and have an afternoon to kill, you might be able to do the job with a standard brace fitted with an extension bit, but your best bet is a big electric drill with a ¾-inch chuck, a lot of torque, and a long bit. To buy one of these monsters (such as the Milwaukee Hole Hawg) new would cost about $300 plus about $100 for a decent bit. That's a lot for a tool you might use twice a year. Your local plumber has one of these rigs in the back of his van right now, and if he is the friendly sort, he might just loan it to you. But come to think of it, I've never met a friendly plumber, especially when I try to borrow his tools. Maybe you'd be better off just renting it.

There are tool-rental outlets in or around most major population centers, and they are definitely the best source for expensive tools that are used infrequently. Big drills, paint sprayers, sand blasters, and arc welders are all available at the local rent-all for a few dollars a day. The one nearest me, a franchise operation with the unlikely name of Grand Rental Station, rents the Hole Hawg and bit combination for $12. If you're a true traditionalist, however, and want to try the hot-iron-rod route, go ahead and have at it. Just make sure you have a fire extinguisher handy and your insurance paid up, and get one of the kids to videotape the process—you might just be a candidate for that TV show that features funny home movies.

KEEP IT SHARP

If you want a quick judge of the skill of a wooden-boat builder, or of any wood-worker for that matter, take a look at his chisels. If they're neatly stored in a leather or canvas tool roll, and if they're unbelievably sharp, you can bet they belong to a good craftsman. If they are anything less, the craftsmanship will be less.

When you buy a new cutting tool, it will never be sharp enough to use. Even the most expensive plane or chisel will have only a rudimentary edge that will require grinding to the proper bevels and honing to a final edge. When you buy a used cutting tool, the edge will likely be in terrible shape and may require extensive grinding to resurrect. However, a dull blade should never deter you from buying a used tool because, once you develop the technique, you can restore a blade to top performance quickly and easily.

The quality of the steel a tool is made from will affect the edge it will take. Most knife blades today are made from one or another kind of stainless steel and are impossible to sharpen. If you do manage to get a keen edge on one of these knives, it won't last. The edge will simply collapse as soon as you use it. A good blade will be easy to sharpen, and it will hold its edge for a reasonable stint of normal use. High-carbon tool steel is best for most edged tools. Carbide and stainless steel are worthless for hand tools.

My old Grandpappy taught me how to sharpen tools when he presented me with my first pocketknife on my eighth birthday. It wasn't just any old pocketknife either. It was a genuine Official Boy Scout model with a can opener, a screw-driver, and a big fat carbon-steel blade that gleamed as bright as an eight-year-old's eyes.

As he showed me how to use an oilstone, he told me in a deep and solemn voice resonant with the wisdom of age and experience, "If ya ever really need yer knife, ya ain't gonna need a dull one." Then he gave me something that, although I didn't realize it at the time, would prove much more important than my first knife. After digging around in the attic for a bit, he came up with the old razor strop he had retired from active duty when the convenience of Gillette Blue Blades seduced him away from his straight razor. He then proceeded to show me the difference between a sharp knife and a really sharp knife: 25 strokes on the rough side of the oilstone—25 on the fine side; 25 strokes on the black side of the strop—25 on the natural side. Then he rolled up his sleeve and, as my young eyes bugged in amazement, effort-lessly shaved a patch of hair from the back of his arm with my new knife.

I don't recall what ever became of that knife, but I used the strop well into my thirties. When I finally wore it in half, I used the ends until there was simply noth-ing left and I was forced to get a replacement.

Since that memorable birthday, I have tried every imaginable technique for sharpening tools that has come along: Arkansas hard and soft stones, Washita stones, India stones, Japanese waterstones, diamond stones, mechanical jigs, special tool grinders, and even a liquid sharpening solution called Razor Sharp that a couple of hucksters put on the market in the 1960s. And it was only just recently that I discovered a sharpening technique that would beat my old Grandpappy's stone-and-hone method. Now I use a 6-inch pink grinding wheel and a hard-felt buffing wheel charged with gray buffing compound. These wheels are mounted on a 6-inch Delta bench grinder that is used exclusively for sharpening tools. With this combination I can put an edge on a dull tool in just a few seconds. The edge is first ground to the appropriate angle until a wire forms all along the cutting edge. Then, moving to the hard-felt wheel, I simply buff off the wire. Then five or six strokes on the strop and I have an edge that would make Grandpappy proud. The whole thing takes less time to do than to talk about.

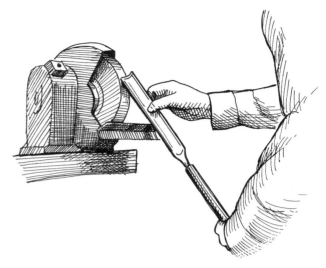

Figure 4-1.
Sharpening a gouge on a grinder.

Just because this grind-and-buff technique works for me doesn't mean it will work for you. In fact, no two craftsmen ever seem to agree on the subject of sharpening tools. One will insist waterstones can't be beat while another will claim oilstones are easier and quicker and better. You must experiment with the various techniques until you find the one that is best for you. Whatever technique you use, it is imperative that you learn to sharpen tools properly. Tools that are anything less than razor-sharp simply won't do what you want them to do.

THE BASIC TOOL KIT

One of the questions I get most often when discussing hand tools with people who would like to start their own tool kit is "What do I need for basic tools?" As with most general questions, the answer is equally nebulous: "It depends."

But the question is sincere, and it deserves a sincere answer. I usually respond by describing my own basic tool kit. Since I do a lot of work on other people's boats, I need a tool kit I can take with me in a dinghy. Ideally this kit would contain everything I need to do a particular job and nothing extra. And over the years I've developed a kit that comes about as close to this admittedly unachievable goal as I ever expect to get.

THE TOOL BOX

I must admit to a strong prejudice against store-bought tool boxes. After all, don't you aspire to be a craftsman equal to the task of renovating a fine old wooden boat, one of the most intricate objects ever fashioned from the trunk of a tree by the hands of man? Don't you continually strive to hone your skills to ever-increasing keenness by approaching projects of ever-increasing complexity? Are you not invigorated and is your spirit not renewed by each new challenge and opportunity to fashion useful and beautiful objects from otherwise useless materials? Of course you are. Then purge your mind of any ideas of buying a tool box. Build your own, and make a statement to the world that you are indeed a craftsman who cares about your tools, and you're proud of your ability to use them.

Tool boxes for use around boats should always be made of wood, and they should always have a tight-fitting cover that latches securely. It doesn't really matter what kind of wood—plywood will do fine—but wood will be much kinder to your tools than any other material. Moisture won't condense inside wood boxes, so tools in a wood box are less inclined to rust, and wood won't chafe the finish or ruin the edge of your cutting tools.

Metal tool boxes have no place around boats for fairly obvious reasons, but it's amazing how often you see them used by people who should know better. Not only are metal boxes quickly consumed by rust, but the tools inside them won't last long either. The sharp corners on metal boxes are forever gouging and scratching decks, and the tools rattle incessantly. Plastic boxes are a little better than metal ones if you must have a store-bought box, but watch out. Even the most expensive plastic boxes condense moisture, and they have ferrous-metal latches and hinge pins that will become gobs of rust in short order.

My personal tool box is modeled after one that had belonged to my great-grandfather. It would be nice to claim that this ancient ancestor of mine had been a world-renowned shipwright who built Baltimore clippers or perhaps Nantucket whalers, but he wasn't. He was a lawyer, and he took the tools in trade for legal services rendered, as was the fashion with legal counselors of 100 years ago. The tools originally in the box had long been scattered far and wide, commandeered by generations of children who preceded me to build treehouses and forts against the constant attacks by the tribe of imaginary savages who lived in the woodlot in back of the barn. In fact by the time I came along, hardly anything was left of the box itself, but my memory of it would later be sufficient to use it as a model of my own tool box.

Whereas the original was built of oak or maybe chestnut, my box is built of solid mahogany and measures 11 inches high by 13 inches wide by 31 inches long. It is heavy and strong enough to do duty as a workbench or a step stool as required. The top is 4 inches deep, and the entire thing has compartments built for specific tools. The corners are joined by hand-cut dovetails, giving it a shippy sort of look that mimics the original. I finished the outside of the box with a simple wipedown of tung oil. But that was long ago, and the present finish is a mixture of sunbaked salt spray and WD-40 that's totally self-maintaining. The box is decorated with an intricate design of scratches, dents, and gouges from a hundred boats and dinghies and docks and from countless trips to here and there and back again in the bed of a pickup truck. It looks like what it is: a tough old veteran that no longer needs to prove anything to anybody and knows it.

The contents of my box are listed in Figure 4-2; most are self-explanatory, but it might be helpful to go over some of the major items.

TOOLS

24-inch bubble level

32-inch Sandvik crosscut saw

25-inch Ulmia bowsaw

Yankee #103 push-type screwdriver

Extra bits for above

Assorted screwdrivers

12-inch carpenter's square

12-inch machinist's combination square

Bevel gauge

Protractor

Stanley #68A 24-inch folding rule

12-foot steel tape

Stanley loose-leg wing dividers/compass

6-oz. Warrington hammer

16-oz. Estwing claw hammer

Stanley #80-702 carpenter's vise

Set machinist's twist drills 1/16 to 1/2 inch

Set Fuller tapered bits w/ counterbores

Bit brace with augers

Set Vix bits

8-inch Vise-Grips

4- and 6-inch adjustable wrenches

Electrician's pliers

Needle-nose pliers

waterpump pliers

Utility knife w/ extra blades

Razor scraper

Small diamond hone

Small Carborundum stone

Set Stanley #60 chisels

Set Buck Brothers gouges

Stanley #60½ block plane

14-inch jack plane

Record #788 rabbet plane

Chalkline

Makita 9.6-volt cordless screwdriver

Dovetail saw

Heavy-duty scissors

Center punch

Drift punches (1/8 & 1/4)

Small cold chisel

10-inch bastard file

8-inch rattail file

Lenox folding hacksaw

1-inch pull scraper

Coping saw

Small combination tin snips

2½-inch slick

6-inch Jorgensen bar clamps

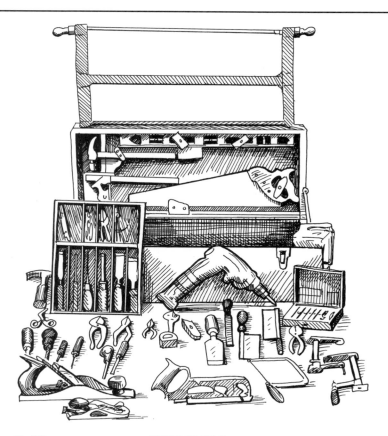

SUPPLIES

Assorted fasteners

Razor blades

Carpenter's chalk

Electrician's tape

Tongue depressors

Sharpie markers

Pencils and notebook

WD-40

Aspirin, Band-Aids

Cutter's insect repellent

Sunscreen

Stainless wire

Epoxy

Contact cement

Rubber gloves

Acid brushes

Disposable paint brushes

**Figure 4-2.
The tools and supplies in Great Grandpappy's tool chest.**

SAWS

The old-time craftsman and well-equipped shipwright usually had a large assortment of handsaws, each with its own specialized function. There were saws with large teeth set for a wide kerf (the cut the saw makes) that would only be used for ripping softwood. Others would have small teeth set fine and would only be used for crosscuts in hardwood. There would be backsaws, bowsaws, tenon saws, dovetail saws and a great little gadget called a floorboard saw designed so it could be used for plunge cuts.

A triangular file and saw set were a standard part of every tool box because these old-timers almost always sharpened and set their saws themselves to match a specific task. A ripping blade might have as few as four teeth per inch (referred to as a *four-point blade*) with a deep gullet and a wide set to facilitate clearing chips and to prevent binding. Crosscut saws would have 12 to 16 teeth per inch, and cabinet saws might have as many as 24 teeth per inch. Frequently if a craftsman needed a new saw, he would simply file all the teeth off an old one and recut the saw to the pattern he needed.

Today's craftsman doesn't need this awesome assortment of handsaws because many of the functions they once performed are now accomplished more quickly with power saws. Ripping that softwood plank, for example, is much easier on a table saw or with your basic 7¼-inch Skilsaw. In fact, I don't know of any company making a true ripsaw anymore, although the Garrett Wade catalog lists a 5½-point saw that would probably do the job very nicely.

Most of today's woodworkers have dispensed with the saw set and file used for sharpening and setting blades. The handsaws of yesterday were made from iron or malleable steel, so they were soft and easy to file. Today's saws are made from much better steel, and the teeth are tempered for maximum toughness and durability. New saws stay sharper much longer than the old ones, but when they finally do get dull, they need to be sent out to a competent tool grinder for sharpening. A file won't touch them.

A fine-tooth backsaw or dovetail saw with about 28 teeth per inch is an exception to this rule. When new, these useful little saws frequently are dull, and most tool grinders don't have a wheel small enough to deal with the fine cut. You must sharpen these saws yourself using a triangular jeweler's file. Usually these saws do not have tempered teeth, but if they do, you can remove the temper by simply heating the edge of the blade to red with a propane torch and letting it cool slowly. These fine teeth are also impossible to set with a standard saw set. I find a small pair of needle-nose pliers and a critical eyeball combine to do a fine job.

Handsaws

Let's quickly discuss the important characteristics of the basic handsaws you should have in your tool box. While "handsaw" is a generic term that applies to any small saw not operated by power, it also applies specifically to the familiar wide-blade saw with a wooden handle. Today, these saws are available in a very limited variety, with 8- and 12-point saws being the most common. Perhaps in an attempt to assuage their guilt for not offering the consumer a wider selection, manufacturers like to call these saws "combination rip and crosscut." Regardless of what they're called, these are crosscut saws that are useless for ripping.

The saw I have in my basic box is a 22-inch Sandvik with a 12-point blade. I've had this little gem for years, and I find it will handle about 90 percent of all my crosscut needs.

Bowsaws

If I had to go through life with only one saw, it would definitely be a bowsaw. Bowsaws have an H-shaped wooden frame with an interchangeable blade on one side and a Spanish windlass or turnbuckle for tensioning the blade on the other. They are available in all sizes from tiny jeweler's saws just several inches long to large bucksaws with 3- or 4-foot blades designed for cutting firewood and other rough cuts. All but the bucksaws have turning blades so long, rips can be made by swinging the handle out of the way of the stock. The middle sizes, with an assortment of thin and thick blades, are versatile and handy for both curved and straight cuts, and they can do practically anything a power bandsaw can do.

Perhaps because many craftsmen feel that various power saws have taken their place, bowsaws seem to have fallen out of fashion in the past 50 years or so. This is a real shame because bowsaws are clean and quiet and very satisfying to use. Many times they do the job in less time than it would take to get out the extension cord and plug in a power saw.

The bowsaw in my kit is 18 inches long, and I always carry both 4- and 7-TPI (teeth per inch) ⅜-inch-wide blades. Because a new blade is cheaper than having the old one sharpened, blades are simply discarded when they get dull.

The simple design of bowsaws makes them the only major tool I ever suggest anyone make themselves. Buy the blade and cut the frame out of any hardwood. Do a good job and your bowsaw will make you look craftsmanlike and will cut just as well as the store-bought saw. Besides, 20 bucks is 20 bucks.

Backsaws

Backsaws are so called because they have a stiff spine of reinforcing steel or brass along the back edge of their rectangular blades. Like bowsaws, they come in all sizes from tiny 6-inch fret saws to large 3- and 4-footers. Regardless of the size, they all have fine teeth, with 15 to 20 TPI being standard. Backsaws were once indispensable for use in miter boxes, but this function has been largely taken over by power miter boxes for all but the most finicky of craftsmen. They still have many uses, however, and are an essential part of any basic tool box.

I have two backsaws in my basic box. A 10-inch, 16-TPI dovetail saw and a little 8-inch job with 17 TPI that Garret Wade calls a Gent's Saw.

Japanese Saws

Japanese or Dozuki saws have gained a large and enthusiastic following among boatbuilders in recent years. Dozukis come in an impressive assortment of shapes and sizes, and their use appears to be as much a matter of attitude as of function. Craftsmen who favor these saws seem to approach their work like a sumo wrestler stalking an opponent. I don't have any objection to these saws. In fact I've traveled to Japan and have seen Japanese craftsmen do amazing things with them. But I do think that, in the same way savage warriors of primitive cultures would eat the heart of vanquished foes to gain their courage, some of us believe we might achieve the skills of those we admire by acquiring their trappings. Thus we're beguiled into spending extra cash for a Jimmy Connors or Chris Evert tennis racket; and Larry Bird makes more money selling sneakers than he does playing basketball.

Since there's nothing I want to do with a saw I can't do with the ones I already have, my box doesn't contain any Dozuki saws. Besides the sandals hurt my feet, and I can't seem to get the little tea ceremony performed before each use right. Don't let me stop you, though. Give them a try. You might like them.

CHISELS AND GOUGES

To the skilled boatbuilder and boat renovator, a good assortment of chisels and gouges is like a lasso to a cowboy or a rifle to a soldier—you just can't get along without it.

There are literally dozens and perhaps hundreds of types and shapes and sizes of chisels and gouges on the market today. We probably have a wider assortment of these tools available to us than did our ancestors, and there just isn't any other type of hand tool you can say that about. Ironically, though, even with this vast assortment of new chisels and gouges to choose from, the best tools are still found in antique stores.

In the past, the best chisels were made with a socket on the end of the blade. A tapered wooden handle fit into this socket, giving the handle and the chisel great strength and resiliency. Today the majority of chisels and gouges have a pointed tang end that fits into a wood or plastic handle reinforced with a ferrule. This arrangement doesn't work nearly as well as the socket, but it's much cheaper and easier for the manufacturers to make them this way. Because of the collector value of the old tools, good socket chisels at reasonable prices are becoming scarce in the antique shops, so a good set of modern chisels may be your only bet.

I'm lucky to have a set of Stanley #40 bench chisels with heavy blades and black plastic handles that are practically indestructible. These chisels haven't been made since the early 1950s, but they do turn up occasionally at flea markets.

A medium-size slick is one of the most useful chisels to a boatbuilder. Slicks have a heavy 2- to 4-inch-wide blade, an 8- to 24-inch wooden handle, and may have a radiused cutting edge. Despite their imposing size, they are kept razor-sharp and used for the finest shaving and paring jobs. Their large size and heft allow precise control when just a sliver needs to be removed from a joint to make a good fit a perfect fit. Many of the old-time slicks you find in antique stores—huge things with 4-inch blades and 36-inch handles, used by builders of the large sailing ships of the last century—are just too big for our purposes, and the collectors have driven the prices of these monsters out of sight anyway. New slicks are available

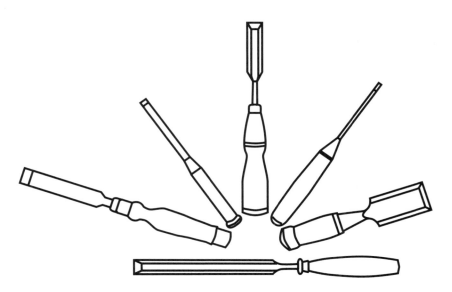

Figure 4-3.
An assortment of
chisels.

from Woodcraft in Woburn, Massachusetts (see Appendix B), but your best bet is to
fashion one for yourself out of a large, old firmer chisel.

Sharpening

To sharpen chisels and slicks, first grind a primary bevel of 25 to 30 degrees,
then a secondary bevel of 30 to 35 degrees on top of that, as shown in Figure 4-4.

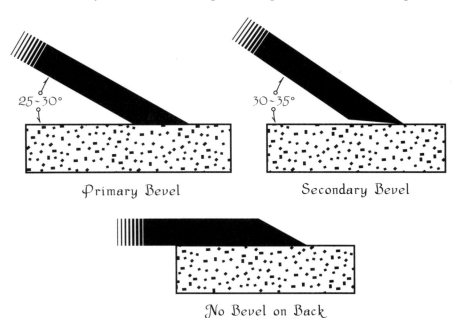

Figure 4-4.
Correct angles for
sharpening chisels.

You will determine the exact bevel you like with experience. A steeper, more blunt bevel gives a heavier, more durable edge that stands up well to hardwoods like teak and oak, while a smaller angle gives a slightly sharper edge that works well with softer woods such as cedar or pine. With chisels, all grinding is done on the bevel side of the blade; never ever touch the back to the grinder. Hone the back on a fine oilstone or waterstone, keeping it flat at all times.

Gouges are sharpened just like chisels except that the secondary bevel is ground on the back of the blade instead of the front.

The Stanley #40s are too heavy to carry around in my basic kit. Instead I have a set of Stanley #60s, the common garden-variety chisels with the yellow plastic handles you'll find in your neighborhood hardware store. These are made from good steel, they work perfectly well, and they cost about half as much as the fancy Marples and Sorbys you get from a tool-supply house. My box contains ¼-, ⅜-, ½-, ¾-, and 1-inch firmer chisels; a 2½-inch slick; and ¾- and 1-inch Buck Brothers gouges. I also carry a couple of old junk chisels that I use for scraping sealant, opening paint cans, and loaning to moochers in boatyards.

PLANES

On those rare days when the words I would write will not come and the sky hangs heavy overhead, when every little noise is a distraction, and every distraction is an annoyance, and every annoyance is a burden, I shuffle myself off to the woodshed, select a fat chunk of seasoned oak firewood and chock it firmly into the bench vise with the flattest side upward. Then, taking my heavy cast-iron scrub plane, I stroke away the torn and broken fibers of split wood until the surface is scalloped like the surface of the sea in the first breeze after a long calm. Then taking my jointer plane with its exaggerated 24-inch bed, I work away at the scallops. And when they are gone and the wood is perfectly flat, I continue moving the plane in long, full strokes, enjoying the pungent odor of fresh-cut oak and the soft hum of the iron, until my arms grow tired with the pleasant ache of exertion and my feet are buried to the ankles in soft, golden curls of wood. After a brief rest, I continue working on the log with my short-bodied smooth plane set to take only the finest of shavings, and the surface of the old piece of firewood is rendered as fine as that on the most extravagant of furniture. In no time at all, the old planes have stripped the ugly, rough surface from the wood and the gloom from my soul. No matter how many times I do this, the newly exposed intricacies of grain and texture are like a wonderful new discovery at the dawn of time. No man, no matter how foul his mood or how dark his thoughts, can perform this exercise without becoming one with his maker and at peace with himself.

Using a sharp and finely adjusted plane is an experience that can't be described with mere words, and most neophytes who have not actually witnessed a skilled craftsman using hand planes have no idea what can be done with them. Even more than other hand tools, they look deceptively easy to use, but attempting to use an improperly tuned and dull plane has to be one of the most frustrating things an aspiring craftsman can encounter.

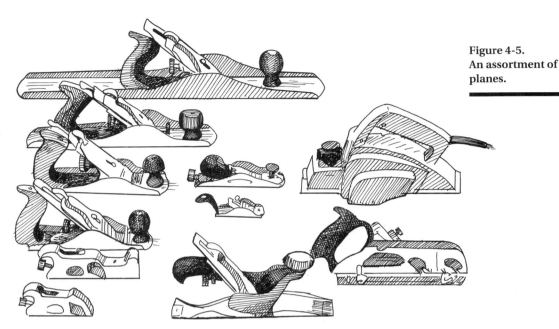

**Figure 4-5.
An assortment of
planes.**

A plane with anything less than an absolutely sharp iron is worse than useless.
It will chatter and gouge and chip and ruin your work. Even with a sharp iron, a
plane not properly adjusted will either gouge your work or will refuse to cut at all.
And then, when you finally do get it squared away with a sharp iron adjusted just
right, your troubles are far from over. Each piece of wood will have a personality all
its own, and any attempt to plane against the lay of the grain is sure to meet with
disaster. You must learn to read the surface of each board you plane, and this can
only be done with practice and experience. Occasionally a board must be planed in
both directions at once, and that, my friends, is a real challenge.

Yes, planes are temperamental and hard to learn to use, but once you master
them, you can make them do things no other tool can do. They are worth the effort.
So hie yourself off to the woodshed, pick out a fat chunk with straight grain and no
knots, and practice.

There are three hand planes in my basic box. Most smoothing work is done
with a venerable 14-inch jack plane of undetermined ancestry that I found in my
father-in-law's garage. It's old and pitted with the rust of neglect, but it works like a
charm. Less demanding work is done with a Stanley #60½ low-angle block plane.
The low angle of the blade and the adjustable throat make this plane useful for end
grain and indispensable for plywood. I also use it for radiusing and chamfering
planks and beams and for making the final, critical fit in joints.

The third plane in my basic kit is a Record #788 rabbet plane (the English call
them rebates) that I use anywhere wood needs to be planed right up next to a
shoulder, such as in a stepped scarf joint for patching plywood hulls (see Chapter
Seven) or for cutting the gains (progressively tapered rabbets) on the ends of a lapstrake plank. The #788 also has a handy provision that allows you to move the iron

all the way forward so it can be used as a crude but effective bullnose plane for planing into corners.

MEASURING AND MARKING TOOLS

Measuring and marking tools are a major part of any boatbuilder's basic tool kit primarily because accurate measuring and marking are such important parts of any job on a boat.

Any tool box will need several rules. The little 24-inch folding job with the brass hinges I mentioned earlier (Stanley #68A) is handy for most linear measuring. If you can't find one of these in an antique store (and you probably can't), a regular carpenter's folding rule cut off at 24 inches makes a usable if woefully inadequate substitute. Measurements longer than 2 feet are handled with a 12-foot steel tape or a 100-foot reel tape.

A proper bevel gauge is an important inclusion. Get the kind with the metal stock and the wing nut on the end; the wooden ones with the wing nut on the side are a nuisance because the nut gets in the way of at least half your measurements. Most boatbuilders make their own bevel boards to use with their bevel gauges. This is nothing more than a piece of aluminum or other suitable material about 4 X 8 inches on which angles from 0 to 45 degrees (in both directions) are laid out and scribed (see Figure 7-14). I keep two or three bevel boards in the shop, but when I travel to a job, I prefer to use a large plastic protractor I borrowed from my son's school bag (he had an extra). It doesn't do much to foster the mystique of the trade, but it works.

I have two squares in my box: a small 16-inch carpenter's square and a 12-inch Starrett machinist's square. The machinist's square measures 45 and 90 degree angles, and with a little notch in the end to hold the point of a pencil, it doubles as a dandy marking gauge.

One of the slickest tools I have in my collection . . . ah . . . er, I mean the case where I keep tools safe from collectors, is an 18 X 27-inch folding square made from birch and brass by F. Gibson & Sons of Glasgow, Scotland. Unfortunately the wood is warped enough to render it unusable, but if some enterprising toolmaker were to make a modern version, it would neatly solve the problem of how to get a large square into a small tool box. I bet they'd sell a ton of them. (Tom Lie-Nielson of Lie-Nielson Tool Works, Inc. [see Appendix B], maker of a line of exquisite hand tools, is considering reissuing the Stanley #68 folding rule and is "intrigued" by the folding square. Ah well, maybe someday.)

There are dozens of other tools in my basic box: a compass, a set of scribes, drill bits, clamps, pliers, hammers, various scrapers, a small pry bar, and a big box of Band-Aids, just to name a few. I don't carry a lignum-vitae mall. I know it's a sacrilege, but when I need to hammer a chisel, I just whack away with the old claw hammer. And unlike many who work on wooden boats, I don't carry a rosewood marking gauge or a try square or a spokeshave or a drawknife. I lugged these things around with me for years and hardly ever used them. They are all useful items that I keep in my shop, but their functions can be served well by other tools, and their weight doesn't warrant keeping them in my portable box.

What you end up with in your basic tool box will reflect the way you work and the kind of work you do. The trick is to acquire tools one at a time and get to know each tool intimately; it will repay your efforts a thousandfold.

POWER TOOLS

Power tools are the primary reason that hand tools are fun to use. This statement seems to be pretty silly at first, but it's a truism. By turning over all the drudgery of heavy, repetitious work to power tools, you're left with the time and the inclination to do your finest work with your hand tools. Drill half a dozen keel-bolt holes through white oak deadwood with a hand auger and you'll soon understand why it's called boring. Sawing out a deck beam with a bowsaw is fun and satisfying work; two deck beams is just work; a dozen is an ordeal. The bandsaw will do the job quickly, and it won't complain a bit.

There isn't room here to go into a detailed discussion of all the power tools on the market—there are entire books devoted to this single subject—but I'll try to hit the high points of the tools you'll find most useful in boat work. My recommendations shouldn't stop you from experimenting for yourself, but power tools are very expensive, so don't buy tools you don't need. And it always bears repeating: Buy the best.

CIRCULAR SAWS

The most popular circular saws are table saws, power miter boxes (popularly called chop saws—presumably because of their tendency to chop off parts of the operator), radial-arm saws, and portable circular saws, often referred to as Skilsaws. The size of circular saws is determined by the diameter of the blade.

Figure 4-6. Checking a saw blade with a dial indicator.

You will definitely need a 7¼-inch Skilsaw, and if you can afford it, a small table saw will pay its own way in short order. An 8-inch table saw is fine, but a 10-inch saw is more versatile and has more guts, and of course, it costs more. The chop saw is most useful for interior work, miters, squaring the ends of stock, and for cutting stock to length.

The radial-arm saw is the best stationary circular saw to have for all-around use as it combines many of the functions of a table saw and a chop saw. I have a 10-inch DeWalt that's a beauty, but it cost over $1,000. The best deal in a radial-arm saw is a used, old-style Craftsman, frequently found in the classifieds for about $200.

When buying a used circular saw, always check to see that the blade runs perfectly true

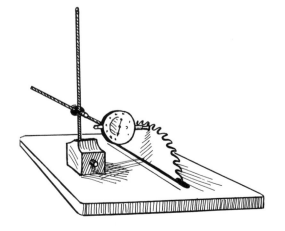

with no wobble. A wobbly blade means the arbor is bent (assuming the blade is flat) and the saw is worthless. The best way to check for wobble is with a dial indicator as shown in Figure 4-6.

Blades

The most important thing about a circular saw isn't the saw but the blade you put on it. You can make do with an inexpensive saw, but never buy a cheap blade. In fact, don't be surprised if the blade actually costs more than the saw. High-quality carbide is the only way to go when selecting a circular-saw blade, simply because carbide will outlast steel better than 10 to 1. Forest blades are first-quality, as are Systematics and DMLs, but stay away from the imported blades: they have attractive price tags, but they're unbalanced, use cheap carbide, and will throw teeth quicker than brides throw bouquets. Freud blades may be a good compromise if you must save money. They use good carbide and a lot of it, but they tend to have balance problems. The average price of a Freud blade can be half the price of the other three types mentioned.

BANDSAWS

**Figure 4-7.
Using a bandsaw.**

If you can only afford one power saw, make it a bandsaw—it will do almost everything other saws will do and more. A good bandsaw will resaw rough timber into planks, planks into boards, and boards into veneer. It will cut curves where you want curves and straight where you want straight. Unlike circular-saw blades, bandsaw blades are inexpensive, so it doesn't cost a fortune to have an assortment of blades on hand to answer different cutting needs—thin blades with fine teeth for intricate shapes and wide blades with coarse teeth for long, straight rips and resawing. For general work, I favor skip-tooth blades—so called because they have every other tooth removed—and with four or six TPI, I don't have to change blades that often.

When bandsaw blades get dull or break, they're simply replaced. You can even buy blade stock in 100-foot rolls and make your own with a small spot-welder if you like.

The Delta 14-inch bandsaw (size is determined by the throat, which is the distance between the blade and the back frame) seems to be the standard by which all others are judged. There are many cheap copies of this saw made under about a dozen brand names (JET and Grizzly are just two) that sell for about half the price of the real thing. These imports are almost all made in Korea where production standards are quite low and quality control is practically nonexistent. They may represent a good value if you're on a tight budget, but don't buy one if you don't have to. Service from the supplier will be lousy, parts will be expensive and hard to get, and when you do get the parts you order, they probably won't fit.

Stay away from the 3-wheeled bandsaws that are on the market, regardless of who makes them. There are some good ones, but they're very expensive, and the cheap ones are worthless. Once again your best deal is an old 12-inch Craftsman from the classified ads in your local paper.

PLANERS

A good planer has always been an essential tool for serious wooden-boat work. When you buy wood (and much more on this in the next chapter) it will either be rough or it will be finished in some nominal thickness convenient to the lumberyard. Four-quarter stock (¾ inch thick) is what is usually available, but this thickness has very few actual applications in boat work. You will be needing stock with a thickness of ½ inch, $^{15}/_{16}$ inch, ¼ inch, and so on. The only practical way to get wood to the thickness you need is to plane it yourself. This way, you'll get just what you want, and you can often save enough money to pay for the planer with just one major project.

One of the most important recent developments in power tools for the boatbuilder or renovator was the introduction of lightweight, inexpensive planers. I bought one of the first ones on the market (a Ryobi) about eight years ago, and I liked it so much that I eventually got rid of the huge Powermatic planer that was taking up about a quarter of the floor space in my shop. The little Ryobi does about 75 percent of the work the behemoth did, and I do the rest with a hand plane or farm it out to a local cabinet shop. The little Ryobi has had constant heavy-duty use for the past eight years, and it's still going strong. And it's light enough to take it right to the job when I'm working in a boatyard.

JOINTERS

Jointers are essential tools for a well-equipped cabinet shop, but they have a more limited application for boat work. Jointers flatten stock and put a straight, square edge on boards. They're certainly handy to have; it's just that in boat work, you need curved beveled edges more often than you need square straight ones, and this is best done with hand planes.

The size of a jointer is determined by the length of the cutter head, which determines the width of the cut. Some cutter heads have two blades; the better ones have three. Since jointers are most useful in boat work for flattening stock, the bigger ones are more useful than the smaller ones, and a long bed is more useful than a short bed. So if you do decide you must have a jointer, get the biggest one you can; 6-inch should be a minimum, but 8-inch is better. Don't bother with the little 4-inch portable jobs—use a hand plane instead.

THE DRILL PRESS

A good, sturdy, floor-stand drill press is a wonderful addition to any shop. It can be used for sanding, grinding, buffing, and with the right attachments, even planing. I've seen drill presses used as milling machines and even as vertical lathes. In a pinch, they can even be used for drilling holes.

One of the handiest attachments for a drill press is a set of mortising chisels designed for cutting the rectangular slots for mortise-and-tenon joints but useful anytime you need a square hole. Any wooden-boat project is going to require piles and piles of bungs of different sizes, so a good set of bung cutters will be essential. Please don't try to cut bungs with a hand drill; you'll ruin the cutter and probably a few fingers to boot.

If you can't justify a full-size drill press right now, at least get one of those bench-top stands that holds a large hand drill so it can be used as a drill press. These actually work surprisingly well, and they'll do many of the things you would otherwise need a drill press to do. They're great for making bungs and they're portable, but don't expect them to handle heavy tasks like cutting mortises.

POWER SANDERS

Sanding is one of the drudgery jobs we all hate with a passion but that we all must face up to if we ever hope to achieve a decent-looking finish on our old wooden boats. And while power sanders don't make the job fast, easy, or enjoyable, they do make it infinitely faster and easier.

The more power sanders you have on hand, the better off you'll be. When friends drop by and offer to help, there will always be sanding to do, and when you're in the middle of a complicated job, it's real handy to have several sanders with different grits of paper mounted and ready to go. This saves time because you aren't continually changing paper, and it saves money because if you glue your paper to your sander as you should, it will usually tear and can't be reused when you remove it.

All power sanders are not created equal. The cheap orbital sanders, those featured in the Sunday-supplement ads for large department stores, have the unlikely ability to hold the sandpaper absolutely motionless while shaking the operator to pieces, they make more noise than a chain saw, and they don't cut at all. Before you buy sanders, make sure you read the little sign you made for your workbench. Buy the best.

Palm Sanders

Palm sanders are orbital sanders that move the paper in small circles (orbits) of about $\frac{1}{16}$ of an inch in diameter at an incredibly high speed—about 1,500 of them every second. They take a quarter sheet of sandpaper, and they are useful for general flat sanding and essential for finish sanding. A good palm sander is the first sander you should buy simply because it's the most versatile. Makita makes one that isn't bad once you remove the silly little dust bag that doesn't work and constantly gets in the way. But the best one on the market is the Porter Cable Model 330. It costs about 10 bucks more than the Makita, but it is quieter, heavier, and it cuts better than any of them. You can figure on spending from $50 to $60 on a good palm sander. If you can afford it, buy two.

Half-Sheet Pad Sanders

Pad sanders are also orbital sanders, but they're bigger, heavier, and usually a little slower (about 1,000 orbits per second) than palm sanders. These are larger, more powerful tools, taking a half sheet of paper and requiring two hands to use effectively. They are unsurpassed for sanding large flat areas with the coarser grits of paper, and they work well with the finer grits. Actually they don't do anything palm sanders won't do, they just do it quicker. Once again Porter Cable leads the pack; their Model 505 beats them all. You can expect to pay from $100 to $125 for a good half-sheet sander.

Disc Sanders

A big, fat disc sander with an 8-inch disc and a heavy-duty variable-speed motor is invaluable for general boat work. This one tool can be used for flattening stock, stripping paint, fairing, and grinding epoxy, as well as for rough sanding and sculpting intricate parts. For removing a lot of stock fast and efficiently, and other rough work, they are much easier to control than a belt sander. Fitted with a foam pad with a ¼-inch plywood disc glued to its surface and 80-grit paper, they will sand perfectly flat without gouging. And when fitted with a lamb's-wool pad, they make fine buffers and polishers.

Makita, Porter Cable, Milwaukee and the Sears Industrial are all good disc sanders. Because this is a heavy-duty tool, outside the realm of the average home handyman, it may be hard to find, and when you do find one, it will be expensive— usually about $200 at discount stores. Watch out for the low-priced Sears model. The one I tried lasted less than a week before the bearings burned out. But to Sears' credit, I got my money back with no questions asked.

A variable-speed hand drill with a sanding attachment in the chuck makes a handy disc sander for small jobs. They're awkward to hold, however, and they can get out of control easily and damage your work.

Random-Orbit Sanders

Random-orbit sanders combine the principles of the disc sander and the orbital-pad sander. They've been around for a long time in industrial applications and as finish sanders in autobody shops, and there are several models now on the market designed for woodwork.

The cutting surface of random-orbit sanders spins like a disc sander while an eccentric counterweight causes the pad to vibrate in tiny circles. This combined action removes stock quickly, like a disc sander, but without the troublesome cross-grain swirl marks disc sanders always leave. Porter Cable was the first to introduce this useful tool for woodworkers, but others are coming on the market all the time.

Belt Sanders

Sometimes I think more good woodwork is ruined by belt sanders in the hands of aggressive boat renovators than by all the dry rot and teredo worms combined. Otherwise rational workers who insist on using belt sanders for finish sanders or for stripping varnish and paint invariably end up with deep gouges and digs that are impossible to remove. Belt sanders cut fast, even with fine-grit belts, and this makes them attractive to those of us who hate sanding and want to get it over with as quickly as possible. But the fast cutting, and the fact that you can't see your work because the belt rollers get in the way, make them difficult to control. If you must use a belt sander, keep it away from your finish work.

One redeeming characteristic of a belt sander is the ability to fasten it upside down and use it as a stationery belt sander. I have a huge—4 X 23 (belt-size)—Makita that I can clamp to a bench or just clamp in the vice. I use this setup frequently for shaping and rough sanding small wooden parts. It works like a charm, and it saves the floor space a real stationery belt sander would demand. The thing is actually too heavy to use for anything else anyway.

Some belt sanders are built so that it's impossible to clamp them down, so check before you buy one.

HAND DRILLS

Hand drills are the handiest of all the small power tools. Notice I used the plural; like pad sanders, more than one will be needed. The inexpensive ¼-inch drill discussed earlier is the first one to buy, and if all you want to do with your drill is drill holes, this one will suffice. However, you'll find dozens of uses for a ⅜-inch variable-speed reversible drill—from stirring paint to sanding to driving screws. When you're driving fasteners, it's handy to have a drill bit and counterbore chucked in the small drill, and a screwdriver bit chucked in the large one. This way, you can drill pilot holes and then drive the screw without having to continually change bits.

One tool that came on the market a number of years ago and quickly established itself as indispensable for boat work of any kind is the heavy-duty, battery-operated electric screwdriver. Although called screwdrivers by the manufacturers, they make dandy drills for light work. They do not replace your regular electric drills, however; even the heavy-duty models don't have enough power for anything but the smallest drilling job. I use the Makita, but Porter Cable and Milwaukee both make good ones.

A ½-inch drill is handy for heavy-duty tasks, especially if you don't have a drill press. It has the guts to drive hole saws and large auger bits. I have several of these large drills, but I go months at a time without using them. They are readily available at tool-rental outlets, so don't buy one if you don't need it.

Drill Bits

One of the seductive temptations that many amateur craftsmen succumb to is the use of cheap drill bits, especially spade bits. If you already have a set of spade bits, they must be reserved for your crudest rough work in softwood. Never use them in hardwood or on any finish work. Spade bits (also called spoon bits or shovel bits) possess the unique ability to make the careful work of a skilled craftsman look like the half-hearted efforts of a hack.

Good drill bits will cost more than the drill you use them in, but they are essential for professional-quality work. I highly recommend a boxed set of six taper drills with countersinks and matching bung cutters made by Fuller that costs about $50 at the discount tool stores. This one set does about 75 percent of all the drilling I do, and it's a permanent part of my basic tool kit. You'll also need a set of machinist's twist drills in number sizes from ¹⁄₁₆ to ½ inch and a set of augers from ¼ to 1 inch. I like the Irwin augers that can be used with either a brace or an electric drill, but they're tricky to use and require a little practice.

For clean finish work and drilling larger holes, or when you need a hole with a flat bottom, nothing beats a set of Forstner bits; they cut fast and they're easy to keep sharp. A few electrician's wiring bits that are about 24 inches long, in sizes from ¼ to ½ inch, will find many uses drilling deep holes and getting into remote places. Brad-point bits are good for finish work, but they're expensive and hard to sharpen. Avoid Chinese-made drill bits, especially the brad-points; they're pure junk.

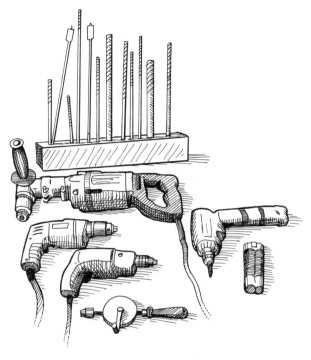

Figure 4-8. An assortment of drills, power and otherwise.

ROUTERS

One of the old tools I keep in the case in my office, safe from the cloying clutches of conniving collectors, is a Stanley #45 combination plane. This fascinating tool is a miracle of complexity with dozens of blades and thumb-screw adjustments that allow it to be used for cutting just about any molding profile you can imagine. The #45, or it's even more complicated big brother, the #55, was once a part of every serious woodworker's basic tool box. Designed to replace the hundreds of wood-bodied molding planes that were required of woodworkers 100 years ago, the old #45 and #55 are, alas, no longer needed, and the pleasant hum of their multiple blades has been replaced by the insalubrious screech of the electric router.

Routers are indeed handy if somewhat unpleasant tools to use. You should have one that will accept ½-inch cutters and has a 1½-h.p. motor—such as the Porter Cable Model 690. Avoid using cutter bits with ¼-inch shanks in heavy-duty routers because the small shank will bend easily; bits with ½-inch shanks don't cost that much more anyway.

The best tool to use for fine work with small ¼-inch cutter bits is a little spe-

**Figure 4-9.
The Stanley #45
multiplane uses
interchangeable
blades to cut hun-
dreds of molding
profiles, rabbets, and
dadoes. Although its
functions have
largely been
replaced by the
electric router, a
multiplane is still
fun to use.**

cialty router called a laminate trimmer. This is, as the name implies, made for trim-ming plastic laminate used on kitchen countertops. It's small and handy, and it has plenty of power to drive small cutter bits without bending the shanks.

The big 3- or 4-h.p. plunge routers are great for big cutters and heavy work, but they are best confined in a router table. Since they're expensive and have limited application, you're probably better off renting one when you need it.

When you buy bits and cutters for your router, don't waste your time on steel. Spend the extra money for high-quality carbide. Teak will knock the edge off a steel router bit in a single pass where carbide seems to go on and on.

Well, we could go on talking about tools forever, but a recent communiqué from my friendly but grievously overworked editor points out that we're a third of the way through this book and we have yet to drive the first nail. He's right, of course, in the manner that ministers and wives and editors are always right. And since, on those odd occasions when they aren't, it's prudent to proceed as if they were, we will press on in our search for the often-promised but heretofore elusive nitty-gritty. But first a brief discussion of the woods from which boats are made is in order. Now in a book on wooden boats, what could be more important than that?

CHAPTER FIVE

Boatbuilding Woods

Where would we be without wood?

Wood is one of the crucial materials that has allowed us to squirm our way out of the primordial slime. From it we have fashioned tools to challenge our creative genius, weapons to vanquish our enemies, habitations to perpetuate our species and nurture our offspring, wheels to rearrange nature, and boats to conquer our horizons and satisfy our endless yearnings for fresh adventure and new experiences. And, given the unbounded resourcefulness of our species—were there not more suitable alternatives—wood would someday take us to the stars.

Chemically speaking, wood is an arrangement of cellulose cells collected in strings or tubes stuck together with stuff called lignin. All woods have cellulose and lignin, but they also have other substances that, depending on the arrangement, shape, size, and proportion of the cells, give different species of trees their unique qualities—some of which make good boats and some of which do not. Since we lack the luxury of the time and space required for an intimate study of the nature of this wonderful substance, we must limit our discussion to the merits and demerits of the woods you're most likely to encounter in renovating your old wooden boat.

The suitability of a wood for boatbuilding is largely determined by its durability and resistance to rot, and its weight, toughness, and resiliency. Some well-known woods, such as pine, birch, and cherry, have some qualities that might make them attractive for boatbuilding, but they all rot away so fast as to make them unusable. Other woods, such as white cedar—which is soft but is used for planking—and Sitka spruce—which rots easily but is used for spars—have many shortcomings but are used anyway because they have redeeming qualities; cedar is rot-resistant, and Sitka spruce has a high strength-to-weight ratio.

Even so, you well may encounter an old wooden boat with white-pine plank-ing or birch deadwood, and I know of one boat with a cherry deckhouse. The fact is, just about every kind of wood in the world has been used to build boats at one time or another because throughout history boatbuilders built with what they had and what they could get. Until fairly recently that meant wood from the trees that grew on the bank of the river where the boat would be launched. Most Gloucester schooners and many other boats built in New England were framed and planked with white oak. That white oak is one of the best woods in the world for frames was incidental to the fact that it was abundant and cheap. Oak wasn't the best wood for planking the schooners, but it was used until supplies of Southern yellow pine became available after the Civil War. More recently, as terms like "economic feasi-bility," "cost equivalency," and "financial viability" became part of the boat-builder's jargon, the physical properties of wood became secondary to the return-on-investment rating on the balance sheet, and suitable wood became affordable wood.

A tree grows from the top up and from the outside out. The center wood of a living tree trunk, called the heartwood, is dead—that is to say, it contains no living cells—and the dead cells of cellulose fill with hardened gums and resins. The outer wood in the trunk, called sapwood, contains a certain number of cells that retain their capillary function and are filled to a degree with sap and water. These cells are, therefore, hollow when the wood is dried. Consequently the heartwood of most species is much harder and more dense and usually has a darker color than the sapwoods and thus is more desirable to a boatbuilder. In fact with some species, such as oak, the sapwood is practically worthless for anything but fire-wood.

GRADES OF LUMBER

All lumber is divided into two general categories—softwood and hardwood—which, interestingly, has nothing to do with the hardness of the wood. Some hard-woods, such as poplar, are very soft, while some softwoods, like Southern yellow pine, are like iron. Softwoods all come from conifers or evergreens, while hard-woods come from deciduous broad-leaved species like oak and cherry. Larch (also called hackmatack or tamarack) is an oddball deciduous conifer classified as a soft-wood.

Grading of wood is a complex art, and the grader at any lumberyard is an important man because he determines the suitability of the wood for different functions. There are many grades of woods, and there are specialty grades for dif-ferent industries like furniture manufacturing and building construction.

The grade of lumber you'll be most interested in is FAS (Firsts and Seconds), which is the top grade for general hardwood lumber. FAS indicates clear, straight grain with a minimum of knots, checks, and splits. The amount of sapwood doesn't affect the FAS grade in most species, so when you buy lumber, you'll have to allow for a certain amount of waste depending on what you're buying—up to 20 percent for oak, less than 10 percent for mahogany and teak.

If you're using a lot of small pieces of wood that can be cut from between knots, or you're building something where knots won't be a problem, the next lower wood grade to consider is #1 Common, which will have substantially more defects than FAS but will also be substantially cheaper. Number 2 Common will have a lot of defects and be a lot cheaper than #1 Common. The last time I bought white oak, FAS was over $5 a board-foot, but I was able to get a load of #1 Common in short lengths and narrow widths for less than $2 a board-foot. True, half of it ended up going into the fireplace, but I still saved a buck a board-foot—and I got a load of firewood out of the deal to boot.

SAWING AND DRYING LUMBER

Generally, there are two ways a mill will saw a log into lumber. Flat sawing, in which a log is sawn into flat slabs or flitches, is the simplest, but it produces boards with varying grain characteristics. Rift sawing, sometimes called quarter sawing, involves sawing boards from the log in a radial pattern so that the grain always lies across the thickness of the board.

Flat-sawn lumber is the most common with most species because it is easier to produce and it yields the most usable stock with a minimum of waste. Flat sawing

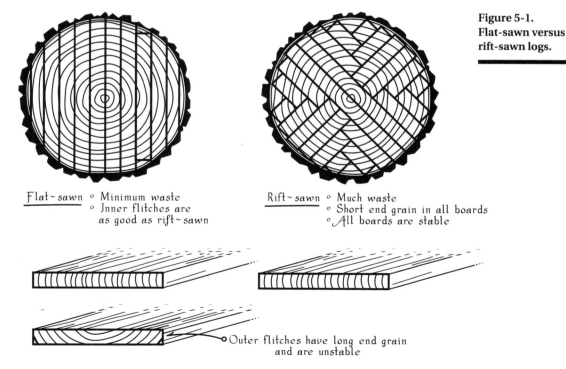

**Figure 5-1.
Flat-sawn versus
rift-sawn logs.**

Flat~sawn ° Minimum waste
           ° Inner flitches are
             as good as rift~sawn

Rift~sawn ° Much waste
           ° Short end grain in all boards
           ° All boards are stable

° Outer flitches have long end grain
  and are unstable

always produces boards of varying desirability from the same log. The three or four flitches taken from the center of the log will produce lumber that is the equivalent of rift-sawn boards, but the outer flitches will contain mostly sapwood with grain structures considerably more unstable than those taken from the center flitches.

Rift sawing produces uniformly stable lumber. Wood movement is most severe perpendicular to the grain, or annual rings, and since these rings are sections of a circle, or arcs, the movement is uneven across the flat surface of a board, causing the board to cup and warp. Rift sawing minimizes the length of the annual-ring arc which, in turn, minimizes cupping and warping.

Rift sawing also produces a uniform grade of lumber with a minimum of sapwood and a uniform quality from a given log. Oak and several other species used for decorative trim benefit from being rift sawn because of the characteristic medullary rays that don't show in flat-sawn boards. Other woods such as fir and Sitka spruce are always rift sawn when used for spars or planking because of the strength and stability this imparts to the wood.

In the old days a boatbuilder would buy green lumber from the sawmill and stack it in drying sheds for a few years until it was dry enough to use. The progress of the drying was checked by weighing a sample of the wood, and when it had lost about half its weight, it was considered dry. Today things happen much faster, and most of us can't stand around waiting for lumber to dry, so drying lumber these days is nearly all done in kilns.

There's a lot of nonsense bandied about in boatyards regarding the relative merits of air-dried wood versus kiln-dried wood. Some old-timers went so far as to use only lumber from logs cut in winter under a dark moon. The moon part was superstition, but the belief that winter-felled logs contain less sap than summer-felled logs persists today even though it has been repeatedly shown to be simple folklore. The only thing that matters is the moisture content of the wood; how it got that way is incidental. This statement is guaranteed to provoke a heated argument anywhere wooden boats are discussed. Kiln-dried wood and air-dried wood do have different characteristics; whether they're beneficial or not is an entirely different argument.

The amount of moisture remaining in wood after it has dried is important. If wood is too dry, it will swell excessively in the damp marine environment, causing a severe increase in internal stress. If it's too green, however, it won't glue or finish well, and it will shrink excessively, opening seams and loosening joints. Hardwood lumber from a lumberyard kiln can contain as little as six or seven percent moisture, which is actually too dry for boat use. A moisture content of around 12 to 15 percent is usually considered about right for most work with hardwoods, and 20 percent is about right for softwoods. Oak that will be used for steam bending must be green, and it must be rift sawn.

RAIN-FOREST WOODS

Everyone knows the rain forests of the world are being destroyed at an astonishing rate and that if something is not done immediately, it will be too late. By some estimates, the great rain forests will be just a memory in as few as 20 years. The doom-sayers tell us if the rain forests go, man as a species won't be far behind, and none but a fool would say with certainty that they are wrong. Even conservative figures put the consumption of rain forests at about 100 acres a minute, which gives the remaining forests a life span of less then 40 years. Anyone who isn't desperately concerned about this situation must be incredibly naive and uninformed, but the problem should be of particular concern to boatbuilders and renovators because so much of the wood we use comes from rain forests—particularly those various woods we know as mahogany and teak.

Although the problems of deforestation are obvious, solutions are not. Separating fact from rhetoric and information from diatribe is nearly impossible without intensive study. And the extent to which lumbering operations contribute to the problem is not at all clear. While some clamor for a boycott of all rain-forest products and for laws that would put mahogany logs into the same category as cheetah skins and narwhal tusks, one lucid argument favors lumber exports from rain-forest countries as a means of increasing the value of the forests.

The jury is still out, and I won't pretend to know the answers—but deforesta-tion should remain an area of concern for all of us who use these woods. In the meantime I continue to use teak and mahogany sparingly and with only a slightly guilty conscience. But let's remember that no rain-forest wood is essential to boat-building. Oak, fir, and cedar are readily available, inexpensive, and can be har-vested cleanly and efficiently from forests in the temperate zones where modern forestry management can ensure a sustained harvest and closely monitor those resources—such as cypress and old-growth fir—that are not renewable. All the world's forests should be treated as a treasured resource, and right now it makes sense to use oak instead of teak and fir instead of mahogany wherever you can. You may not save the world, but you will save some cash, and the product of your labors will look just as good. (One boatbuilder I asked about any moral problems he might have with using rain-forest woods said it didn't bother him at all because he never used wood from trees that hadn't already been cut down. That's like saying you would never eat a whale that wasn't already dead.)

The woods you're most likely to encounter in your old-wooden-boat renova-tion are oak, mahogany, teak, cedar, Sitka spruce, and of course, plywood in all its varied guises. Let's discuss each of these, and some others, individually.

OAK

The American white oak (*Quercus alba*) and the English white oak (*Quercus petraea*) are both specific types of trees. But like mahogany and several other woods, the white oak you buy at the lumberyard is a generic type that might come from any of dozens of different species found around the world. White oak is one of the heaviest and hardest woods in general use today and one of the toughest and most durable as well.

If there's any such thing as a traditional boat wood, it's white oak. For cen-turies it was the backbone of the world's military and merchant navies. The British

Empire was built on keels of English white oak, and the boats that finally sent them scurrying for cover were built of American white oak, in American history books anyway. And oak continues as the material of choice for knees, frames, keels, and stems in new traditional boat construction. It may also be used for planking and decks and for trim such as caprails, rubrails, and grabrails. Because of its light color, low cost, and good machining qualities, white oak is becoming popular as an interior finish wood. In fact it's possible to build an entire boat of white oak, except for the spars, and not go wrong anywhere.

Red oak, a distant cousin to white oak, also is harvested from a variety of species of trees. It's great for floors and furniture—but in your house, not on your boat. Red oak is porous with a coarse and open grain structure, and it isn't weather or rot resistant. Quite a bit of red oak is used in boats, but it shouldn't be. White oak is common, inexpensive, and such a superior boat wood to red oak that there is no real reason to use the red stuff.

White oak steam-bends very well, it takes glue well, machines well, and has very good compression strength. Many boatowners are surprised to learn it's heavier and stronger than teak and nearly as weather resistant (although not as rot or bug resistant). It also has a higher resiliency than any other commonly used boat wood, which is to say that it is tougher. And white-oak heartwood is impermeable to liquids, even alcohol, which is why it's used for whiskey barrels.

But nothing is perfect. White oak is a favorite meal for insects such as beetles, termites, and teredo worms. It splits easily, so it can't be nailed without predrilling the holes. It contains very high levels of tannic acid, which can devour iron fittings and shorten the life of bronze and stainless fasteners. And its great weight argues against using it for planking. It also has one glaring fault that makes it secondary to teak for trim: It's boring. White oak is plain and ordinary, and nothing about it is exotic. As for teak, well, teak is teak.

TEAK

To my way of thinking, teak is the most overrated wood used in modern boatbuilding. It's not that it doesn't have many properties that make it a good boat wood—it's resilient, tough, highly resistant to insects and rot, and when properly finished, it looks terrific. But there are so many problems with its use and so many suitable woods to use in its place that I see no need to use it at all.

In the first place, most high-grade teak comes from Burma or Thailand, which between them account for some of the most odious politics in the world. In Burma the government has been cutting its teak forests as fast as it can to finance its war against insurgent rebels. The rebels, in turn, have been cutting teak as fast as they can to buy guns with which to overthrow the government. Meanwhile there is a thriving black market in teak logs, and smugglers have been cutting teak as fast as they can to take advantage of the high prices before the supply collapses entirely.

Bob Keiver of Keiver-Willard, a major importer and wholesaler of boat lumber, has predicted that teak will continue to rise in price and decline in quality into the foreseeable future until the supply is exhausted. Burma has already initiated a ban on exporting teak logs in the hope of increasing its sale of milled lumber and teak products. So far the ban has been unenforced due to political strife, but it's obvious that an end to hostilities won't do anything to increase the world supply of teak.

The one bright spot for teak comes from new teak plantations in South and Central America. Costa Rican teak is just coming on the market, and Bob reports that it is surprisingly high in quality. The major problem with plantation teak is that it's all short lengths and narrow widths—a situation that's bound to improve as plantation trees mature. But the very economics that make teak an attractive plantation crop argue against its use from a practical perspective; it is horrifically expensive. The price of teak is approaching $12 a board-foot at this writing and destined to go even higher.

The advantages of teak as a material for exterior trim are consistently misrepresented by boat manufacturers and misunderstood by the boating public. Yes, teak is very weather resistant, but so is white oak. And teak does indeed turn gray when left to weather, but so do most other woods. Besides, most people I know prefer the look of oiled teak, and varnished teak is best of all. So why do builders insist on using it? Because the switch to teak for exterior trim on boats saved the modern boatbuilding industry a bundle in production costs.

How can that be? you ask, when except for the real exotics like purpleheart, rosewood, and bubinga, teak is one of the most expensive woods you can buy. Before the wholesale switch to teak, the favored wood for exterior trim on pleasure boats was mahogany. It looked great, and it was strong and weather resistant. But mahogany required careful sanding and varnishing, which involved a lot of time and highly skilled labor—the two most expensive elements in the boatbuilding equation. Teak, on the other hand, because of its natural oils, retains a nice color when milled or machined, and it need not be sanded smooth. This color will last several months when exposed to the elements—just long enough to get the boat sold. So without the finishing steps, raw-teak trim costs a fraction of what finished-mahogany trim costs.

What seems to be lost on a lot of boatowners is that, except on decks, weathered teak doesn't look any better than any other kind of wood that has been neglected. And varnishing or oiling teak is actually trickier and a lot more work than doing the same thing to oak or mahogany.

MAHOGANY

When we say mahogany, we're actually talking about dozens of species of trees indigenous to almost all the world's tropical areas. The highest grades of mahogany were originally from Cuba and several other Caribbean islands, and by all accounts it must have been wonderful stuff. But it's gone now, harvested into oblivion by greedy men with small minds. The highest grades of mahogany available today are from South America and are usually referred to by their country of origin, such as Honduras or Colombia. African mahogany, a product of the Khaya family of trees, is also of a high grade. Lauan or Philippine mahogany—actually a species of cedar—has the lowest grades commercially available to boatbuilders.

Species	Type	Uses	Hardness	Source	Rot Resistance	Weather Resistance	FAS Price Bd/Ft 1992
Ash	HW	Frames, LM Knees, INT	Very Hard	Temperate Zone	Moderate	Moderate	$4.25
Cedar	SW	Planking	Soft	Temperate Zone	Very Good	Good	$3.75
Cypress	SW	Planking	Mod Soft	Temperate Zone	Very Good	Good	Special Order
Douglas Fir, Rift-sawn	SW	Decking, Spars, LM Planking, Backbone	Mod Soft	Temperate Zone	Good	Good	$5.95
Larch	SW	Planking Decking, Knees	Mod Soft	Temperate Zone	Poor Untreated	Poor	Special Order
Lauan	HW	Planking, Trim	Mod Hard	Tropical	Good	Poor	$2.95
Mahogany, Honduras	HW	INT, Trim, Knees, Planking, LM	Hard	Tropical	Good	Good	$4.65
Mahogany, Philippine	HW	INT, Trim, Knees Planking, Trim	Hard	Tropical	Good	Good	$3.50
Oak, red	HW	INT, Trim	Hard	Temperate Zone	Poor	Very Poor	$4.25
Oak, white	HW	Bent Frames, INT, Knees, LM, Backbone	Very Hard	Temperate Zone	Very Good	Very Good	$4.35
Sitka Spruce	SW	Spars	Soft	Temperate Zone	Poor	Poor	$8.00
Teak	HW	Decking, Trim Planking	Very Hard	Tropical	Very Good	Very Good	$12.00
White Pine, Clear	HW	Planking, Decking	Very Soft	Temperate Zone	Very Poor	Very Poor	$5.95

KEY: HW=HARDWOOD; SW=SOFTWOOD; LM=LONGITUDINAL MEMBERS; INT=INTERIORS

Figure 5-2.
Properties of boat-building woods.

With the exception of a few from Southeast Africa, all the species that comprise the woods we know as mahogany have one thing in common: They make excellent boat woods. They are strong, straight grained, and range in density from moderate to quite hard. They all machine and finish very well, although the lesser grades tend to fuzziness if tools are not kept sharp. And the lighter grades of lauan are quite economical—typically less than $3 a board-foot—and make excellent planking. The more expensive grades and types of mahogany (about $4.50 a board-foot for Honduras) are usually reserved for brightwork and varnished interiors, where their superior color and attractive grain make higher prices acceptable.

CEDAR

Many old wooden boats that are in good enough shape to warrant your attention will be planked in white cedar, a soft wood that grows in swampy areas all along the East Coast. It's called swamp cedar down South and juniper in other areas. White cedar is great for planking because it's light and highly rot resistant. It's not very strong, however, so it is just about useless for anything else.

Western red cedar is sometimes used for planking because of it's great resistance to rot. It's harder than white cedar, but because it is very brittle and not very strong, it's not used that often. Port Orford cedar was used a lot for planking boats built on the West Coast. It is slightly harder than white cedar and just as resistant to rot, but it's now hard to get. Eastern red cedar is used for closet linings and for making pencils and has little use in boatbuilding.

The last time I needed a small quantity of white cedar for a hull repair, it wasn't available, and I had to substitute cypress. It seems that most of the large stands of marketable cedar had been cut to satisfy the demand from the people who make precut log cabins. The stands that were left were in inaccessible swamps and couldn't be harvested without running afoul of laws designed to protect our wetlands. White cedar is now available again, but since it is more important to have cedar swamps than cedar logs, periodic shortages will probably occur—even though most of the log-cabin companies have either gone out of business or switched to spruce or pine.

CYPRESS

Like white cedar, cypress grows in swamps, and there is a similar problem in harvesting logs. Cypress is used a lot in the South, and a substantial portion of the older shrimp boats are planked with it. It is much like cedar in rot resistance and strength, but it's harder and tougher. The one big drawback to cypress as planking is it soaks up water like a sponge, making for a very heavy hull.

SITKA SPRUCE

Sitka spruce is a conifer that grows along the Pacific Coast of the U.S. and Canada. It has very light, soft white wood that's not particularly tough. In fact it isn't really a spruce at all but a pine, and like all pines, it's very susceptible to rot and insect infestation. However, because of its light weight and high compression strength, Sitka spruce is unsurpassed for spars. Unfortunately for boatbuilders, it is also unsurpassed for making soundboards on musical instruments, and the vast majority of the Sitka spruce that is harvested goes straight to Japan as logs. Bob Keiver says spar-quality Sitka spruce is available, however, and Fred Bolter of Bolter Plywood in Somerville, Massachusetts, keeps enough on hand to satisfy most needs. At $8 a board-foot, Sitka spruce is not quite as dear as teak, but the last time I priced a new 30-foot-long, 8-inch-square mast, nearly $800 worth of wood was involved. That makes any Sitka spruce spar a substantial investment, but if you want wooden spars, no other wood works quite as well.

DOUGLAS FIR

Douglas fir grows in Washington and Oregon and is one of the most important lumber crops in the country. It's used extensively in building construction and is the wood most used in structural plywood. It has many uses in boatbuilding, and it's about the only wood to even consider as a substitute to Sitka spruce for spars. Douglas fir that is rift sawn as boat lumber looks like an entirely different species than the ugly, coarse wood you see in construction lumber and on fir plywood. It has long, straight grain, great compression strength, and it finishes nicely. In fact it is far superior to Sitka spruce as a boat wood because it's harder, stronger, and more resistant to rot. The only thing that makes it less suitable for spars is its heavier weight.

Other places you might find Douglas fir used on your old wooden boat are in the planking; in the deadwood; as clamps, rails, and stringers; and in strip-planked and laid decks.

LARCH

Larch (hackmatack or tamarack), the only deciduous softwood, as we mentioned earlier, grows in Maine and in most of Canada. It was once a critical wood to boatbuilding in New England because its roots were the primary source of naturally bent knees used in bracing deck beams. Its great durability is attested to by its use as railroad ties and telephone poles. It is also an excellent wood for planking, and occasionally you'll find it used for this on older hulls.

PLYWOOD

Some wooden-boat extremists (affectionately called scary-eyed granola crunchers in some quarters) say "plywood" with the same guttural sneer of contempt usually reserved for "fiberglass." But this is being grievously unfair. Plywood has been around since the days of Cleopatra. And since efficient waterproof glues became available after World War II, plywood has been used in just about every boat built. Waterproof plywood opened up an entire new world to backyard boatbuilders. And the combination of plywood and epoxy-reinforced fiberglass can create one of the strongest hulls modern materials can build.

Plywood has many different forms, of course, and it has several important advantages over sawn lumber. All plywood is constructed in layers (plies), and the grain of each ply runs perpendicular to the adjoining plies. This alternating grain gives plywood far greater dimensional stability than lumber because it cancels cross-grain movement caused by changes in temperature and moisture content. Alternating plies also make plywood stronger than lumber by canceling the tendency of most woods to split along the grain. It also makes for much more efficient use of scarce and expensive woods because the costly woods can be used on the outside plies while the inside layers can be a low grade of a cheaper wood. Since the outer plies always have grain going in the same direction, plywood always has an odd number of plies.

The standard size for plywood panels is 4 X 8 feet, but supply houses such as Bolter Plywood and Harbor Sales in Baltimore, Maryland, both of which cater to boatbuilders, can supply panels in just about any size you need. In fact the maximum size they can provide is determined more by shipping restrictions than their capabilities. Oversize panels up to 5 X 10 feet are available from the mill that makes the plywood. Larger sizes—up to about 28 feet long—are made of smaller panels joined with strong scarf joints. (Bob Weiss of Harbor Sales says the largest single panel of plywood he has ever shipped was 40 feet long!)

Plywood manufacturers use a bewildering number of grading systems to classify their products, depending on what the plywood is intended to be used for and where it comes from. But the marine grades and exterior grades are the ones of most interest to us. Exterior grades of plywood are those manufactured with waterproof phenolic-formaldehyde or resorcinol glues for use in any wet environment—as building siding or for outdoor signs, for example.

Exterior plywood is available in many types of wood, from very rough Douglas fir known as CDX, commonly used as a base for roofing shingles, to the finest exotic hardwoods. It is the wood used for the best surface ply of any plywood that determines the type, the grade, and the cost; thus plywood that has six plies of lauan covered on one side with one ply of teak is teak plywood even though less than 10 percent of the total wood is actually teak.

The quality of the plies is indicated by a letter code. A and N are the highest grades, indicating a virtually flawless surface with a limited number of repairs (N has no repairs), and D is the lowest grade commonly available. An AB grade on a panel of plywood indicates one surface of the highest-grade veneer and the other surface ply of a slightly lower grade. The quality of plywood is also determined by the number of plies and the type of wood used in the core and by the number of butt joints and gaps or voids they contain.

MARINE PLYWOOD

Marine-grade plywoods are exterior plywoods that are manufactured to the highest standards, and naturally the price reflects these high standards. Right now, ¾-inch AC exterior fir plywood is $22.50 per sheet, while ¾-inch marine-grade fir is $65. Currently plywood in marine grade is available in Douglas fir, Philippine mahogany, teak, and Okoume (sometimes called Gaboon). The least expensive marine plywood is Douglas fir, which is still approximately three times as expensive as the AC exterior grade Douglas fir plywood you can get at the local lumberyard. The fact that the kind of wood and the glue are identical in both marine and exterior grades of fir plywood has led many authorities on building and repairing boats to recommend using the lumberyard stuff as a means of saving money. And it isn't unusual to find construction-grade fir or spruce plywood used liberally in low-priced production boats. The argument is not as simple as it might seem, however, and it deserves a closer look.

It is true that construction and marine grades of exterior plywood use the same phenolic and resorcinol glues, and they may even use the same types of wood. They may even look exactly the same on the surface. But if you look at the edges of sample pieces of the two grades that are ¾ inch thick, you'll see that the biggest difference between them is in the quality of the cores. Construction-grade plywood will usually show five plies and a core made of low-grade wood with a lot of knots and voids. The edge of the marine-grade sample will usually show seven plies with a core of high grade wood and virtually no voids.

If you're building a new vanity for the head, the quality of the core in your plywood matters very little. But if you're about to replace a piece of your hull or put down new decking or a new cabin sole, all those little voids and holes in construction-grade lumber can cause you a world of problems. Each void creates a weak spot in your structure that won't stand much pressure without breaking through; screws driven into the voids will pull out, and if the wood gets saturated with water, the voids become little reservoirs that leach out just enough moisture to ensure that rot gets established in record time.

Construction-grade fir plywood has one other glaring fault that to me makes it unusable as a boat wood—it's ugly. Maybe it's all those little football-shaped patches, or perhaps there's something about the grain structure of fir, but even after several coats of paint, fir plywood always looks like fir plywood, and it looks . . . well, it looks amateurish. I've seen fir plywood used on so many crudely built boats, and not all built by amateurs either, that I have an instinctive reaction to it that says "cheap boat." I don't even like the way it looks on the inside of lockers and cabinets.

So what do you do? How do you get a classy-looking job without going broke buying marine-grade wood? Well, for decks and cabin soles and major hull repairs there is no substitute. You should bite the bullet and buy the marine-quality stuff without question. But what about interior bulkheads, cabinets, and shelving that obviously don't need void-free, marine-grade wood? For varnished surfaces you can use hardwood plywood, but for painted surfaces, that's a waste. Besides, the stuff usually costs more than marine grade anyway because of the expensive hardwood veneers used.

THE AFFORDABLE ALTERNATIVE

The answer to this dilemma lies in a product called underlayment-grade lauan, available at larger lumberyards that cater to contractors rather than homeowners. It's manufactured in thicknesses from ⅛ (called door skins) to ¾ inch, using all-lauan (Philippine mahogany) plies and waterproof glue. It is intended to be used under carpeting or tile floors and has an essentially void-free core. It has all the attributes of marine-quality plywood, but (get this folks) it usually costs even less than construction-grade fir.

The one drawback to underlayment-grade lauan plywood is that the surface plies can be pretty crude—usually B or C quality with no voids but lots of patches. However, most lumberyards don't mind if you pick through their pile of stock as long as you promise to stack everything back up as you found it, and every stack will have several pieces with beautiful, smooth surfaces and grain that will match the best Honduras mahogany. If you're looking for wood to paint, even rough-surfaced lauan will sand out smooth with very little effort, and unlike fir, it will take paint beautifully.

My standard procedure, which I highly recommend to you, is to purchase a quantity of ¼-inch lauan mahogany with as nice a face ply as I can find and use this for the majority of my nonstructural plywood needs. True, most of your projects will call for ½-inch plywood, and some, such as shelving, will require a thickness of ¾ inch. You can handle this by simply laminating the ¼-inch sheets with epoxy until you get the thickness you desire. We will discuss the mechanics of this technique in detail later on, but for now, suffice it to say it's quite easy to do, and it has many benefits.

The foregoing is all very good, but what if you don't want to paint the stuff and you don't want mahogany? You may want something with a little more class like bird's-eye maple or bubinga. Well, you can easily do that too, using the fairly simple expedient of veneers.

VENEERS

Up until about 20 years ago, veneering wood was an art form acquired only through much practice and involved techniques passed from master to apprentice through the centuries. Skilled veneerers used esoteric tools (special presses, tiny saws, rollers, and veneering hammers), and today the old ways are still the best for most of you with the time and inclination to learn them. The rest of us can do a surprisingly acceptable job using new paper-backed veneers, contact cement, and a heavy ink roller. Paper-backed veneers are available in just about every wood imaginable from Boulter Plywood and Woodworker's Supply, Inc. (see Appendix B). You can get contact cement at your lumberyard, and most art-supply outlets sell the rollers. If you want to try the real thing, Garrett Wade (see Appendix B) sells the necessary tools, and a terrific little book called *Techniques of Wood Surface Preparation* by David Hawkins, probably available at your local library, will tell you how to do it.

CHAPTER SIX

Just for the Hull of It

That the hull is the essence of a boat seems to be a ridiculously obvious statement at first, but it is really quite profound when you think it over. Designers and builders will tell you that the cost of the hull is but a small part of the total cost of any complete boat—as little as 10 percent, but seldom higher than 20 percent. If we agree on a compromise average of 15 percent, you can easily see that the hull is practically insignificant in terms of the total cost of the boat. However, if we also agree with the even more elementary definition of the hull as the part that keeps the water out and your feet dry, it's obvious that its importance is far greater than its proportional cost.

It's also interesting to note that if you were to disassemble most any boat and place everything that could be removed—rigging, rudder, engine, et cetera—in a pile next to the bare hull, then brought in any kid off the street who was in reasonable control of his faculties and asked him to point to the boat, he would invariably point to the hull, not to the pile of stuff that represents 85 percent of the cost. Thus we can safely conclude that the hull is, in fact, the boat, and the rest of the stuff remains just stuff, regardless of its cost, until it is reinstalled. Furthermore, if anyone would like to argue with the conclusion that the hull is the most important part of any boat, I challenge them to sail a boat without one.

DEFINING TERMS

A great many readers of this book will have a good working marine vocabulary and know full well that a keel rabbet is not the furry little critter that eats the clover under your boat at the boatyard and that a butt block is not an offensive move in a football game. Furthermore, it can be annoying to try to read material in which the author repeatedly stops to define terms. The beginning renovator, however, usually needs a little help with esoteric terms like *horntimber*, and just what the hell is a garboard anyway? So in order to get everyone across the line on the same tack, a few definitions that may be helpful are provided in the accompanying sidebar. You'll find a more comprehensive glossary at the back of the book.

A Few Helpful Definitions

Battens: Resemble stringers but are mounted on the *outside* of the frames (and usually let into them). Battens are used to reinforce the seams of plywood construction and on carvel planking where extra strength is required.

Breasthook: A triangular block much like a knee that reinforces the bow where the clamps and shelfs (never say shelves) attach to the stem.

Bulwarks: The continuation of the hull planking above the deck of a boat to provide a protective rail.

Butt blocks: Blocks used to reinforce butt joints in planking.

Caprail: The top trim of a bulwark.

Clamp: Attached to the inside of the frames to carry the deckbeams.

Garboard: The lowermost plank (sometimes called garboard plank or garboard strake) adjacent to and on each side of the keel.

Plank: A single piece of material that is fastened—pinned, riveted, bolted, nailed, screwed, glued, or (in days of yore) sewn with sinews of beasts—to frames or other planks to form the outer skin of the hull. A plank that is *edge set* is sprung sideways to fit the adjacent plank. An *edge-fastened* plank is attached to the adjacent planks, usually by nailing or gluing or both.

Rabbet: The collective term for the groove cut into the stem and keel to receive the ends of the planking and the inboard edge of the garboard. The *garboard rabbet*—also called the *keel rabbet*—is a longitudinal groove cut into the sides of the keel to receive the garboard; the *stem rabbet* is cut into the stem to receive the ends of the planking.

Scarf: A long, tapered joint designed to maximize the contact-surface area between two pieces of wood. Scarfs are designated by a ratio of the length of the taper to the thickness of the material being joined: a 12-to-1 scarf would be 12 inches long for every inch of thickness in the stock.

Sheerline: The profile of the top edge of the hull where it meets the deck or bulwarks.

Strake: A plank, plain and simple.

Stringers: Longitudinal members fastened to the inside of the frames and used to stiffen the hull and to carry or distribute the weight of other parts of the hull.

HULL REPAIRS

If the old wooden boat you've selected for your renovation project has a sound hull that needs no repairs, you are indeed fortunate; most boats that have been neglected will need some structural attention. If extensive hull repairs are necessary, your surveyor should have advised you against buying the boat, and you probably should have listened to him.

Massive repairs to a wooden hull are usually not worth the effort—not in economic terms anyway. Of course your old wooden boat could have some intrinsic value other than monetary—sentimental value perhaps, or it may be just the boat you always dreamed of owning. Or maybe you intentionally bought a boat with a deteriorated hull because of the challenge it represents to your woodworking skills. All of these reasons are just as valid as financial ones for saving a boat as long as you go in with your eyes open and your feet on the ground. Otherwise you could be kissing a frog, thinking of reforming her into a princess, only to find yourself—after the honeymoon is over—married to a frog.

Major structural defects in a hull would encompass such things as a completely rotted or broken keel or stem, lots of broken ribs, totally deteriorated fasteners, major areas of rot, bad initial construction, or (often worse) bad restoration efforts by previous owners. Most likely, if the hull is in bad shape, some combination of these conditions will exist, and they can make efficient repairs a tough beat to weather.

However, if you listened to your surveyor and bought wisely, you have a basically sound hull that will require some repairs. Refastening is one of the most common requirements of old wooden boats. Replacing a plank or two shouldn't intimidate anyone handy with basic tools. Repairing one or two cracked frames is something every owner of a traditionally built wooden boat will have to face some day. (*Rib* and *frame* are used interchangeably, but ribs are generally lightweight, bent frames; it's OK to call ribs frames, but anyone who calls frames ribs is not to be trusted.) Replacing a few floors and repairing a bit of rot in the deckhouse won't be any problem. A rotted or broken stem or transom is going to be a challenge if you haven't done it before, and replacing a keel section is work that requires the skills of an expert boatwright.

How you proceed in making repairs will depend on the type of hull that's under your old wooden boat. More than likely it is carvel planked, strip planked, lapstrake, or plywood. It's much less likely to be cold-molded or stressed-panel construction, but we will discuss these as well, just in case.

CARVEL PLANKING

Carvel planking is the most common type of traditional wooden planking. It is equally suited to larger yachts and heavy workboats like the Gloucester fishermen and to smaller boats like the lovely Crosby catboat and the graceful Friendship sloop, and even to tiny boats like the Peapod dinghies.

A carvel-planked hull has wide, heavy planking that lies flat against the frames.

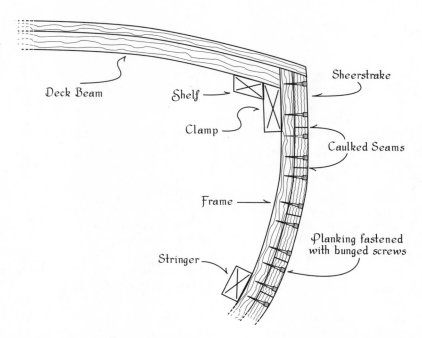

**Figure 6-1.
Carvel planking.**

Except for the garboard, which is fastened to the keel rabbet, planking is fastened only to the frames and to the stem and sternpost or transom. The planks are placed edge-to-edge with slightly open seams that are caulked to form a smooth hull. Carvel planking allows the easy use of stealers, triangular-shaped strakes that don't run the full length of the boat, which gives the designer the flexibility to increase sheer and rocker (the hull profile at the keel).

A fairly common variation of the carvel-planked hull is the double-planked hull, which uses two layers of thin and narrow carvel planks, one over the other. The seams of the outer layer of planking are laid out to fall in the center of the planks on the inner layer. The garboard is usually a single plank equal to the thickness of both inner and outer planks combined, and it has a deep rabbet that serves as a starter for the alternating seams. Usually canvas or heavy muslin is placed over the first layer of planking and painted or doped, in the manner of an old-fashioned canvas canoe, prior to the installation of the second layer of planking. On many boats the double planking runs from the garboard to just above the waterline, and the topside is covered with conventional single-layer planking.

Double planking requires a skilled boatbuilder who can fit tight seams. Long planks are required on the outer skin since butt blocks can't be used effectively. Usually the inner planking is about half the thickness of the outer layer, and the individual strakes have no allowance for caulking. The combination of tight seams and the painted canvas provides a watertight hull. This construction is particularly useful in medium to heavy powerboat hulls subject to heavy pounding and torsion that would tend to open up caulked seams. It is found on many of the older production boats like Elco and Chris-Craft.

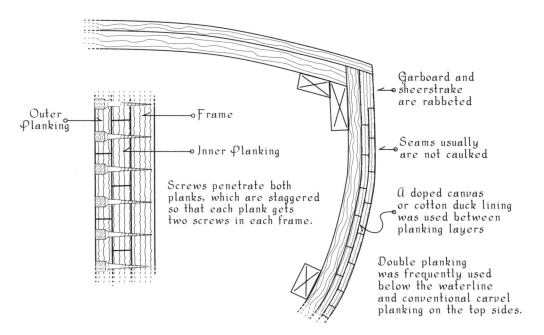

Outer Planking

Frame

Inner Planking

Screws penetrate both planks, which are staggered so that each plank gets two screws in each frame.

Garboard and sheerstrake are rabbeted

Seams usually are not caulked

A doped canvas or cotton duck lining was used between planking layers

Double planking was frequently used below the waterline and conventional carvel planking on the top sides.

If the hull of your old wooden boat is carvel-planked, your surveyor should have pulled a few bungs and checked the condition of the fasteners in his initial survey. If he didn't, take a close look at the seams in your hull. If they're tight and the paint doesn't crack over the caulking in the course of a normal season, you can bet that the fastenings are all snug and in good condition. If the paint over the seams is cracked, the seams are working, which indicates the fastenings are becoming loose or deteriorated or both. And while a certain amount of this working is tolerable and even unavoidable in heavy boats, the condition will gradually worsen until recaulking and refastening are necessary.

Figure 6-2. Double planking.

STRIP PLANKING

Strip planking is essentially carvel planking using narrow pieces of wood that are edge set and edge fastened to form a seamless hull. However, the similarity is only superficial because the construction techniques, structural requirements, and repair procedures are all quite different.

The wood used for strip planking is cut into thin, frequently square strips that are nailed and sometimes glued *to each other* and only lightly fastened to the frames. With this technique the planking contributes much more to the strength of the hull, which allows the boat to be constructed with fewer and lighter frames, and the need for caulking is eliminated. A strip-planked hull is easy to fair and finishes perfectly smooth. Where carvel-planked hulls are usually planked over the frames, strip-planked hulls are often constructed over molds and the frames are added after the planking is complete.

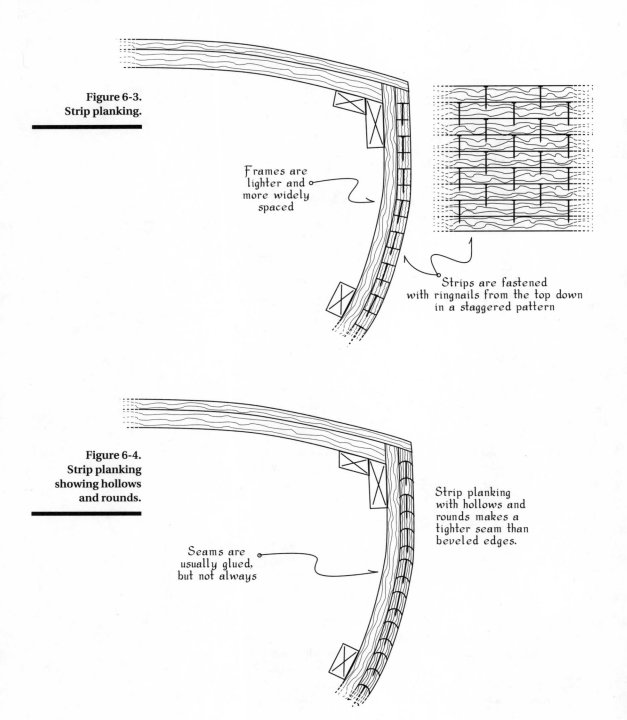

**Figure 6-3.
Strip planking.**

Frames are
lighter and
more widely
spaced

Strips are fastened
with ringnails from the top down
in a staggered pattern

**Figure 6-4.
Strip planking
showing hollows
and rounds.**

Strip planking
with hollows and
rounds makes a
tighter seam than
beveled edges.

Seams are
usually glued,
but not always

Strip planking is horrendously time-consuming. Each strip must be individually formed because on a curved hull none of the edges of adjoining strips will be parallel. Some builders compensate for the curvature of the hull by hollowing one edge of each strip and rounding the other so that they nest together, forming a tight seam that can be faired smooth, but milling the hollows and rounds is also a lot of work. Depending on the design, achieving the desired sheer can be another problem that will require a lot of energy to solve: A builder can work stealer strips into the planking pattern, or each strip can be individually tapered as it is installed. Some builders trim the ends of the strips along the garboard or the sheerstrake, or both, leaving the bulk of the strips in the center parallel.

Epoxy adhesives have been a great boon to the builder wanting to strip plank a hull. Prior to epoxy, resorcinol was the only practical waterproof glue, but this thin adhesive required heavy clamping and a perfect fit between strips; otherwise, it would run out of any gaps, resulting in a weak bond and voids that were sure to leak. Epoxies, on the other hand, require only light clamping, and they can be thickened with additives that will keep them from running out of poorly fitting joints. When an epoxy-glued strip-planked hull is combined with a layer or two of epoxy-saturated fiberglass cloth, an incredibly strong, tough, and beautiful hull results.

Until epoxy came along, the repair of a strip-planked hull was a real nightmare, since any patch was difficult to fit and impossible to fasten properly. Now, patching is quite easily done using epoxy. We will discuss the specific technique a little later.

LAPSTRAKE PLANKING

To me, nothing conjures up the notion of romance and adventure quicker than the lapstrake hull. From the unmatched grace and beauty of the Viking longboats, built over a thousand years ago, to the comparatively modern Old Towns, Lymans, and Thompsons of the 1950s, to the modern versions of the lapstrake rowing skiff—the Rangely Guideboat, the Swampscott dory, and the Whitehall are but three examples of lapstrake pulling boats currently "in production" in widely scattered one- and two-man boatshops—a lapstrake hull is what I think of first when I hear the word boat. It was in a lapstrake skiff powered by an ancient outboard that I first ventured out alone into the steep chop of Buzzards Bay searching for bluefish and

Figure 6-5.
Swampscott dory.

finding the fraternity of adulthood. My first adventures with those strange and frighteningly wonderful creatures of the opposite sex occurred in a lapstrake boat. And when my days on Earth come to an end, I can think of nothing better than to be sent off to whatever comes next in a lapstrake hull—just the way the Vikings were.

The best lapstrake designs are more than boats—they're an art form. If some evil and vindictive force were to visit mankind and erase from our collective memories every concept of every type of small-boat construction save lapstrake hulls, we would lose little but convenience and utility. If it were to erase the concept of lapstrake hulls and leave the rest, mankind would be as impoverished as if Renaissance art or modern jazz were taken away from us.

Lapstrake hulls differ from other plank-on-frame hulls in several important ways. The planks are frequently quite wide, and of course, they overlap each other. The wide strakes are substantially thinner than other types of traditional planking, and combined with lightweight bent frames, they form a hull that's not only beautiful to look at, but surprisingly light in weight. The doubled planks at the laps and the way they are fastened have the same strengthening effect as stringers, making a lapstrake hull stronger for its weight than any other type of traditional construction. But this lightweight construction has one important disadvantage: Because lightweight boats don't stand up to abuse and neglect as well as carvel or strip-planked boats, a greater proportion of lapstrake boats on the market will actually be beyond repair.

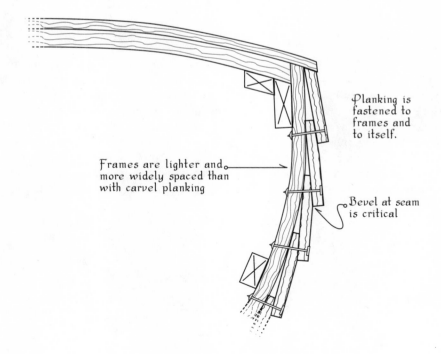

Figure 6-6.
Lapstrake planking.
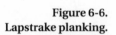

Planking is fastened to frames and to itself.

Frames are lighter and more widely spaced than with carvel planking

Bevel at seam is critical

Lapstrake planking is often of hardwood, such as mahogany, although pine and cedar and just about every other kind of wood are also used. Production boats with lapstrake hulls are frequently planked with plywood.

Each strake in a lapstrake hull requires careful beveling where the overlapping strakes come together. At the ends, this beveling is increased dramatically to form gains, the flat area at the ends of a plank that allow it to lie flush in the stem rabbet or flat against the outside of the transom. Frequently, these gains are in the form of long tapered rabbets and occasionally, on boats using heavier planking, the entire overlapping edge is rabbeted to reduce the reveal—the amount of the edge of a plank that is visible on the finished boat.

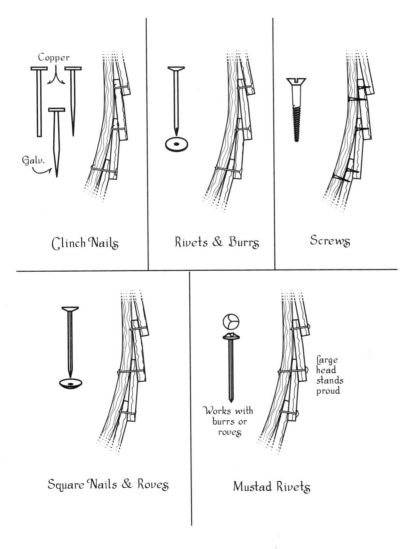

Figure 6-7.
Five methods of fastening lapstrake planking.

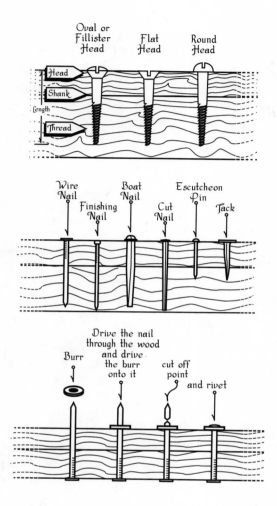

As with strip-planked hulls, lapstrake planks are fastened to adjoining planks and only lightly fastened to the frames. Most fasteners in lapstrake hulls are of a type that penetrates both planks, such as rivets or clinch nails; screws and even bolts are sometimes used with thicker planking. Some of the Viking longboats were actually laced together with rawhide or heavy cord.

Older boats are frequently clinch-nailed using copper or galvanized boat nails that are bent over and set back into the inside surface of the wood by driving them against a bucking iron. When round copper nails are used with a washer known as a *burr*, they're cut slightly proud of the burr, then peened and bucked to form a rivet. In newer boats and in production boats, riveted planking is more common, using square nails and *roves* that work on a principle similar to pop rivets. When properly done, riveting makes a strong seam that requires neither glue nor caulking to be watertight.

PLYWOOD

Plywood is one of the best things that has happened to the backyard boatbuilder . . . and perhaps one of the worst. It's a boon to the amateur builder in that it is strong, inexpensive, and very easy to work with; and it's a plague because it may even be too easy to work with. Its simplicity has resulted in a plethora of bad designs that run from the ludicrous and comical to the outright danger-

Figure 6-8. Just a few of the many types of fasteners used in planking tradition- ally constructed wooden boats.

ous. A great many plywood boats should never have been conceived, much less built, which is a real shame because bad designs and poor construction have given plywood a bum rap that is totally undeserved. Now it seems that any boat with a chine is suspected of having been built from plans purchased from the back pages of *Mechanix Illustrated* in the backyard of some guy in Peoria who had never before seen a handsaw, much less an ocean.

The fact is there are some wonderful designs from the boards of talented architects for boats constructed of plywood. And a boat's having been built in some-one's backyard is not an automatic indication of inferior construction. In fact just the opposite is often the case. A skilled home builder is free from the constraints of the profit motive that shackle commercial builders to a time schedule and a budget. The amateur can spend years fussing over details and getting things just right, and the result can be a boat that is more solidly built than any production boat.

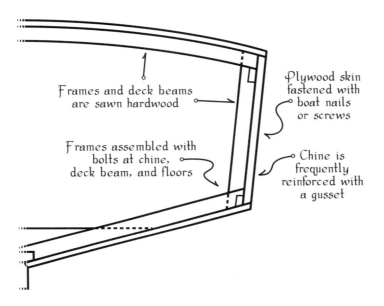

Figure 6-9.
Chine construction.

Frames and deck beams
are sawn hardwood

Frames assembled with
bolts at chine,
deck beam, and floors

Plywood skin
fastened with
boat nails
or screws

Chine is
frequently
reinforced with
a gusset

I mentioned earlier that one of my favorite designs is the venerable Jim Brown Searunner trimaran. Jim Brown himself has pronounced the design outdated, but similar pronouncements have been made about the schooner rig and about any boat with a full keel. Outdated or not, the Searunner design is a true classic in every sense of the word, and the hulls are constructed from marine plywood covered with fiberglass and epoxy.

Another classic designed for plywood is the Newporter Ketch. She is 40 feet on deck and weighs in at a little over 14 tons. She sports a full keel and a traditional clipper-bow that manages to avoid the gaudiness of the Asian-built boats that have given this genre a well-deserved bad name. Over 125 Newporters were built in California by C. E. (Ack) Ackerman. Several other builders have built versions of the Newporter, and who knows how many were home built.

Figure 6-10.
Jim Brown
Searunner.

While plywood has many advantages as a boatbuilding material, there are a few disadvantages as well. The ungainly look of the worst plywood designs is largely due to the inability of plywood to bend in more than one plane; if it's bent in one direction, it can't be bent in the other direction. But designers like Brown and Phil Bolger, the modern guru of plywood construction, manage to use this characteristic to their advantage, and both have come up with some really appealing, seaworthy, and practical plywood hulls.

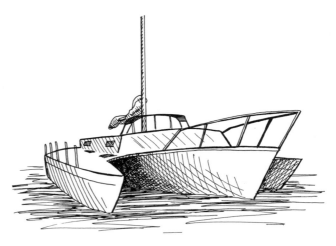

Most plywood boats have the telltale chine or multi-chine hull constructed over sawn frames with batten seams. Many are covered with fiberglass and polyester, but the strongest are those covered with fiberglass and epoxy. One thing that works in favor of the used-boat buyer contemplating a plywood boat is that bad designs and construction are usually painfully obvious and therefore easy to avoid. Defects such as rot and delaminated wood are hard to hide; anything that will harm plywood seems to be totally traumatic to the wood and shows up with startling clarity even under a fiberglass skin.

COLD-MOLDED HULLS

Cold-molded hulls superficially resemble the double-diagonally planked hulls favored by a few builders of powerboats through the 1950s.

Figure 6-11. Newporter 40 Ketch. Thin strips of wood, usually cedar or mahogany, and sometimes even plywood, are formed in layers over molds and frames, with the grain of each layer perpendicular to the previous layer. In double-diagonal construction, there are two layers of comparatively heavy stock, ¼ inch or more, with a painted fabric liner in between. The layers were sometimes glued and sometimes clinch-nailed together. Cold-molded hulls use three to five layers of thin stock that is little more than a veneer. Each layer is saturated and bonded with epoxy. Double-diagonal hulls require frames while some cold-molded hulls do not.

A similar form of wooden hull you might encounter is the stressed-panel hull. This is similar to cold molding but instead of using thin strips of wood, large sheets of thin veneers are saturated with epoxy and vacuum-bagged over molds to form curved sections that are then assembled into a hull.

In effect, a builder using double-diagonal, cold-molded, or stressed-skin hull construction is laying up his own plywood with any required compound curvature built in. The result is, in fact, a plywood hull, but the characteristic hard chine and slab-sided look of conventional plywood construction is avoided. When properly faired and painted, these plywood hulls are hard to tell from fiberglass hulls.

CHAPTER SEVEN

Hull Repairs

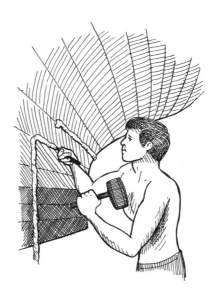

Hull repairs can be grouped into three broad categories: frame repairs, planking or skin repairs, and backbone repairs. (Backbone includes, for our purposes, the stem, the keel, the deadwood, and the transom or sternpost.) Most renovations will require work in several areas since a damaged hull is likely to need attention to both planking and frames. As we clearly don't have the space to discuss the details of every type of repair to every type of hull, we will focus on the areas where you're most likely to find problems. You can find additional help in the recommended books listed in Appendix A.

EPOXY

Before we plunge headlong into the nitty-gritty of fixing boats, let's take just a few paragraphs to talk about epoxy. Such a discussion has to start with the Gougeon brothers—Jan, Meade, and Joel—of Bay City, Michigan, who are probably the best thing that's happened to old wooden boats since bottom paint. While experimenting with wood and plastic composites that would make their iceboats lighter, more efficient, and faster, they developed and pioneered most of the technology used today for the manufacture and repair of wooden boats. And their company, Gougeon Brothers, Inc., is one of the largest suppliers of epoxy and other space-age materials useful to boatbuilders and repair shops. In fact, in the same manner that the word *Coke* means soft drink to a lot of people, *WEST* (System), their brand of epoxy, has almost become synonymous with epoxy in general.

Epoxy is truly miraculous stuff for fixing boats. It sticks with the tenacity of a life-insurance salesman to practically anything (except some plastics like polypropylene). Reinforced with fiberglass or strips of wood, it can be shaped and tooled into practically any part, from a winch base to an entire hull. Epoxy—and the techniques for its use developed by the Gougeon brothers—has been responsible for saving thousands of terrific old boats from the trash heap, boats that would be just too expensive or too time-consuming to repair otherwise.

The word epoxy refers to a group of products that are polymerized from a variety of viscous liquids and tough, brittle solids, most of which are hydrocarbons derived from petroleum distillates. The scientific name for the specific epoxy we use on our old wooden boats, regardless of the brand name, is *digylcidol ether of bisphenyl A*, which is pretty meaningless, but I thought I'd throw it in to try to class up the book.

The two products I'm familiar with in addition to Gougeon Brothers (WEST System) are System Three of Seattle, Washington, and LBI, Inc. of Groton, Connecticut. All three seem to work fine, and the only discernible difference is the mixing ratio of the resin and hardener. And I've never had any problem mixing products from one company with products from another (don't try to mix hardeners, however), even though all three warn against it. Epoxy, it appears, is epoxy, no matter who you buy it from, but I do highly recommend Gougeon Brothers simply because of their helpful attitude and their service-oriented approach to business. If you ever have to call them about a problem with one of their products, they seem to take it personally and won't rest until you're satisfied and the problem is resolved.

Epoxy is not the easiest stuff in the world to use; in fact it can be downright tricky (and more than marginally hazardous, about which more later). To activate the curing process, a small amount of resin is mixed with an appropriate amount of hardener. WEST System epoxy is mixed at a five-to-one (resin-to-hardener) ratio, and you must use a set of calibrated pumps they supply. System Three and LBI epoxies use a two-to-one mix that can be measured with pumps or with measuring cups.

Once mixed, the pot life of the epoxy will vary considerably with several factors. All three manufacturers make a fast and a slow hardener for use in low and intermediate ambient temperatures. System Three and WEST System also make a high-temperature or "tropical" hardener. (In addition, WEST System offers a special hardener for use with clear finishes under varnish.) Cool temperatures will greatly extend the pot life of all three epoxies, and high temperatures will accelerate hardening dramatically.

Epoxies cure by exothermic reaction; that is, they generate the heat required for curing internally. This means that the type of container the epoxy is mixed in will directly affect the pot life. A large-diameter shallow container that provides a large surface area for heat to escape into the atmosphere will keep the epoxy cooler and result in a longer pot life than a small-diameter deep container allowing a smaller surface area. The difference the mixing container can make is startling. One of the first mistakes a novice often makes is to mix too large a batch in too small a container and then turn his back on it for a moment or two, only to return and find it smoking hot and bubbling and turning solid right before his eyes. This happened to a kid I once hired to help out around the shop, and it frightened him so badly that he emptied an entire 50-pound fire extinguisher onto about 6 ounces of epoxy.

The exothermic nature of epoxy also means that it must be applied in thin layers and coats. I once drilled a ¾-inch hole in the wrong spot in the stem of a lobster boat on which I was working, and instead of pegging it as I should have, I poured it full of epoxy. I figured the epoxy would fill the hole and keep it from filling with water. Instead the epoxy started to boil internally, and in about two minutes I had a miniature volcano on my hands, spewing hot epoxy all over the interior of the boat.

Another thing that affects the pot life of epoxy is the temperature of the material before it's mixed; in warm weather it's not unheard of to keep the hardener, the resin, and the mixing container in the refrigerator.

Once epoxy is mixed, it can be used as is or it can be thickened with any of several thickening agents. There are three reasons for thickening epoxy: to increase its tensile strength; to increase its bulk; and to decrease its tendency to flow. Chopped-strand fiberglass is the most popular additive for increasing strength, but if a finer mix is needed, milled glass fibers can be used. To give epoxy more bulk so it will go farther and to improve its finishing qualities, microballoons (microscopic hollow glass spheres) or WEST System Microlight can be added, but my favorite bulking agent is a big handful of sawdust off the shop floor: 'taint fancy, but the price is right. Bulking agents all weaken the tensile and compressive strength of the epoxy, but they're fine for fairing and filling, and they make sanding a lot easier. When you need to use a filler in epoxy but don't want to sacrifice tensile or compressive strength, you should thicken with Cabosil or colloidal silica.

It's perfectly all right and frequently desirable to mix any and all of these additives, and as you gain experience with the stuff you'll undoubtedly develop your own favorite recipes for specific applications. For example, for filling screw holes I always mix half colloidal silica and half Microlight to the consistency of peanut butter. Nothing else seems to work as well.

To judge the degree of thickening required for any given task, the Gougeon brothers long ago established the standard of comparing the epoxy to the viscosity of various foods. I prefer catsup, mayonnaise, and peanut butter. And since no one, to my knowledge, has been able to improve on this system, and as far as I know it's not copyrighted, I'm going to borrow it for this book.

An important characteristic of epoxy that you must keep in mind, especially for work on boats, is that it's subject to photodegradation. Ultraviolet radiation will reduce cured epoxy to a useless white powder in a matter of months if it isn't protected. The best ultraviolet protection for epoxy, or anything else for that matter, is a thick coat of white paint. But other colors also work, as do varnish and polyurethane, provided they contain a strong ultraviolet shield.

Here's another important characteristic of epoxy that you'd *better* keep in mind: It may be a boat-saving miracle-in-a-can, but it's a miracle with demonic overtones. To placate the beast, picture Charlton Heston on the Mount, and follow these Commandments:

- Never ever work with epoxy without wearing protective clothing—latex gloves, disposable Tyvek coveralls, barrier cream (shop the epoxy section of your local chandlery), safety glasses.
- When you're working with epoxy, ventilate, ventilate, ventilate.
- If you're the particularly sensitive type, wear a fume-filtering mask when playing with uncured epoxy. *Everyone* should wear a dust mask when sanding cured epoxy, or when mixing thixogens (microballoons and the like) into liquid epoxy.

If you manage to annointeth yourself with epoxy, clean it off—quick. The Gougeons and others sell various barrier creams and cleaners; waterless hand cleaners sold to keep auto mechanics marginally presentable work, too. Never ever use acetone, lacquer thinner, or other volatile solvents to clean epoxy off your skin.

- Be sensitive about disposing of waste epoxy. The best method is to let it cure before disposal. Check with your local environmental authorities for instructions.

I don't mean to scare you away from using epoxy; it truly is a miracle worker. Just be careful, follow the epoxy manufacturer's directions to the letter, and you'll have no problems.

Enough about epoxy. Let's get back to the subject at hand—hull repair.

HULL FLEXIBILITY

When undertaking any repairs to an old wooden boat, it's important to keep the flexibility of a wooden hull in mind. Boats that were stiff when newly built will loosen considerably over the years and can become quite flexible. In fact, almost any traditionally built hull will have a degree of flexibility that must be considered when making repairs.

Epoxy is wonderful stuff, as we have previously conceded, but those making repairs on old boats often overuse it—to the detriment of the integrity of the entire hull. If a hull that has a great deal of flexibility is repaired in a way that doesn't incorporate that flexibility, and the repaired area is made stiff through the use of epoxy, the forces that cause the boat to flex will be transferred from the repair to the adjacent unrepaired area where they will be substantially magnified. Frequently a boat that is incorrectly repaired with epoxy will have an adjacent piece fail for no apparent reason. The cause is directly related to the repaired section being unable to absorb its share of the flexing burden. Instead of flexing and absorbing the forces, it simply passes them on to its neighbor, which can't bear the additional load and breaks.

Unless you want to epoxy the entire hull, the safest approach in any repair is to use epoxy to join only pieces that were originally made out of a single piece of wood, such as knees and frames. Fasten them to the rest of the boat the way the original part was fastened, and let the boat flex a bit.

REFASTENING

Refastening hulls is one of the most common tasks we, as owners of old wooden boats, must face, and one that our brethren of the plastic craft don't even have to think about. So let's talk about it first, even though frame repairs and replacing planks, if needed, would logically come before refastening.

We've already talked about flexibility, about how the movement between the various structural parts of a wooden boat increases as the hull ages. As the hull works, the fasteners loosen and corrode, which lets the hull work even more, which loosens the fasteners even more, and so on—a continuous cycle that, if not corrected, will eventually destroy the hull. Refastening is necessary when the fasteners loosen, when they are destroyed by corrosion, or when the wood surrounding the fastening is destroyed by rot or electrolysis. Most frequently, some combination of all three conditions is involved.

How long hull fasteners will last in a particular boat depends on many factors: the environment in which the boat is used, the electrical system, the kind of wood used in planks and frames, the size and structure of the boat, how well it was built and how it has been maintained, and the type of fastener and the material from which it is made. No metal, with the possible exceptions of gold, platinum, and a few others that don't make good fasteners, is immune from galvanic corrosion, but generally the higher the metal is on the galvanic scale, the longer a fastener made of it will last. When many old wooden boats were planked, modern formulations of stainless steel and silicon bronze weren't available, so galvanized iron and naval bronze were the order of the day, both of which will disintegrate under the right conditions even with the best of care.

Once you've determined, through your surveyor or by other means, that your boat needs refastening, there's no need to panic. Unless the planks are actually springing loose from the frames (as they do in severe cases), you can refasten your hull over a period of time, doing a section every haulout.

The Boatyard Way

Refastening a hull is always something you should do yourself. To do a proper job is, on one hand, quite easy, and on the other, very time-consuming. If you have a boatyard do it for you, you can bet that they will take shortcuts to try to save time, and that they will assign the task to their lowest-paid and least-skilled workers (still, of course, charging you $45 an hour). This is not so much a reflection on the boatyard as it is on economic reality. To remain competitive, commercial boatyards must do this kind of work in a slapdash manner—they simply can't afford to do the job right.

The favorite boatyard shortcut to refastening a hull is to simply install a new fastener right next to the old one, or to sink new fasteners in each plank between the old ones. This might work for a while on an old fishing trawler with 3-inch oak frames, but on the kind of boat you and I are talking about, it's an abomination. The new holes drastically weaken the ribs and the planking. And the old fasten-

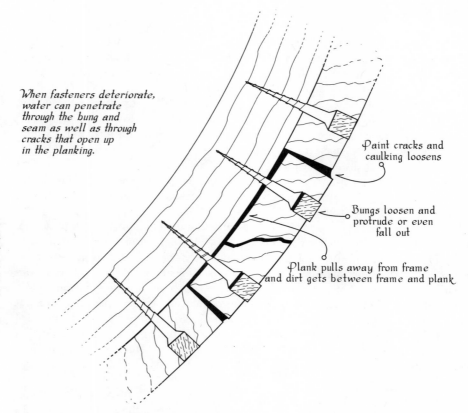

When fasteners deteriorate, water can penetrate through the bung and seam as well as through cracks that open up in the planking.

Paint cracks and caulking loosens

Bungs loosen and protrude or even fall out

Plank pulls away from frame and dirt gets between frame and plank

Figure 7-1. Deteriorated fasteners—threat or menace. These will want careful attention on most any old boat.

ers—still in the hull—will continue to waste away, eventually leading to chronic rot and leaking.

The Proper Way

The only proper way to refasten a hull is to remove the old fasteners and replace them with new ones. I like to work in an area of about two square feet, removing all the bungs and fasteners and replacing the fasteners in that area before moving on to the next. You can wait and replace the bungs all at once, but if you remove too many fasteners at one time, there is a danger of the planks springing out of position.

Remove the bung by drilling out the center with a drill bit roughly half the diameter of the bung. Then collapse the bung in on itself with an awl or ice pick. Don't pry the bungs out with the awl, and don't remove them by driving a screw into them like some authorities who should know better recommend; both of these methods are sure to damage the planking.

Where the fasteners are screws, especially large screws, the best way to extract (and to drive) them is with a screwdriver bit in a hand brace, or with the mechanic's equivalent, a speeder wrench. When the screws have badly deteriorated, removal

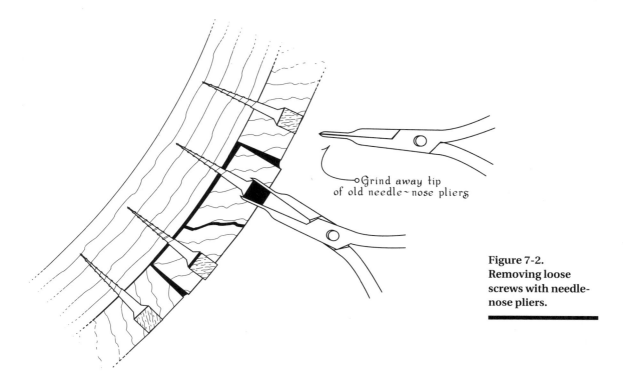

**Figure 7-2.
Removing loose
screws with needle-
nose pliers.**

can be frustrating because both the threads and the screwdriver slot are usually gone. I find an old pair of needle-nose pliers that have been ground extra thin can extract the screws with a minimum of damage to the planking.

If the hull is fastened with rivets, don't bother trying to re-buck them: It simply doesn't work. All you'll do is crimp the shank, and the retightening won't last even one trip around the buoys. Cut or grind the head off the old rivet from inside the boat and drive it out with a drift punch, then replace it with a new one.

Replacing Screws

When replacing screws, it's usually best to use a replacement the same length as the original but one or even two sizes larger: If the original was 1¼ X #8, replace it with 1¼ X #10 or #12. You can tell as you install them if they're holding; if they aren't, you need to move up another size.

In the past I would squirt epoxy into each screw hole, using disposable syringes WEST System sells for just this type of thing. Recently I've switched to 3M-5200 simply because it's easier to work with, and I like the idea of having a little extra flexibility between the planking and frames. As a hull works, the planking will sometimes pull away from the frames just enough to allow dirt and detritus to get between them, causing a large enough gap to admit moisture. This residue is impossible to remove without removing the plank, so the purpose of the sealant, epoxy or polyurethane, is not to hold the screw but to seal this gap.

Figure 7-3.
Injecting
polyurethane
sealant into the hole
before replacing a
fastener.

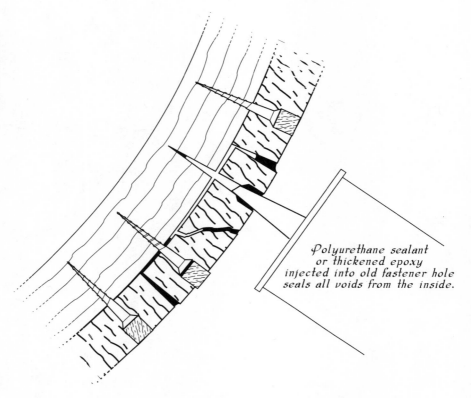

*Polyurethane sealant
or thickened epoxy
injected into old fastener hole
seals all voids from the inside.*

Bolts

When replacing rivets, it's a lot easier to remove the old rivet and replace it with a silicon-bronze machine bolt and washer. The bolts hold better than rivets, they draw the planks better, and you can control the tightness. Bolts are also useful for replacing screws where the wood in the frame has deteriorated to the point that it won't hold a screw. Always use a washer under the nut on a bolt and use fender washers if the wood is bad. Use sealant under the bolt, and after the bolt is tightened, cut the shank flush with the nut. The best tool for this is a pair of farrier's (horseshoer's) end nippers because it makes a blunt cut, and the idea is to upset the threads above the nut so the bolt won't loosen. The only drawback to using bolts instead of rivets, besides their appearance—which could be a problem in some cases—is their cost: Silicon-bronze bolts and washers cost substantially more per fastener than any other type.

Square Nails and Roves

Another type of fastener you might encounter, especially in lightweight lapstrake construction, is the square nail and rove. They resemble rivets, but they work on a different principle—something like that of a pop rivet. You can remove the old rove and nail the same way you would remove a rivet, but to install the new

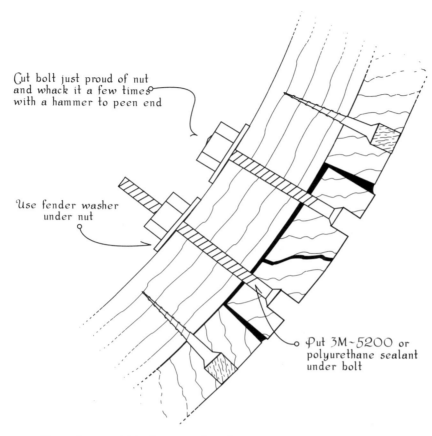

Cut bolt just proud of nut and whack it a few times with a hammer to peen end

Use fender washer under nut

Put 3M-5200 or polyurethane sealant under bolt

**Figure 7-4.
Fastening planks to
the frame with bolts.**

one you'll need a special hollow punch called a rove set. (Roves, square nails, and rove sets are all available from The Wooden Boat Shop in Seattle, Washington. See Appendix B.) The nail is inserted from the outside of the hull and backed with a bucking iron while the rove is driven onto the nail from the inside with the rove set. Believe it or not, you can actually do this by yourself on a small boat by holding the head of a masonry hammer against the nail with your thigh while you reach inside and drive the roves. Notice that I said you "can" do it this way, not that you should; it's much easier with a helper. If you do try it alone, make sure you wear hard-toed shoes; you're going to drop that hammer on your foot at least once for every rove you set.

Bungs

When you replace the bungs, do not epoxy them in place. Use varnish or paint or plain old carpenter's glue; the final paint job will seal the bung in place. If you cut all your bungs from one piece of wood and install them with the grain going in the same direction as the grain in the plank, paring them off flush with a sharp chisel will be much easier than if you install them in a random manner.

FRAME REPAIRS

The frames of your old wooden boat are, most likely, sawn or steam bent. Regardless of how they're made, frames are subject to rot and to fracture from impact. They are also frequently destroyed by ignorant owners who saw them in half to make room for plumbing or electrical lines. Steam-bent frames are particularly subject to stress cracking and breaks.

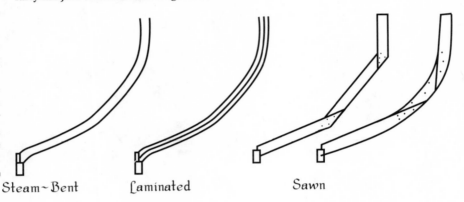

Steam~Bent   Laminated   Sawn

Sistering

The traditional method of repairing cracked or broken frames or ribs has been to *sister* an identical member next to the damaged one. While this method is quite often satisfactory, it isn't completely free of dangers, and it isn't the best way to proceed. Sistering effectively doubles the cross section and the strength of a broken frame along the entire length of the sistered section—except for the small area where the break occurred. Since the old frame is broken, this section has only the strength of the sister, so the frame is now doubly strong except where we need the strength the most. If the hull is working at all, the new double-strength section of the frame will now be twice as capable of transferring stresses back to the area of the original break. It's the same as trying to repair a broken hockey stick by attaching a new section of handle beside the old one. Twice as strong and half as flexible as it was, except where it broke, the repair is much more likely to break again in exactly the same spot.

If your boat has sistered frames, it's likely that the sisters will show signs of stress right next to the original break. If they don't, don't mess with them, but if they do, it's best to remove the sister and repair the frame properly.

Replacing a Frame

The best way to repair any damaged frame is to replace it with a new one that you make as identical to the original as you can. Remove the old frame by carefully removing all the fasteners. More than likely the frame is fastened from the outside by screws or rivets with their heads hidden under bungs. Sometimes, if your hull is working excessively, the bungs will show through the paint, but usually the paint

Figure 7-6.
**Removing fasteners
with a hole saw.**

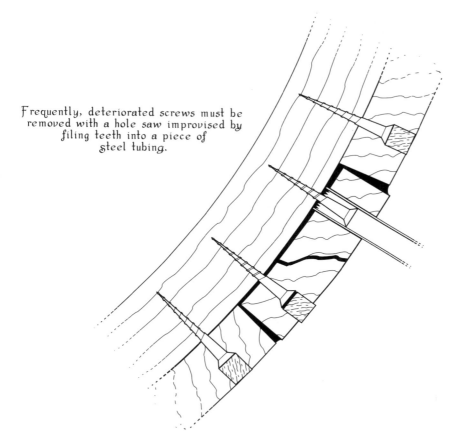

Frequently, deteriorated screws must be removed with a hole saw improvised by filing teeth into a piece of steel tubing.

must be removed to reveal their location. Remove each bung by drilling out its center and collapsing it in on itself.

If the fastener is a screw, it should back out easily. If it is deteriorated to the extent that it's loose but it can't be removed with a screwdriver, you might be able to get it out using the modified needle-nose pliers described above. Large screws that are tight will probably have to be drilled out. (Loose screws will simply spin.) Another possibility is to make a small hole saw by filing a few teeth into one end of a piece of steel tubing slightly larger than the screw but smaller than the bung and use this to cut through the planking around the screw. This approach leaves the screw in the frame to be removed later with Vise-Grips. It also leaves a large hole in your planking, so use this method only for an occasional screw or where the plank is going to be replaced.

If the planking is fastened by rivets, simply grind off the head of the rivet down to the burr on the inside of the hull with a disc sander and tap out the shank with an appropriate drift punch. Don't let the rivet punch out the bung because this too will damage the planks: Always remove the bung first.

Once the planking fasteners are removed, the frame must be freed from the clamp and from any stringers, and then removed from its socket in the keel, if it has one.

Graving In New Wood

In most cases where one or two frames need repairs, they will be in areas where they can't be removed without removing the covering boards (the outermost planks on the deck) or doing other major work that it's best to avoid if you can. Fortunately most sawn frames can be repaired in place simply and quickly without resorting to sistering by *graving in* a new piece and securing it with screws and epoxy.

Sometimes called a Dutchman repair, graving involves chiseling away the damaged wood and carving a new piece to fit the cavity. First remove the planking fasteners from the area of the repair and, using a sharp chisel, remove from the damaged frame a wide, shallow V-shaped section (the angle isn't important; a 2-to-1 slope is fine) that includes all the damaged wood. Chisel the old wood away slowly and carefully: You can be sure you've missed at least one fastener, and it's lurking in the wood ready to ruin the edge of your chisel. Next, hold a piece of new wood of the same type as the original next to the cut-out area, taking care to match the direction of the grain, and scribe the V-shape on the new wood with a pencil.

**Figure 7-7.
Repairing a sawn
frame in place.**

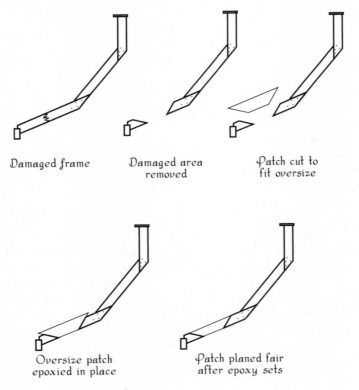

Damaged frame

Damaged area
removed

Patch cut to
fit oversize

Oversize patch
epoxied in place

Patch planed fair
after epoxy sets

Cut away the waste with a handsaw. Coat the cut-out area with carpenter's chalk and trial-fit the new piece; the chalk will transfer from the frame to the new wood, showing the high spots. Use your block plane to take them down until you have a perfect fit. You have, in effect, cut two long scarf joints in the old frame. Coat the planed surfaces of the new piece with silica-thickened epoxy and hold it in place with shores (braces) on the inside of the hull while you replace the fasteners from the outside. When the epoxy has cured you will have a repaired frame that is equal to but not stronger than the original.

Steam Bending

This repair technique works well on sawn and built-up frames. Bent frames require a slightly different approach. First, unless you want to try it just for the experience and to be able to say you've done it, get any idea of steam bending a replacement frame out of your head. I get a big kick out of people who say steam-bending wood is easy. Either they have never really done it and are just passing on what they've read, or they're full-time boatbuilders who have actually done it often enough so that it really is easy—for them anyway. For me and you, laminating frames will be easier, and we won't have to worry about some Rube Goldberg steaming contraption torching the garage, or having plastic surgery to reconstruct scalded flesh.

True steam bending is a complex art that requires a lot of practice and an understanding of wood dynamics you don't get from reading about it. Properly steamed, a piece of ash or white oak several inches square will be rendered temporarily as flexible as an overcooked noodle. To bend successfully, the wood used must be rift sawn with perfectly straight grain, and most woods steam best when dead green. Unless you have an uncle who owns a sawmill, just obtaining decent steaming wood can be a major headache. If you have a lot of frames to replace, or if you just want to try steaming wood, both Robert Steward and Howard Chapelle will give you enough information to get started. But it makes a lot of sense and will save you a lot of time if you can get an experienced boatbuilder to show you how to do it. Better yet, take a course in framing technique at any one of a number of good schools that teach boatbuilding courses.

LAMINATING BENT FRAMES

Besides being much easier to make in small numbers, laminated frames are stronger and more stable than steam-bent frames. Bent wood wants nothing more than to straighten out again, and left to their own devices, steam-bent frames will do just that. Frames laminated into a curve are locked into that position forever and don't need the rest of the hull to hold them in shape.

Occasionally I read someone's advice to avoid laminated frames because they will eventually delaminate, but I've never seen a single example of wood properly laminated with epoxy coming loose even under the most extreme conditions. In fact, as an informal experiment I once tossed a few cut-off ends of laminated oak frames into an old galvanized bucket full of water. I covered it with a scrap of plywood weighted with a hunk of lead, stuck it out in the garage, and forgot about it until the bucket rusted through several years later. The wood was a mess, but the glue joints were as strong as new.

Making a New Frame

Replacement frames can easily be laminated outside the boat, providing of course you have enough room to install them once they're built. You'll need a duck board, which is nothing more than a scrap of plywood with a bunch of 90-degree brackets (called ducks because they resemble lofting ducks used by boatbuilders in laying down lines) screwed to it to make a form and serve as a clamping surface (Figure 7-8).

The wood for the new frames should be the same type of wood as the original frames. Cut the wood about a foot longer than the finished product and slightly wider, then rip it into strips on your table saw. The thickness of the strips will depend on how sharp a bend you need and the properties of the wood you're bending, and is best determined by trial and error. You want the wood to bend easily, but you also want as few laminations as possible. Usually stock ⅛ to ¼ inch thick works well.

Figure 7-8.
A duck-board setup.

If you were able to remove the old frame intact, use it as a pattern to lay out the ducks. If not, use a heavy piece of copper wire to make a pattern of the curve, and use this pattern to transfer the curve to the ducks. Screw the ducks down securely over a piece of waxed paper to prevent dripping epoxy from permanently bonding

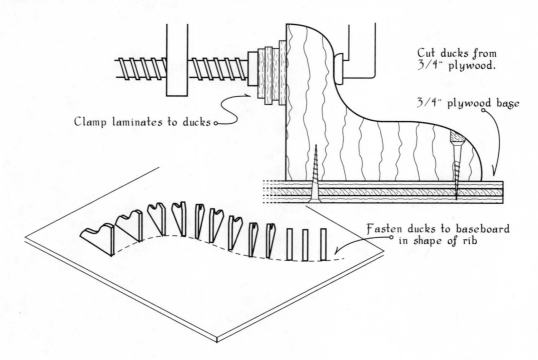

Clamp laminates to ducks

Cut ducks from
3/4" plywood.

3/4" plywood base

Fasten ducks to baseboard
in shape of rib

your ducks to the board. You can use the mold flat, but it's usually better to mount it vertically by screwing it to a wall or clamping it in a vice. The vertical board makes it easier to clamp up thin strips of stock made slippery by epoxy, and it makes cleanup easier because the drips fall clear.

If the finished frame is to be varnished, rip all the strips from a single piece of stock and keep them in order. When they are glued up and finished, the grain in the laminations will match perfectly, the seams will be invisible, and the new frame will look just like a single piece of wood.

Repairs in Place

In most cases it will be a lot less work to laminate repairs to a bent frame without removing it from the boat—especially in the case of a cracked rib where only a section of the original need be replaced. Remove the fastenings as before, and using a sharp chisel or gouge, carve away a section of the old frame until the entire cracked, broken, or rotted area is removed. Next, simply epoxy strips of the same kind of wood as the original into the section you removed until the original thickness of the frame has been exceeded slightly. The laminates curve to fill the cutout. Do not epoxy the frame to the inside surface of the planking but reinstall the planking fasteners as soon as you can, preferably before the epoxy sets.

Since clamping is usually impossible, holding the strips in place while the epoxy cures can be tricky and is best done with shores, depending on the access

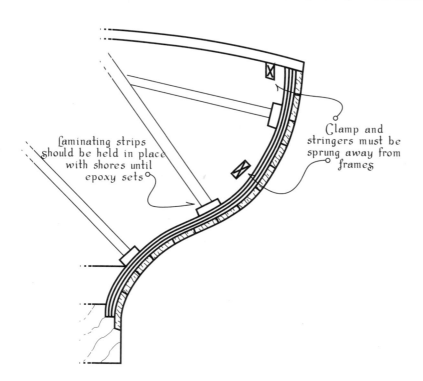

Laminating strips should be held in place with shores until epoxy sets

Clamp and stringers must be sprung away from frames

Figure 7-9. Laminating frames in place. See Figure 7-7 for an alternate method.

and other limiting factors. Sometimes it's easier to laminate the strips one at a time, shoring each in place only long enough for the epoxy to set. In this case replace the fasteners only after the last strip is laminated. It is, of course, possible to laminate an entire frame in place using this method, provided you can devise an effective means of clamping or shoring the strips together securely.

The most difficult part of laminating repairs or replacement frames in place is finishing the patch after the epoxy has cured. The compound curves of some repairs will take a lot of tedious work to get them looking just right, but it's always worth the effort even if the repair won't normally be visible. My old Grandpappy used to say, "If it don't look fixed, it ain't fixed." Usually some combination of sanding, scraping, and block planing will do the job. If you have a radius plane, it will make short work of the inside curves.

Knee Repairs

If your old wooden boat has bent knees that need repair or replacement, laminate them the same way you would bent frames. Sawn knees are inherently weak because there is always cross grain in an awkward spot, which is why the old-timers used natural knees cut from spruce or larch roots. I usually make replacements for sawn knees out of plywood to eliminate the problems with the grain. If the knee will show and you want to varnish it, plywood won't look right. Laminate the replacement out of two thicknesses of solid stock, each half the thickness of the original knee. Epoxy the two pieces together with their grains perpendicular. You'll have a very strong knee, and no one will notice that it isn't a single piece.

Figure 7-10.
Laminated knees.

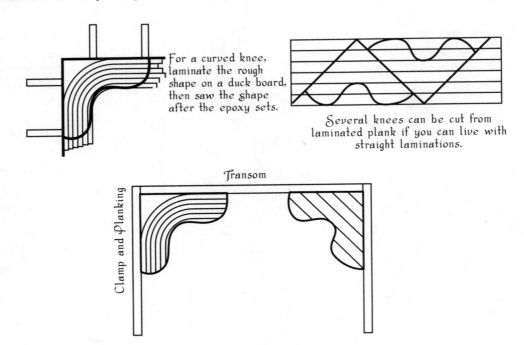

For a curved knee, laminate the rough shape on a duck board, then saw the shape after the epoxy sets.

Several knees can be cut from laminated plank if you can live with straight laminations.

Transom

Clamp and Planking

PLANK REPAIRS

Replacing one or two planks isn't beyond the skill of anyone who is moderately handy with tools, although it may seem a bit intimidating at first. Proceed slowly and carefully and don't worry if something goes wrong; there's nothing you're going to do that can't be done over if it doesn't come out right the first time.

If the planking on your old wooden boat is so far gone that she needs a whole new bottom, you're going to need outside help. A replanking job is really beyond the scope of this book, but once you remove the old planking and repair any frames that need it, replanking isn't dramatically different from planking a new hull. Several good books cover the subject, including, of course, those by Steward and Chapelle, and all the boatbuilding schools offer seminars on planking.

SPILING

One of the big differences between a boat carpenter and a run-of-the-mill cabinet-maker is the ability to make accurate reproductions of complex shapes using tick sticks and spiling battens. We will deal with tick sticks later, but in order to make planking repairs, you must be able to make an accurate spiling.

Most authorities on boatbuilding recommend the use of dividers or a compass for spiling, but the method I use and the one I'm going to describe to you uses neither. It was taught to me by an accomplished boatbuilder named Paul Ton That who worked in my shop in Beverly and taught for a while at the Northwest School of Wooden Boatbuilding in Port Townsend, Washington.

All spiling starts with a proper spiling batten, which is any thin, flexible piece of scrap stock cut slightly smaller than the plank you want to replace. My favorite batten material is ¼-inch Melamine-surfaced plywood I mooch off of a local cabinetmaker. It's flexible and the white surface takes a pencil mark readily; and the marks erase just as readily, so the batten can be reused many times. But don't worry too much about the material; any thin stock will do fine.

You also need a spiling block—a wood block the same thickness as the planking material and measuring about 1½ X 3 inches. All surfaces of the block should be finished and dressed square.

After the old plank you're replacing is removed and the dirt, flaky paint, and old caulking has been cleaned from the opening, attach the batten to the exposed ribs using tacks—or clamps, if you have room. It is critical that you get the bat-

Figure 7-11. Using a spiling block.

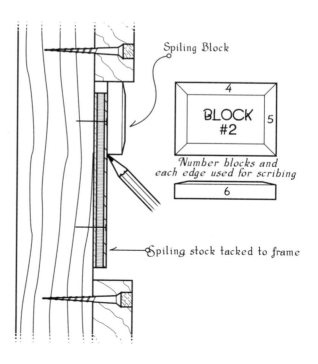

Figure 7-12. Marking a spiling batten for a replacement plank.

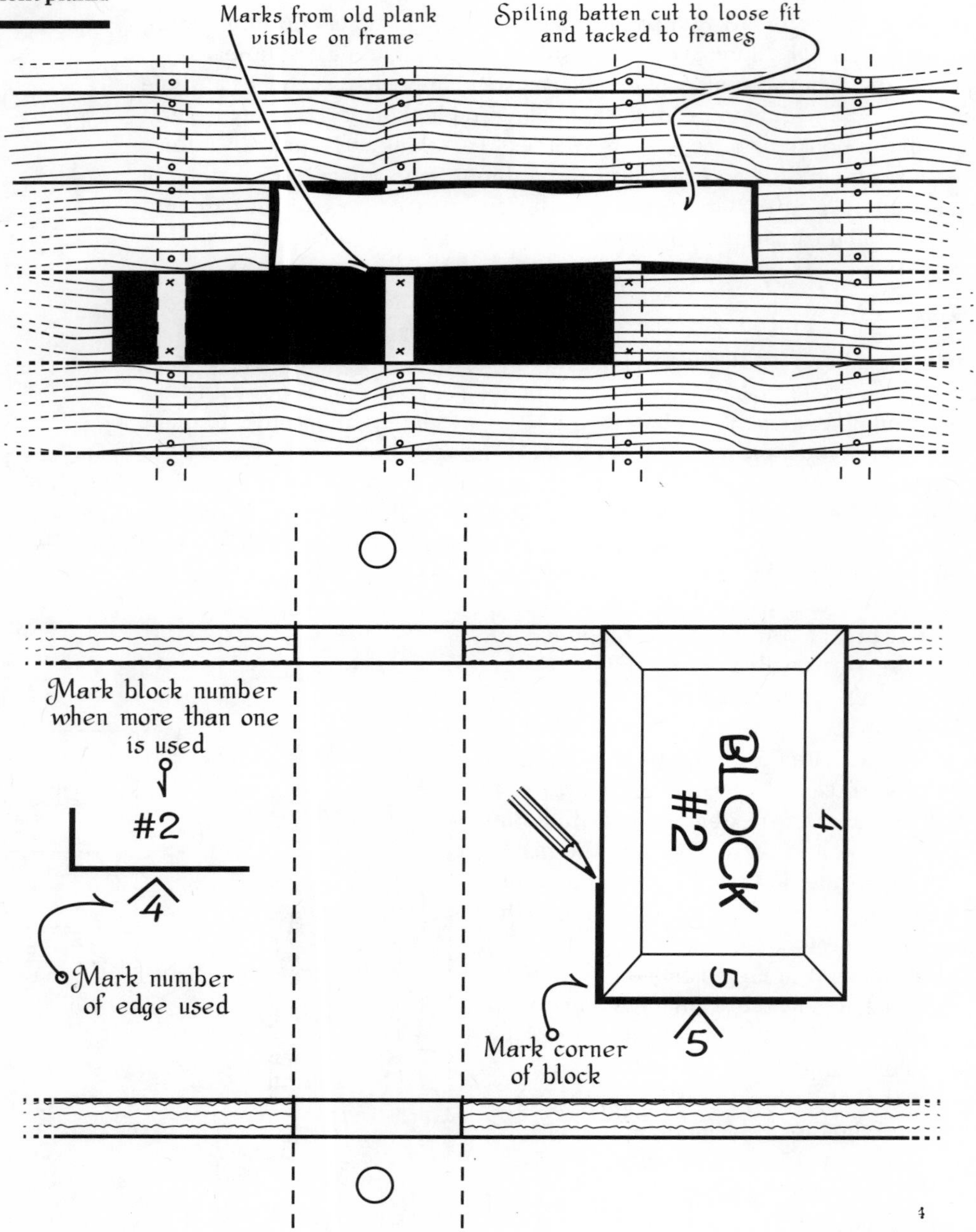

Marks from old plank visible on frame

Spiling batten cut to loose fit and tacked to frames

Mark block number when more than one is used

#2

4

Mark number of edge used

BLOCK #2

4

5

5

Mark corner of block

ten to lie perfectly flat against the frames; if it's sprung, the resulting plank won't fit. Make a mark on the batten showing the location of each rib; this will help orient the new plank when it is installed.

Using a Spiling Block

Starting in the middle of the batten, hold one end of your spiling block flush against the lower edge of the plank above the batten and scribe a line along the bottom end of the block and up one side for about ¼ inch. Slide the block a few inches to your right and repeat the marking process. OK, you have the idea. Just continue this marking procedure all the way around the batten until you get back to your first mark. Take special care in the corners, and it's perfectly all right to lay the block on its side or even to use several blocks of different sizes if that will make the job easier. If you're using more than one block, number them and note the number of the block used by each mark on the batten.

Once the marking is complete, remove the batten from the boat and tack it lightly to the planking material. Now simply reverse the marking sequence. Mark the location of the ribs first, then place the block back on the batten right on the first line you made and scribe a line on the new plank, using the upper edge of the block as a guide. Repeat this procedure until you have scribed a mark on the planking for each of the marks you made on the batten.

Put a 4d finish nail in every 12th mark or so, slightly off to one side or the other (be consistent) and just far enough into the wood so that they're sturdy. I have a bunch of ice picks I use instead of nails, but they are kind of hard to find these days. Make a fairing batten out of any straight-grained, flexible piece of wood and spring it around the nails so that it touches at each of the marks. Hold the fairing batten in place with a few more nails (ice picks if you have them) and scribe a line on the new plank. Repeat for each dimension of the plank, and you'll have a perfect pattern of your new plank ready for your bowsaw.

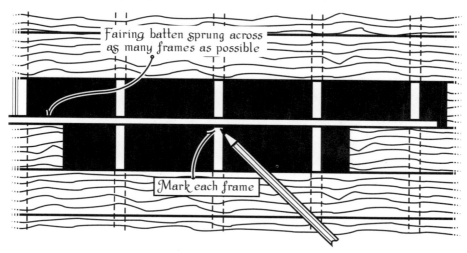

Figure 7-13.
Using fairing batten.

If your repair involves more than one plank, you won't be able to spile the lower edge of the top plank because there is no adjacent edge to spile against. The width of the old plank is usually obvious from the mark left on the original frames by the seam. If it isn't, the planks must be laid out on the frames using a fairing batten sprung between the ends of the remaining planks. Set your dividers for the width at each frame and transfer it to the corresponding frame marked on the new plank. Spring a batten over the marks, and you have your lower edge.

There are several advantages to using spiling blocks to mark the batten instead of dividers or a compass. In order for the spiling to be accurate, the compass or dividers must remain on the exact same setting for the entire marking procedure. I always seem to bump the damn things, which means resetting them if I notice it and a total disaster if I don't. Using dividers also forces you to do the entire job with one setting. With the block, you automatically have three settings (length, width, and thickness) just by turning the block and using a different edge, and it can't get bumped out of adjustment. Try it both ways and see which one you like best. I guarantee it will be the block.

If the old plank was in good shape and fit well before it was removed, sometimes you can use it as a pattern to make a new one. But if it isn't in such good shape and the fit isn't all that great, it's always better to spile a new one. At other times the old plank will have such a curve to it that it's impossible to make it lie flat on the new stock. If you attempt to force it straight, it will simply snap into pieces at the fastening holes. Besides, spiling is an important boatbuilding skill you should develop by practicing every chance you get—until your planks fit perfectly on the first try every time.

**Figure 7-14.
Using a bevel gauge
and a bevel board.**

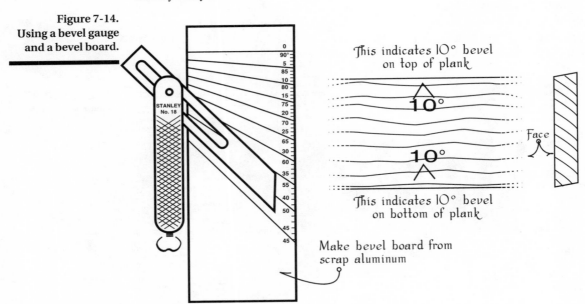

Beveled Edges

There is one more thing to do before you cut out your plank. There's a good chance that the plank you removed doesn't have square edges but is beveled in one direction or the other, or even in both directions. Use your bevel gauge and angle board to measure the bevels and write them on your new plank. Don't assume the bevel is consistent: It isn't. You should check the bevel at every rib, or at least every foot or so, and mark it on the new plank accordingly. Be sure to mark the direction of the bevel. I do this with arrows that show the direction of the bevel at the top of the plank, but whatever system you use, make it easy to read and consistent so there is no ambiguity.

Boatbuilders use many methods of cutting bevels in planks. Some use a bandsaw with a floating table, and with the angles marked on a far wall, cut by eye. I like to cut the plank square to the large dimension and then do the bevels with a hand plane: It takes longer and would be very tedious if you were building a boat, but with only a few pieces to do in an average repair, it's a lot less risky.

Carvel Planking

Repairing or replacing a carvel plank on an average-size pleasure boat is a straightforward exercise in precision carpentry. (On a big dragger it can be a monster, but that's not what we're talking about.) First remove all the old fasteners and carefully remove the old plank. Take particular care not to damage the edges of adjacent planks and resist the temptation to pry the old plank out with a chisel or screwdriver. Rake out the dried compound and caulking with the bent-over tang of an old file and tap the old plank free from inside the hull if you can get at it. Clean up the opening and inspect the surfaces of the adjoining planks, and check the bearing surface of the frames for hidden damage or rot. Don't be surprised if the removal of a plank reveals unexpected damage in adjoining members—it happens all the time, and it's just part of the joy of wooden boats. At this point, assuming the wood has not deteriorated enough to require replacement, I usually saturate all the exposed frames with epoxy and fill any cracks and all the old fastening holes with epoxy thickened with Cabosil to the consistency of peanut butter. Since we want all structural repairs to be as strong as possible, when I call for thickened epoxy, I invariably mean thickened with Cabosil or colloidal silica unless otherwise noted.

Make a spiling pattern of the opening and carefully cut out the new plank, using a frame saw or a bandsaw. Even when there are no beveled edges to cut, I always saw just outside the pencil line so that the sawn plank is about $\frac{1}{16}$ inch oversize; then I make the final trim using a hand plane. This procedure gives a better fit and a cleaner edge than trying to saw right up to the line. It also leaves a little margin for error and later adjustment. If your spiling was accurate, the new plank should fit just right, not snug or tight but not loose either, and only a small amount of final planing will be needed.

Fitting

If the plank is a bit snug, don't force it. Put a little carpenter's chalk around the opening and put the plank in place as far as it will go. The chalk will transfer from the opening to the plank and show where the high spots need to be taken down. Actually, lipstick works better than chalk, but Susan always gets inexplicably hostile when I try to borrow hers. And if I try to keep it in my tool box, the guys at the boatyard look at me funny, and it always melts or gets loose and makes an incredible mess.

Most planks, even those with square edges, benefit from a 5- or 10-degree bevel three-quarters of the way across the thickness to allow access for the caulking and the iron. Check the other planks on your boat and use your judgment.

Laminating a Plank

Occasionally you can encounter thick planking with a radical curvature that's difficult or impossible to spring into place. Professional boatbuilders working on new boats will either steam these planks or force them into place with a fearsome assortment of shores and wedges and a liberal application of sledgehammer blows. Pounding on an old wooden hull with a sledge is bound to invoke the law of diminishing returns, and you're likely to cause more damage than you're fixing. You could steam the plank, of course, but the simpler way to make a difficult bend in a replacement plank is to resaw it on the bandsaw into several thinner planks. These are easily bent into position one at a time and laminated with epoxy as they're

Figure 7-15. Replacing a heavy plank by laminating thinner planks in place.

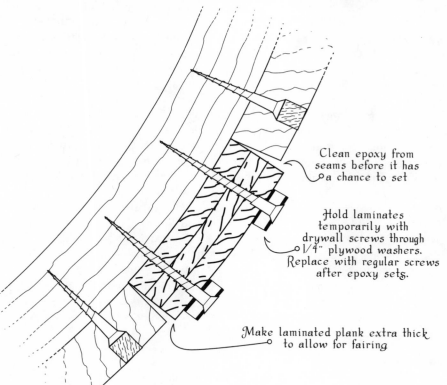

Clean epoxy from seams before it has a chance to set

Hold laminates temporarily with drywall screws through 1/4" plywood washers. Replace with regular screws after epoxy sets.

Make laminated plank extra thick to allow for fairing

installed. This will give you a stronger repair, and it's easier than trying to force a big plank into position with shores. Remember not to epoxy the plank to the frames or to adjoining planks.

Regardless of the thickness of the plank or sharpness of the curve, never give in to the temptation of trying to draw the plank into the frames with the fastening screws. Almost every amateur will try this on his first plank, only to learn firsthand that it just doesn't work. At best you'll strip the screws out of the wood, requiring the plank be removed to repair the frame. At worst you'll break the new plank at the pilot holes. Always get the plank in tight and held securely with clamps and shores before you drill the pilot holes.

Fasteners should be countersunk by no more than a third the thickness of the plank; you don't want to weaken the plank, but you need enough counterbore for the bungs. The Fuller counterbores and tapered drill bit combinations are perfect for this job because they drill the pilot hole and counterbore in one operation. When I drill a new pilot hole into old wood that is slightly spongy, I usually inject epoxy into the hole with a hypodermic syringe. The epoxy saturates the wood and firms it up. Put a little Butcher's wax on the screw so you can remove it later and drive it into the wet epoxy. If the screw won't hold, don't worry about it; let the epoxy set around the screw and tighten it after the epoxy has hardened. But remember not to use epoxy to install the bung; use varnish or carpenter's glue.

Caulking

Dana Story, a noted marine historian and author of several fascinating books on the building of fishing schooners (see Appendix A), describes how the resonant crack of caulking mallets striking making irons echoed continuously up and down the banks of the Essex River for more than 200 years. The ring of the mallets was as much a part of that environment as the sounds of automobiles passing on the roads is for us today. And he tells wonderful stories about the itinerant caulking crews that frequented his father's boatyard in Essex, Massachusetts, when he was young. He describes them as being aloof and remaining detached and distant from the other tradesmen who worked at the yard: They had a sinister quality that was a bit scary to a small boy.

When I was growing up around the Chesapeake Bay in the 1950s, caulking seams was a full-time trade for many people. In those final days of the dominance of wooden pleasure boats, no one would even think of caulking their own seams—at least no more than they would today think of painting their own car. When you had caulking to be done, you called a caulker.

Caulking seams is another one of those things that you don't learn from reading about it in

**Figure 7-16.
Caulking tools.**

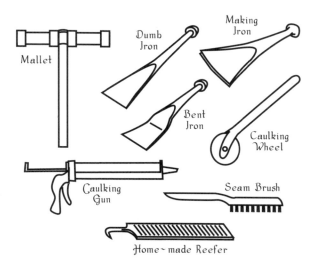

books; in fact, I'm convinced that many people who are otherwise handy with tools can't learn to do it at all. It's a tricky business with numerous variables. Take the tools you should use, for example. Caulker's mallets are wonders of evolution. As I mentioned earlier, they look something like sawed-off croquet mallets with thin, supple handles and elongated heads reinforced with iron bands. Handles were made from live oak or ironwood, and the best had heads made from black mesquite. They ranged in size from giants with 5-foot handles and heads as heavy as sledge hammers to small finish mallets with heads only about the size of a silver dollar. A caulker would have an assortment of mallets of several different sizes. Today nobody I know of makes caulking mallets, so unless you can locate one in an antique shop (you can't), you'll have to make do with a lignum vitae mall. These work surprisingly well, however, and they're much easier to learn how to use than the traditional mallet.

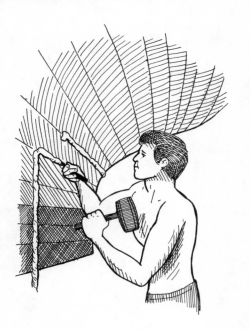

Figure 7-17. A student at the Landing School learns to caulk seams.

Then there are the irons; the old-timers had dozens of them. Most used were the making irons with fan-shaped blades grooved to set the oakum or cotton or sisal soaked in coal tar into the seam just so. Making irons were gauged by the thickness of their blades at the tip and ranged from $\frac{1}{32}$ inch (called wicking irons) to $\frac{1}{2}$ inch or more in thickness. And every caulker had an assortment of dumb irons that acted as wedges for opening seams without removing wood. Bent irons of every conceivable size and shape for reaching into all the nooks and crannies where leaks might occur completed his collection.

The next time you get a chance to inspect a set of old caulking irons, either in a museum or an antique shop, notice how smooth the shanks are. And try to imagine the caulker standing on a plank staging next to the hull of a new fishing schooner. The iron was held loosely in the circle of the forefinger and thumb of the left hand and struck with the mallet so that it bounced in the seam. The bounce of the iron was very important in judging the set of the caulking and was the reason for the exaggerated length and resilient oak or mesquite in the head of the mallet. The blows made cracking sounds like small-caliber gunshots and were struck in a regular cadence of about one every second . . . crack . . . crack . . . crack . . . for ten hours a day . . . crack . . . crack . . . crack . . . for six days a week . . . crack . . . crack . . . crack . . . for a lifetime . . . crack . . . crack . . . crack. That's why the shanks are so smooth.

Today you might get lucky and find some old irons in an antique shop. The Wooden Boat Shop often has an assortment of old irons on hand, and they carry new making irons in three sizes: #00 ($\frac{1}{32}$ inch), #0 ($\frac{1}{16}$ inch) and #1 ($\frac{1}{8}$ inch). Jamestown Distributors also has a small selection of new irons.

The third variable in the seam-caulking equation is the material that's used to fill the seam: Traditionally this has been any one of several fibrous materials such as cotton, jute, sisal, cannabis, or oakum. Over the years, I have been called on to repair a lot of amateur caulking jobs, and what I find stuffed into the cracks between the planks never fails to amaze me. String, clothesline, and stuffing-box packing are popular, but matchbooks and newspaper also have a following, and on one memorable occasion I pulled the elastic top from a pair of Jockey shorts out of a leaking garboard seam.

Amateur caulkers are fortunate in having a ready supply of caulking materials—jute, cotton, and wicking—readily available from several suppliers including Jamestown Distributors and The Wooden Boat Shop. Wicking is thin, like heavy kite string, and is used for caulking the narrow seams in the thin planking usually found on small boats; jute or oakum is used on thick planking with wide seams. The material of the most interest to us is caulking cotton, which is sold in one-pound bales. The cotton comes in folded strands and must be unfolded, twisted loosely, then rolled into a ball before you can use it. Frequently, two strands are twisted together for use in wider seams, but if a seam requires more than two strands, you should switch to a heavier fiber like jute.

I suspect that caulking a new boat that has been properly planked is a lot easier than recaulking either an entire hull or a repair. On a new boat, the seams should be clean and of a reasonably uniform width. On a repair, however, the seams between the old planks and the new ones are usually imperfect and the width of a seam can vary greatly. To compensate for erratic seam widths, you'll need to leave loops of cotton hanging as you tap it in place (called starting) between the planks. On new boats, the caulking material is sometimes started with a caulking wheel (a 3- or 4-inch brass wheel mounted in a wooden handle), but these are useless for most repairs.

Before caulking, prime the seam with any good primer, then stuff the cotton loosely into the seams using the making iron to form heavier loops to fill wider sections and lighter loops for the narrower sections. After you have the cotton started, go back and set the cotton into the seams by striking the making iron smartly with your mall or mallet. If the iron wedges in the seam or drives the cotton through the seam and out the other side, either the seam is too wide, the iron is the wrong size, or your loops of caulking are too small—retreat, reformulate your attack, and try again. When you get it right, the iron will set the caulking about halfway into the seam just tight enough so that the iron will bounce from the blow.

Getting just the right touch on the making iron is only learned from experience, lots of it. If you're following the foregoing instructions, you can't do a lot of harm by caulking a small repair yourself, especially where you can do it over if it doesn't come out just right the first time. But if you have a big caulking job to do, bite the bullet and hire a professional boatbuilder (a real boatbuilder, not a plastic boatbuilder) to do it. Or, even better, take a course at a boatbuilding school. Trying to caulk a hull or a major hull repair yourself with no experience or instruction is practically guaranteed to lead to disaster.

Once the caulking is set, give the seam another coat or two of primer, making sure the cotton is soaked with paint. After it dries, plane the repair fair and give it a final sanding. Now fill the seams with any good seam compound. I use Calahan's Slick Seam below the waterline and Interlux above the waterline. The old-timers would sometimes hollow the seam compound slightly with their fingertip so that when the planking swelled, it would push the compound out to make a perfectly flat surface.

In recent years polysulfide and polyurethane sealants have become popular for use on old boat seams. These products are all right for plywood construction where the seam is backed by a batten (as long as the seam is scrupulously clean), and I'm told that some, like Boat Life and Sikaflex 241, work OK on new boats (I wouldn't know—I've never caulked a new boat), but they're a disaster on old boats. The problem with using these products for repairs is that over the years the old planking absorbs oils that make the wood repellent to new sealants. To make matters worse, it doesn't happen over the entire length of a seam; if it did, the sealant would simply fall out. Instead, the sealant fails to adhere in spots here and there and sticks tenaciously everywhere else, so that after a while the hull leaks like Eliza's bucket. And now, getting the stuff out of the seams to fix the leaks is a real chore. If you feel you must use polysulfide or polyurethane, use them as a seam compound over traditional caulking.

Short Section Repair

In the past it was considered bad practice to replace a short section of a plank. Butt blocks were required to back up the butt joints, and they were weaker than the plank itself. When a plank was damaged, it was better to replace the entire plank rather than a piece of it. With the advent of epoxies this is no longer true, and it is perfectly all right to grave in a small section of plank using long scarf joints.

Figure 7-18.
Butt blocks—a prime
spot for rot, and a
frequent spot to
repair.

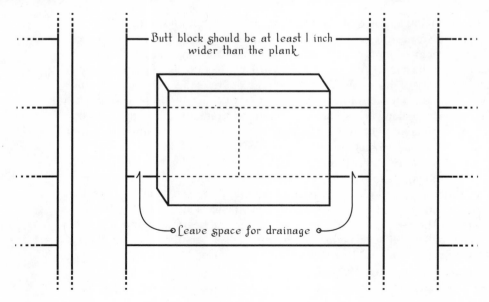

Butt block should be at least 1 inch wider than the plank

Leave space for drainage

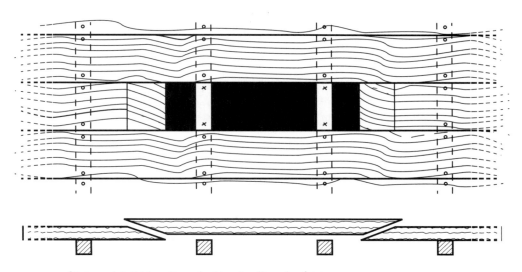

° Make patch thicker than planking to allow for fairing
° Hold in place with shores until epoxy sets

Lay out the patch so that at least two ribs will support the repair and remove the planking fasteners within the area of the repair. Carve out the bad section of the hull with a sharp chisel, leaving the ends of the planks tapered to form scarfs that are at least five or six times as long as the hull planking is thick. Make the cuts by eye, and if the tapers don't exactly match, don't worry about it. Clean up the opening and patch up the frames with epoxy as before.

Spile the replacement section for the width of the plank, letting the ends run long by ½ inch or so. Now plane matching bevels on each end of the repair piece until you get a rough fit and the patch stands proud by about ¼ inch. Cover the tapers on the existing planks with carpenter's chalk and press the repair firmly in place. Remove the repair piece and plane off the chalked high points. Do this over and over until the repair sits flush with the old planks and you have a perfect fit on the ends. Coat the scarfs with thickened epoxy and secure the patch by screwing it to the frames. Once again, avoid gluing the patch to the frames or to adjacent planks. Fair the patch with a hand plane, and you are ready to caulk and finish it.

A plank repaired in this way avoids the use of butt blocks. In fact the entire repair can usually be completed from the outside of the hull, so you won't have to remove any of the internal furniture. And the patched section of the hull will look like new and will actually be stronger than new.

Figure 7-19.
A scarfed patch is the quickest and easiest way to repair a small section of damaged planking.

LAPSTRAKE PLANKS

The trickiest part of replacing a lapstrake plank is getting the old one off the boat without damaging adjacent planks. The edges of the overlapping planks are most often riveted or clinch-nailed together with fasteners spaced every few inches, and the planks are nailed or screwed to the frames from the inside.

Rivet Removal

If the planks are fastened with rivets, you can sometimes cut off the heads from the inside with a grinder or disc sander and punch them out individually. If the rivets are countersunk and the heads can't be removed without affecting the wood in the plank or the frame, you'll have to drill the heads off from the outside and punch the rivet through to the inside. A spring-loaded automatic center punch will neatly dimple the heads of the soft copper rivets and make keeping the drill in the centers of the heads much easier. As a last resort, you can cut the fasteners by forcing a hacksaw blade into the seam and sawing them in half, but be aware that this is an excellent way to damage the planking; use it only in extreme cases where other more conventional methods have failed.

The ends of the planks are usually attached with screws into a rabbet in the stem and lap the transom if there is one. Remove these fasteners very carefully because the ends of the planks will have gains in the form of a steep bevel or a tapering shiplap. It's easy to split these gains if you don't remove the planks with care.

Plank Removal

If the joints between the planks are sealed with a polyurethane sealant, heat a thin, flexible putty knife with an electric heat gun and slide this into the joint to melt the sealant after the fasteners are out. A propane torch will also work, but it will be a lot harder to torch the boat using a heat gun. You may have to repeat this procedure two or three times before the plank comes loose because as soon as you move the putty knife, the sealant cools and reseals itself. Just keep repeating to yourself "plenty of patience and persistence pays prodigious premiums," and if you don't win a free trip to the Happy Valley Rest Home first, the plank will eventually pop loose.

If your boat is much larger than a small skiff, it is likely your plank will have a scarf joint in it since lapstrake builders hardly ever use butt blocks. This scarf was formed before the plank was installed, and it will be held together with rivets and glue that will defy removal. Removing just one end of a scarfed plank is difficult, and it's always better to replace the entire plank. If you must replace only a section, cut away the old scarf and recut a new scarf downstream a bit from the original, making sure the scarf on the section you remove goes on top of the section you're leaving, even if this means reversing the direction of the original scarf. This will make it a lot easier to replace the plank.

Since lapstrake planking is often much thinner than other types of conventional planking, the old plank can usually be made to lie flat on the new planking stock to serve as a pattern. This is just as well because spiling a replacement plank is complicated somewhat by the gains on the ends, and it's much easier to just copy the old plank. Clamp the old plank to the new stock or hold it in place with weights. I keep four or five 25-pound bags of birdshot handy just for this sort of thing; you can buy bags of birdshot at any large gun store, and they work much better than sandbags. It is important to copy exactly the bevels in the sides of the plank where the planks overlap.

Installing the New Plank

Being careful to fit the bevels and the ends as well as you can, reinstall the plank. A plank on a double-ender will have to be sprung into place where the stems are rabbeted, and it will require some fitting with carpenter's chalk and a block plane. Once the plank fits just right, drill a hole in the top and the bottom of the center of the plank using the old holes in the adjacent planks as guides. Fasten the new plank to the old ones using machine bolts and fender washers. Usually #6-32 bolts work well, but any size that fits the hole will do fine. The purpose of the bolts is to clamp the planks together while you drill the remaining holes. Drill from the center toward the ends and install additional bolts as they are needed.

Once all the holes are drilled, remove the plank and run a thin bead of polyurethane sealant (Sikaflex 240 or 3M-5200 are both fine) around all the mating surfaces of the plank. Purists will say sealant isn't necessary if you fit your new plank properly; I say purists aren't necessary. The sealant will be invisible, it won't do a bit of harm, and it's good insurance against leaks just in case you didn't get the joints just right. Do not, however, use epoxy in the joints unless you're prepared to epoxy the entire boat.

Reinstall the plank and reinstall the bolts to draw the planks together and set the sealant. The rivets will draw the planks, but it's much better to draw them with the bolts and not depend on the rivets. Install the same type of rivets as the originals, working from the center toward the ends. Bucking rivets will require a helper to hold a heavy steel bucking block against the head of the rivet. The bucking block can be a short section of railroad track unless the rivets are countersunk, in which case you'll need a specially ground block with a head the same diameter as the rivet.

If you're using square nails and roves, buck the nail from the outside of the hull while you drive the rove onto it from the inside with a rove set. If you're fastening the planks with round copper nails with burrs, cut each shank slightly proud of the burr and upset it with a rivet set or a sharp blow with a ball peen hammer.

Clinch Nails

If the planks are fastened together with clinch nails, replacement is a little more difficult. I prefer to use bolts at about 2-foot intervals to draw the planks and set the sealant. Nail between the old holes where the wood is sound and undamaged. After the planks are nailed, remove the bolts and fill their holes and all the old nail holes with epoxy thickened to peanut-butter consistency.

Like riveting, clinch nailing on a large boat requires two people: one on the inside holding a bucking iron and one on the outside doing the nailing. Do yourself a favor and drill pilot holes one or two sizes smaller than the nails you're using. This will prevent splitting the wood in the old planks, and it shows the guy on the inside where the nail will be coming through.

After all the rivets or nails are installed, replace the screws in the stem and transom, reattach the planking to the frames, and you're ready for fairing and finishing.

STRIP PLANKING

I don't know of any way to repair or replace an individual plank in a strip-planked hull. With the strips edge-nailed and glued, the nails are completely buried in the hull, and there's no way to remove them. And even if you could get them out, you would still have to contend with the glue. It's best to treat the entire repair area as an integral unit and approach the repair in the same manner as you would a fiberglass or plywood hull.

Cutting Out the Damage

Mark off a square, diamond, or rectangle on the hull that incorporates the entire area you want to replace. Lay out the repair so that all straight sides of the patch intersect the existing planking on a diagonal, as shown in Figure 7-20. Since the entire hull is studded with invisible nails (I did once run into a strip-planked boat that was fastened entirely with steel *screws*), you shouldn't attempt to use any of your good cutting tools. Instead, get a 7¼-inch carbide nail-cutting blade for your Skilsaw from any good contractor supply house. Nail cutters look like someone's mistake because the teeth have a reverse rake to them and lean backward away from the rotation of the blade, but this lets you cut nails without having your saw throw broken teeth around the boatyard the way Wyatt Earp threw bullets around the OK Corral. You should use nail cutters any time you're cutting into a deck or hull that might harbor hidden fasteners, which makes them particularly good for cutting into strip planking.

Set the depth of cut on your Skilsaw to the exact thickness or slightly less than the thickness of the planking and carefully cut out the rectangle you scribed on the hull. Be sure to wear safety glasses and heavy gloves; pieces of cut nail flying about can easily penetrate unprotected eyes and skin. Cut a little past each corner, and the area of the hull you want to replace should fall right out. Now bevel the edge of the planking surrounding your opening. The bevel on the edge of the opening should be about 45 degrees or less and is best cut with your 7-inch disc sander fit-

Figure 7-20. Lay out the repair on a strip-planked hull as a polygon with all sides as straight lines.

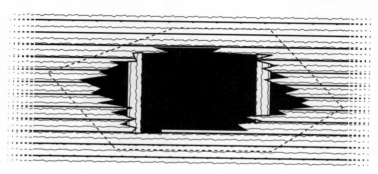

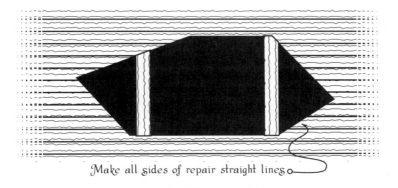

Make all sides of repair straight lines

Figure 7-21.
Cut out the repair area leaving the edges square.

Bevel at 45° or less (30° is better)

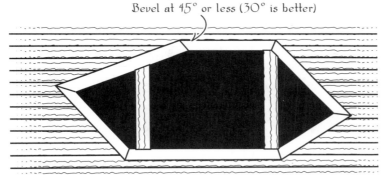

Figure 7-22.
Bevel the edges of the opening.

ted with a carbide disc, which will cut through the nails and the wood with ease. Make the bevel as neat as you can with the sander, then clean it up with a medium double-cut mill file.

Installing New Wood

Use strips of the same kind of wood as was used in the hull to glue up the patch that will go into the opening you just cut. Making up the patch this way gives the repair the same internal dynamics as the original, so that differential expansion and contraction won't crack the paint on the seam. Make the patch about ½ inch thicker than the hull to allow for any hull curvature that will be sculpted after installation. Glue up the patch with epoxy regardless of what was used on the original hull. Don't edge-nail the strips: The epoxy will be plenty strong enough without the nails, and you'll want to use your hand planes to fit the patch. Carve out the hollow to match the inside curvature of the hull and sand the inside surface of the patch smooth. Leave the outside rough for now.

Cut the rough bevel on the patch with a table saw so the patch stands proud of the hull by about ¼ inch. Complete the fit using chalk and a block plane. Saturate all the beveled edges in the hull and on the patch with unthickened epoxy, then glue the patch in place with epoxy thickened to peanut-butter consistency. It's not necessary to wait for the saturation coat to set before applying the patch. Replace the fasteners in the frames, if there were any, or hold the patch in place with shores

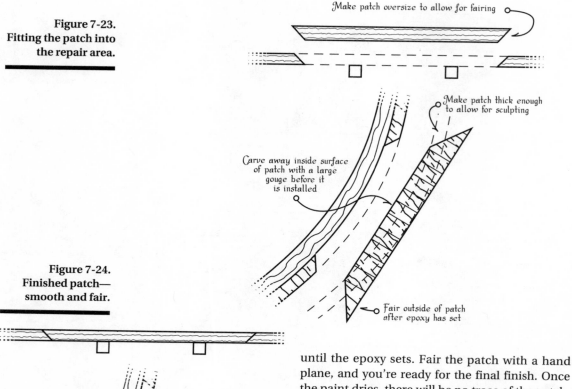

**Figure 7-23.
Fitting the patch into
the repair area.**

Make patch oversize to allow for fairing

Make patch thick enough
to allow for sculpting

Carve away inside surface
of patch with a large
gouge before it
is installed

**Figure 7-24.
Finished patch—
smooth and fair.**

Fair outside of patch
after epoxy has set

until the epoxy sets. Fair the patch with a hand plane, and you're ready for the final finish. Once the paint dries, there will be no trace of the patch, and you can give yourself another well-deserved pat on the back.

PLYWOOD

Many people are intimidated, it seems, by the prospect of having to patch a plywood hull. One reason might be that there is so little instructional material available on how to go about it. Even worse, the few sources I've seen are just plain wrong, invariably calling for a difficult procedure that will surely result in a weakened hull and a highly visible and ugly patch.

The problem with plywood is that, unlike repairs to other types of planking, you can't make up a patch in advance thick enough to allow for fairing after installation because you must use plywood for the patch that is the same thickness as the hull. Any planing or grinding on the patch after it is installed will cut through the plies and substantially weaken it. If you try to use a beveled patch as you would for a strip-planked hull, you must achieve an exact fit, and this, in my experience, is

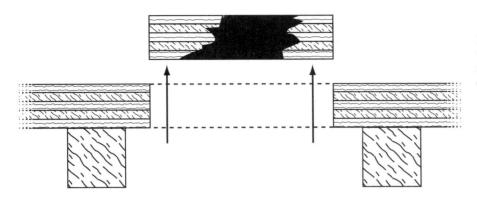

**Figure 7-25.
Cutting damage
from a plywood hull.**

practically impossible. Fortunately this is one of those rare cases where the right
way is much easier than the wrong way.

Start by marking out the area to be repaired with straight lines. The patch
doesn't have to be in any particular shape, but it should incorporate the entire
repair, and the sides must be straight. With the blade of your Skilsaw set to the hull
thickness, cut out the area to be repaired and remove it from the hull—just as you
would begin a repair to a strip-planked hull.

The Routing Template

Lay the piece of the hull you removed flat on a scrap piece of ¼-inch plywood
and scribe around it with a soft pencil, making a pattern of the cutout. Next deter-

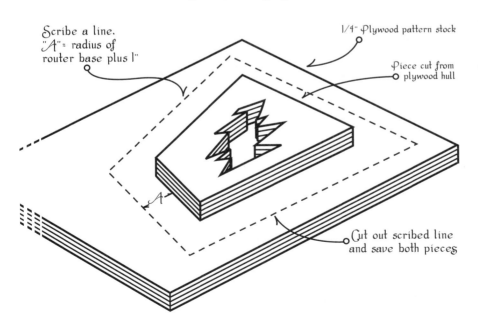

Scribe a line.
"A" = radius of
router base plus 1"

1/4" Plywood pattern stock

Piece cut from
plywood hull

A

Cut out scribed line
and save both pieces

**Figure 7-26.
Making a routing
template.**

mine the radius of the base of your router by measuring from the center of the collet, or bit holder, to the edge of the base. Add 1 inch to this measurement and, using
the result, scribe new lines on the scrap, parallel to the lines on your pattern. For
example, if the radius of the base on your router is 4 inches, you would scribe new
lines parallel to and 5 inches outside of the outline you made of your cutout, giving
you a square or rectangle that is 10 inches larger than your pattern. Cut out this
larger area with your jigsaw and retain both pieces. The outside piece will serve as a
template for routing the hull, and the inside piece will serve as a spiling batten for
cutting the patch.

The next step is to attach the plywood template with small nails to the outside
of the hull, making sure the template is centered exactly over the cutout. If your
hull has a fiberglass skin over the plywood, as many do, it will resist nailing. In that
case, attach the template with a thermoplastic glue from a hot-melt glue gun.
Remove any wax from the hull and the thermal glue will form a secure but temporary bond; any residual glue is easily removed with a putty knife when you're finished.

Rabbeting the Hull

Fit your router with a ¼-inch straight cutter, or better yet a ¼-inch machinist's
end mill, and adjust the depth so that it will cut exactly halfway through the plywood in your hull. If there is a fiberglass skin, you must use a carbide bit and set the
router to cut a little deeper to compensate for the thickness of the skin. Rout out a
rabbet all around the cutout using the template to guide the router. Since the
radius of the cutter is ⅛ inch, you should now have a rabbet that is 1⅛ inch wide all
around the edge of your cutout and exactly half the thickness of the plywood in
depth.

Shaping the Patch

Figure 7-27. Rout matching rabbets in the hull and the patch.

Trim just enough from the piece you cut out when you made the template so
that it will fit inside the routed area of the repair. You don't need to be fussy about
the fit—just tack it in place and use it to spile a pattern of the routed opening.
Transfer this pattern to your new plywood, as described earlier, and cut it out. The

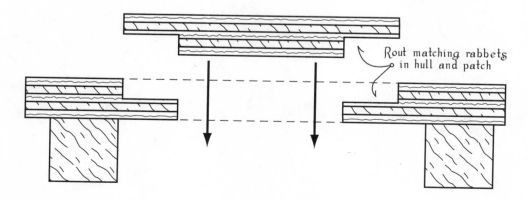

Rout matching rabbets
in hull and patch

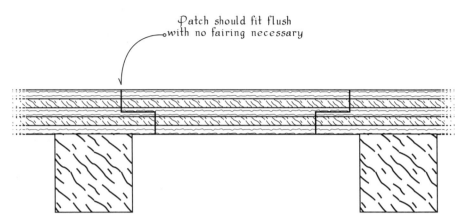

Patch should fit flush
with no fairing necessary

Figure 7-28.
The finished patch.

patch should now fit the routed area of the hull exactly and stand proud by half the thickness of the hull.

The next step is to rout a matching rabbet in the patch. This is best done on a table saw fitted with a dado blade (those of you both cheap and adroit can use an artfully wielded router). Set the saw fence 1⅛ inch away from the opposite edge of the blade and set the depth of cut to exactly half the thickness of the plywood. Since most dado blades are only ⅝ inch wide, you will need two passes along each edge to cut the rabbet to full width.

Now the patch should fit the hull cutout and lie perfectly flush with the plywood in the original hull. If it doesn't, use chalk and a rabbet plane until it does. The fasteners should be enough to hold the patch in contact all the way around, but in some cases you may need a few shores. When the epoxy is set, you'll be ready for fairing and finishing.

Laminating a Curved Repair

Occasionally you'll need to patch an area of a plywood hull that has a radical curvature. Since it's much easier to bend a large piece of plywood than a small one, you will have difficulty bending your patch to match the hull. In this case, it's easier to laminate the patch out of thinner layers of plywood and build it up gradually to the desired thickness.

Start by cutting out the repair area the same as before, but this time rout a stepped rabbet in the hull corresponding to the layers of the thinner plywood you're using for the repair. In other words, if your hull is made of ¾-inch plywood and you want to patch it with three layers of ¼-inch plywood, cut two rabbets—one ¼ inch deep and the other ½ inch deep. (Cutting the ½-inch rabbet first will make it easier to cut the ¼-inch one.) Naturally you'll need another template, but you don't need to be too fussy about it since the internal joints will be filled with epoxy. Because of the curvature of the hull, you may find that your router won't remove enough stock from the apex of the radius; if so, clean it up with a sharp chisel.

The next step is to back the opening with temporary battens that run perpendicular to the radius of the bend. Treat the battens with Butcher's wax (or other

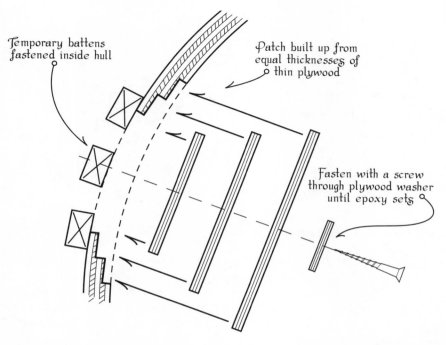

**Figure 7-29.
Patching a curved or
flared plywood hull.**

Temporary battens
fastened inside hull

Patch built up from
equal thicknesses of
thin plywood

Fasten with a screw
through plywood washer
until epoxy sets

paste-type floor wax with a high carnauba content) or mold release compound (available from Gougeon Brothers and other suppliers) and screw them into the hull from the inside where they will support the patch until the epoxy cures and can then be removed. If access to the inside of the hull is restricted, you can attach the battens with screws from the outside and just leave them in place when the repair is done, but it's better to remove them if you can.

Apply the patch one layer at a time, holding the layers in place with shores or with screws into the battens. If it's a particularly difficult repair, you can let the epoxy set between layers, but usually it's easier to put all three layers in place at once. To ensure there are no voids, use plenty of thickened epoxy between layers and let it squeeze out as you apply pressure to the patch.

If your plywood hull has a fiberglass skin, patch it with fiberglass and epoxy regardless of what type of resin was used originally. You may have read that you should use polyester resin to patch polyester hulls. I hear this all the time, but it's a prime example of folk knowledge, and it's pure bilge water. Epoxy should always be used for patching fiberglass hulls simply because it sticks to nearly everything, including cured polyester, about 10 times better than polyester does.

FIBERGLASSING WOODEN HULLS

Occasionally an old wooden boat will come along that's in good enough shape to warrant saving but has loosened up to the extent that the leaks can't be stopped with anything short of a complete refastening and substantial replanking. An option to this traditional approach *might* be to give the hull an outer skin of fiberglass below the waterline. That's an awfully big might, however, and any plan to fiberglass a hull should be given considerable thought.

It is, of course, possible to encase an entire hull in fiberglass. For small boats, up to about 20 feet, this is often the best approach, and the techniques for this process are detailed in Chapter Ten. For boats larger than 20 feet, the magnitude of the job gets well beyond the space we have remaining in this book. And since I've never done a complete fiberglass job this big myself, it would be presumptuous for me to advise you on how to do it. If you're considering this approach, I recommend—no, I insist—you read Allan Vaitses' book *Covering Wooden Boats with Fiberglass* (see Appendix A), which details the techniques he pioneered in his boatyard in Mattapoisett, Massachusetts. Vaitses advocates the use of polyester resin, which I don't agree with, but the man has forgotten more about wooden boats than you and I will ever know, and anything he has written is well worth reading.

Since most leaks occur below the waterline—rack up one more profound observation on the part of the author—a fiberglass bottom to your old wooden boat can make a lot of sense. If the topsides planking is so bad that it also requires fiberglassing, the boat is probably so far gone that it's not worth the trouble. If the boat is a real antique, or is otherwise valuable despite bad planking, then it probably deserves a proper replanking job. Fiberglassing the bottom of a large boat is extremely hard work, but the techniques are easy to master, and the job is well within the capabilities of an average worker.

Covering a boat below the waterline is a much easier job than doing the entire boat. For one thing, you need much less material, making the job reasonably economical and easier to handle. And working below the waterline, you don't have to be quite as fussy about the quality of the final finish as you would be working on the topsides, although you will naturally want to do a workmanlike job. Another important advantage is that all the added weight is below the waterline, where it will lower the center of gravity (CG), increasing the boat's stability rather than detracting from it.

Considerations

The most difficult step in covering a hull with plastic is deciding whether to do it. If you have a plywood or strip-planked hull the decision is easier. These hulls are dimensionally stable, and they take fiberglass and epoxy very well. A fiberglass skin over plywood or strip planking will add considerable strength to the hull with a small increase in weight. The only questions you must ask yourself are if your boat really needs fiberglassing and whether it is worth the effort.

If you have a lapstrake hull, your decision is also easy: you shouldn't consider fiberglass. I have seen it done several times, and in every case the hull was ruined. The glass adds too much weight and bulk to the planking, and the result looks terrible. An exception, of sorts, are those powerboats manufactured in the late 1950s and early 1960s with lapstrake topsides and plywood bottoms. Most were built when companies were desperate to cut costs, and many of them were so poorly constructed that it's unlikely you'll find one worth bothering with. A few, such as the Chris-Craft Cavalier series built in the 1960s, were fairly rugged, and you'll still see them in good enough condition to warrant some attention. Their plywood bottoms are good candidates for fiberglassing, if they need it, but treat the topsides with conventional repairs.

So with plywood hulls and lapstrake hulls the answer to your dilemma is fairly easy. (Yes, fiberglass plywood hulls. No, don't fiberglass lapstrake hulls.) But if you have a carvel-planked boat, there are several things to consider carefully. Carvel planking is very sensitive to moisture content. When a carvel-planked boat is launched after having been out of the water long enough for the planking to dry out, it will usually leak badly until the planking absorbs enough moisture to swell and seal the seams. The total expansion of a 6-inch plank can be upwards of ³⁄₁₆ inch or even more, depending on the wood and how it is sawn. As long as the wood absorbs water evenly, this expansion causes no problems and is, in fact, beneficial because it's what makes the hull watertight.

When a piece of wood is epoxied, water absorption is restricted. If all surfaces of the wood are coated, the wood stops absorbing moisture altogether and becomes dimensionally stable; this is one of the great benefits of epoxy in boatbuilding. If, however, only one surface of the wood is coated, water will be absorbed unevenly, upsetting the dynamics of the wood. The effect can be dramatic and catastrophic: moisture entering one side of a plank can cause the wood to cup toward the epoxied surface and the plank to crack and self-destruct. To demonstrate this, take a piece of dry wood about ¾ inch thick and 6 inches wide, coat one side with epoxy, put the wood into a bucket of water for a day or so, and observe the results. The wood will be so badly cupped that it will be rendered worthless. It's not hard to imagine this scrap of wood being a plank in your hull. The cupping can yank the fasteners right out of the frames.

Detractors of fiberglass skins on carvel-planked hulls will use this experiment in wood dynamics as proof that a fiberglass skin on a carvel-planked boat is a foolish thing to do. Yet I know of several boats that have had fiberglass bottoms for more than 10 years without any problems at all. (One of these, a Marblehead 30 power cruiser owned by Frank Lima of the Bass River Yacht Club, has had a plastic bottom for more than 30 years without a single maintenance problem.) I also know of other boats that have been ruined by poorly applied fiberglass. The lesson here is clear: If you do it right, a fiberglass bottom can add years of life to a hull that would otherwise not be worth saving; if you do it wrong, you can destroy your boat. Let's talk about how to do it right.

The *Duchess* is a good example of an appropriate use of fiberglass on a carvel-planked hull. When purchased, she was structurally sound, but she was starting to hog in the stern, and she leaked incessantly right at the two or three planks that formed the outer curve of the bilge aft. Several attempts by previous owners to repair her, including sistering 13 frames, replanking, and refastening, afforded only temporary relief even though the repairs were expertly done at professional yards. The problem was obviously one of design. With a flat run and no deadrise, the turn of the bilge was just too sharp for the cedar-on-oak construction that was used. The only answer to a permanent repair was a fiberglass and epoxy skin over the old planking.

We're talking here about boats that are too large to invert easily (small boats are discussed in Chapter Ten), so you'll probably have to resign yourself to working upside down. If there is any way to careen the boat without distorting the hull, you should do so because applying fiberglass to the bottom of a boat while lying on your back in the weeds and gravel must be one of the nastiest jobs ever conceived. If you do careen the boat, you can complete one side, flip the boat the other way, and do the other side. Getting the boat under cover will also make the job a lot easier; keeping the wood dry in the initial stages is critical.

Preparing the Hull

All the through-hull fittings must be removed—the rudder too, if this is practical—and the hull stripped down to bare wood and sanded with 40- or 60-grit paper. For more detailed instructions on stripping paint, see Chapter Eleven. Rake all the caulking from the seams with the bent tang of an old file ground to fit the seams, and let the planking dry out for at least several weeks. While you're waiting for the hull to dry, make any repairs to planking and frames, and replace any fasteners that are deteriorated or loose.

Now give two coats of epoxy to the entire area that will be covered, making sure the seams are well coated. The first coat can be thinned about 10 percent with lacquer or epoxy thinner, but the second coat should be straight. These first coats of epoxy will be absorbed by the dry wood and will seal the hull, preventing the wood from sucking the epoxy out of the fabric when you wet it out.

Next, fill all the seams with epoxy thickened to peanut-butter consistency. You need not wait until the seal coats set to start filling the seams. Just make sure the putty is thick enough that it will stay put and not run out of the seams before it has

Make a reefing tool by grinding and bending the tang of an old file.

Figure 7-30. Preparing the hull for fiberglass.

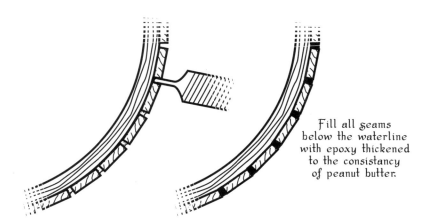

Fill all seams below the waterline with epoxy thickened to the consistancy of peanut butter.

a chance to set. Force the putty into the seams with a putty knife and fair the outside as you go along; epoxy with Cabosil dries very hard, and the less you have to sand off, the better. Let the epoxy set overnight, flush with water to de-wax, and sand the entire hull smooth with 80-grit paper mounted on your half-sheet pad sander. If the epoxy clogs the paper, you either need to de-wax more thoroughly or you need to let the epoxy cure a little longer.

Fabric Selections

After years of experimentation with other synthetic materials (Dynel, trade name for an acrylic which looks like the stuff from which onion bags are made, caught on for a while in the 1970s; Kevlar and carbon fiber [graphite] are popular today with builders who need great strength, light weight, and a quick way to dispose of large amounts of cash), fiberglass has proven itself to be a superior material for reinforcing resinous plastics like polyester and epoxy. It is reasonably light, incredibly strong, economical, and readily available in several forms of interest to boatbuilders.

Chopped strand. Chopped strand is simply loose fiberglass fibers that have been cut into lengths of an inch or so. It's used primarily in the construction of new plastic boats, where it is applied to a female mold with a chopper gun—an ingenious device that chops long ropes of fiberglass into short pieces, mixes them with the matrix (usually polyester), and blows the resulting slurry onto the mold with compressed air, all in one operation.

While the chopper gun has become an important tool in plastic boatbuilding, it has little if any use in boat repair. However, chopped-strand fiberglass does come in handy on occasion for use with epoxy as a thickening agent for filling large voids and fairing areas that need a little more strength than Cabosil provides. To use chopped strand as a filler, simply mix it into the epoxy until the epoxy won't accept any more. This mixture is often called *mishmash*, and it's usually molded into place with a tongue depressor or a plastic trowel. The hardened mishmash will be difficult to smooth and will usually need to be faired using epoxy thickened with microballoons or WEST System Microlight.

Fiberglass tape. Fiberglass in the form of woven cloth tape is one of the handiest materials available for wooden-boat repair. It can be used for reinforcing the seams of plywood hulls and scarf joints; repairing small dings, breaks, and rotted areas of wooden parts; and as tabbing to fasten parts together where conventional fasteners are inconvenient or can't be used. Cloth tape is available in various widths from 1 to 12 inches.

Fiberglass cloth. Fiberglass cloth is a woven cloth available in weights of 4 to 12 ounces (most fabrics are graded by weight, usually the actual weight of a square yard of the material; thus 4-ounce cloth is quite light and thin while 12-ounce cloth is heavy and thick) and in widths of up to 60 inches. The lightweight cloth is excellent for finishing brightwork that will receive a lot of wear because it virtually disappears when wet-out with epoxy. The heavier weights of cloth are a good choice for reinforcing decks, hulls, and cabintops because of the way they hold the resin and are easy to finish. You'll often hear the terms *warp* and *weft* used in conversations about fiberglass cloth. Warp refers to the yarns or threads that run lengthwise through the cloth, and weft refers to the shorter yarns or threads that run across the cloth.

Unidirectional fabric. Technically, unidirectional fabric shouldn't be called a cloth because it's all warp and no weft; it's simply fiberglass fibers all oriented in the same direction and lightly stitched to hold them together until they are imbedded in the matrix. This has two important advantages: first, it puts all the strength of the fiberglass into one dimension or direction; and second, it eliminates or lessens the crimp factor—the tendency for glass fibers to break when they are bent, as when they're woven into cloth. Typical uses of unidirectional fabric are in reinforcing spars and reinforcing cross-grain sections of hull planking.

Woven roving. Woven roving is simply cloth that is loosely woven out of much heavier yarns then fiberglass cloth. It is useful for areas where strength and bulk are needed, but it's hard to finish. If a finished surface is required over woven roving, it's usually best to cover it with cloth—or just use several layers of cloth to achieve the same effect. Woven roving comes in weights up to 24 ounces.

Bi-ply. Bi-ply, or biaxial fabric, is simply two layers of unidirectional fabric that are stitched together with the strands of each layer oriented perpendicular to the other layer. The strands are all oriented on the bias so that they run diagonally to the length of the cloth. Bi-ply is one of the best materials for reinforcing carvel-planked hulls below the waterline because vertically placed panels reinforce the planking more across the seams and the grain of the planks where all the stress occurs, and less where the stresses are minimal.

Mat. Fiberglass mat formulated for epoxy is composed of fiberglass fibers oriented randomly and lightly stitched together into a fabric. It is used where bulk is important but tensile strength is less critical. Frankly, I've found few uses for mat in repair work, but there are those who swear by it. I have, however, used it under a layer of bi-ply to reinforce a plywood hull where impact resistance was the most important factor. If you're using mat with epoxy, watch out for the stuff that is stuck together with a white powdery binder; the binder dissolves in styrene, the primary solvent in polyester, but not in epoxy.

Choosing Cloth

If you plan to use conventional cloth, two layers of 10-ounce fabric should be a minimum for a large boat, and I find the 60-inch width to be the easiest to work with. Since we're working below the waterline, seams in the cloth need not be butted but can be lapped and faired, which makes working with small pieces of cloth easier than working with large pieces. I apply the cloth vertically from the boottop to the keel, letting the end lap the keel by a foot or so. With two layers of cloth, this gives four layers on the keel where it's needed most. After the hull is complete, I run a 12-inch strip of additional cloth the full length of the hull, locating its top edge at the top of the boottop. This serves to fair the top of the glass and neaten it up, and it gives an added layer of protection right along the waterline.

Applying the Fiberglass

Start your application of cloth at the stern and work toward the bow. There are two ways to apply the cloth. One way is to coat an area slightly larger than your piece of cloth with epoxy resin applied with a foam roller and then apply the cloth to the hull, letting the epoxy hold it in place. Or you can staple the cloth in place, then wet it out with epoxy. When you must work upside down, the second approach is usually less frustrating than the first. Whichever method you use, apply the first layer on the transom or the sternpost and trim the cloth with a pair of scissors so that it overlaps the edges about 4 inches. Wear good rubber gloves and

Figure 7-31.
The first layers of fiberglass cloth should go over the transom.

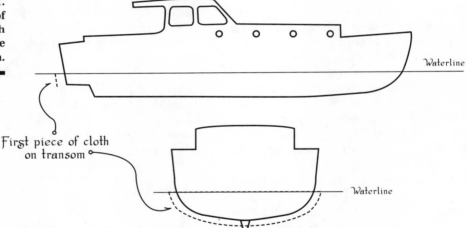

smooth the cloth with your hands once it's in place, cutting darts around the edges where they are needed. A special laminating roller will help work the cloth into tight areas.

Put the first layer of cloth on the hull planking so that the aft edge is even with the stern and runs from a few inches above the waterline to just past the keel. Trim the cloth to fit the angle of the transom. If the boat isn't careened and is sitting on an even keel, repeat the process on the other side of the boat. With conventional cloth, you'll want at least two layers, and the second layer is best put on over the first before the first cures. This is not as critical as it is when working with polyester, but it does save the work of having to de-wax the cured epoxy.

When the first layer on the transom is tack-free, put the second layer of cloth over the transom. Next cut a piece of cloth the proper length for the next layer over

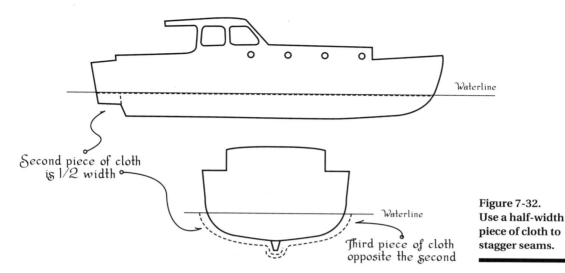

Second piece of cloth is 1/2 width

Waterline

Third piece of cloth opposite the second

Waterline

Figure 7-32.
Use a half-width
piece of cloth to
stagger seams.

the planking, then cut it in half lengthwise and apply the halves to opposite sides of the hull over the first layer, keeping the edge even with the transom. These half-width pieces of cloth will serve as the starter for the second layer, assuring that the seams for subsequent pieces will be staggered.

Now place another layer of glass forward of the first, letting the edges overlap by an inch or so, and repeat the process on the other side. You will then have the transom covered and 2½ pieces of cloth covering the planking on each side of the hull. Place the next piece of cloth so that it laps the half sheet and covers half of the

Figure 7-33.
Layering sequence
for cloth pieces.

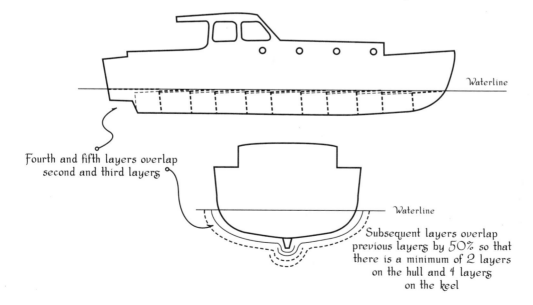

Waterline

Fourth and fifth layers overlap second and third layers

Waterline

Subsequent layers overlap previous layers by 50% so that there is a minimum of 2 layers on the hull and 4 layers on the keel

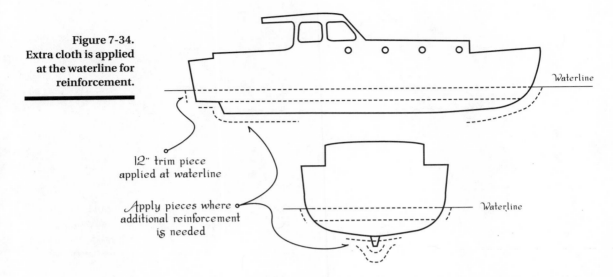

Figure 7-34.
Extra cloth is applied
at the waterline for
reinforcement.

Waterline

12" trim piece
applied at waterline

Apply pieces where
additional reinforcement
is needed

Waterline

second sheet. Simply progress down the hull alternating layers of glass cloth until you reach the bow.

There is a bit of contention with the lapped seams that result from the way I apply fiberglass. These seams would obviously be unacceptable on the topsides, but below the waterline they're barely noticeable once they're faired. I feel that the double layers of glass act as external ribs, stiffening the hull where it needs to be stiffened most. If you are a neatnik, however, and the slight irregularity in the hull caused by the seams bothers you, or if you're using biaxial fabric that results in even more obvious seams, it's quite simple to butt the seams. Wait for the epoxy to set tack-free (usually about 20 or 30 minutes, depending on the temperature, type of hardener, and a few other things) and run a sharp utility knife down the center of the seam. Peel back the cloth and remove the cut sections, then replace the cloth and roll out the seam with fresh epoxy, and you'll have an invisible seam.

When the entire hull has been covered with two layers of cloth placed vertically, run a 12-inch-wide strip of cloth longitudinally right at the waterline or boottop. At the same time, run a similar piece of cloth over any area you feel might benefit from some extra support. The stem, rudder support, through hulls, and keel are just a few possibilities. Remember, it is very difficult to get too much glass on your boat. It's easy not to use enough.

Finishing the Job

After you've finished applying the cloth, give the entire hull one more coat of resin to fill the weave. This last coat should leave the hull with a shiny surface with none of the texture of the fabric showing through; if it isn't perfectly smooth, roll on additional coats until it is. Let the epoxy cure and carefully inspect the hull for any pinholes or bubbles. The pinholes can be filled with resin, but you must make sure you get them all; it is amazing how much water can leak through the tiniest hole.

Bubbles require more drastic action to repair. They will show up as light-colored areas under the cloth and will have a hollow sound when you tap them. To repair a bubble, first grind it off with your disc grinder, feathering the edges into the surrounding fiberglass. Next laminate two patches of cloth over the bubble. The first piece should be about 1 inch larger than the bubble and the second about 3 inches larger. Roll out the repair with plenty of fresh resin.

Sand and fair the cured hull, being careful not to cut through the glass. I like epoxy thickened with WEST Microlight for a fairing compound; it trowels on easily and sands out very well. If you insist, you can get away with using Bondo as a fairing compound. If it falls off, it'll look like hell, but it won't do the boat any harm. Bondo does have the advantage of rapid cure whereas the epoxy product must cure overnight before you can finish it. Even a purist like me will resort to using it when time is a critical factor. When it's fair and smooth (get your eye right down next to the hull and look for dips, dings, and other uglies—preferably in strong sidelight), reinstall the rudder, through hulls, and other hardware, and you're all set for bottom paint.

By applying the fiberglass skin in this manner, you have effectively locked the wood into a single, cohesive unit strong enough to resist the planking's tendency to expand and contract with changes in moisture content and temperature. You can now enjoy the best of both worlds—a wooden boat from the waterline up and on the inside where it counts, and a fiberglass boat on the outside below the waterline where no one can see it. In fact, no one need know about it but you and me, and I would never tell.

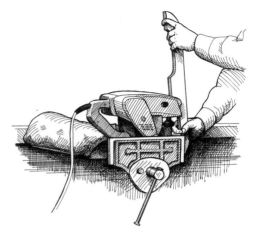

CHAPTER EIGHT

All Hands on Deck

When we are cruising in the old *Duchess* and finally get the hooks out after a long day, I always make a ritual of lifting the cabin sole and checking the bilge for leaks. And, as if she were concerned that my efforts be for naught, the old girl always obliges with just enough greasy water splashing about to affirm that, even with her new fiberglass bottom, she is indeed an old wooden boat. Late at night, as I lie half awake, happy to have eluded sleep for a few precious moments, I listen as the gentle splashing of the bilge water joins the groaning of the timbers and the creaking of the anchor rode in a syncopated lullaby of peace and serenity. About once every other day the mechanical hum of the automatic bilge pump lets me know the time for renewal is at hand, and we begin the game again.

Once, a long time ago, I bought a new plastic boat that didn't leak, and it was a most unsatisfactory experience. The waves slapping against the sides of the hull were loud and harsh, like drumbeats with an arrhythmic cadence, and a poor substitute for the peaceful sound of sloshing bilge water. The pounding waves would frequently wake me, and I would rise in the night to adjust the hatches in a futile attempt to evacuate stale air reeking of styrene. Perhaps that boat and I would have gotten along better if I had drilled a tiny hole in her bottom, just big enough to allow a few quarts a day to seep in. But I didn't. I sold her instead, and now I know better than to ever buy a boat that doesn't leak at least a little.

DECK LEAKS

If the hull of your old wooden boat has a few leaks, get an extra bilge pump, lean back, relax, and enjoy the reassurance that your planking will never be overdry. As long as they remain under control, minor leaks in a hull are no big deal. Leaks in the deck or deckhouse, however, are an entirely different matter.

An unwritten but universal corollary to Murphy's Law states that if decks *can* leak, they *will* leak. Furthermore, when they do leak, they will always leak right over your bunk and always in the middle of the night. A few small leaks in your hull will serve as quiet reminders of the imperfection of man-made things and will teach you to cope graciously with minor adversity. But the smallest leak in the deck will make you rue the day you ever thought of buying a boat and will shortly have you reading the help-wanted columns in the *Death Valley Daily Bugle*.

If your old wooden boat has a plank deck, you already know what I'm talking about because it surely leaks. (If for some reason it doesn't leak now, it soon will.) Painted-canvas decks can be quite tight, but they're usually reserved for the top of the deckhouse where there's little traffic to break them down. Plywood decks are like plywood boats—they can be tight and look great, but once they have deteriorated, they're a disaster.

THE FIBERGLASS OPTION

The answer to most deck problems in old wooden boats is fiberglass cloth and epoxy resin. This is more heresy, of course, and is bound to get the name Trefethen vilified among wooden-boat true believers. But hold off with the verbal abuse for just a bit and let me explain. Our stated objective is to get your old wooden boat seaworthy, safe, and comfortable with as little expense and fuss as possible, and we've agreed that she must look good when you're done. The easiest and quickest way to do this is with plastic, and if you want to take a little extra care, no one will even know there's fiberglass anywhere near your boat.

Realistically, if your deck is not in excellent shape to begin with, the only option other than fiberglass is to strip the deck down to the deck beams and build a new one. Every repair technique I know of involves tedious and time-consuming work that is very frequently ineffective. This is especially true of planked decks, where just removing the old caulking can be more work than installing a watertight fiberglass skin.

The Brightwork Question

What about that nice mahogany deckhouse with lovely varnished sides? Well, I've already gone on record as being in favor of painting over brightwork. In most cases a neatly painted deckhouse is so far superior in appearance and practicality to a shabby varnished one that messing with brightwork just isn't worth the trouble. But I'll concede that many of you reading this aren't going to buy my argument and will want to keep the sides of your deckhouse bright no matter how much trouble it will cause you. Well, this is one time you can have your mahogany and eat it too, to mix a metaphor.

Brightwork on a deckhouse or deck that must remain bright can be handled in two ways. It can be coated with epoxy and finished with varnish as is described in detail in Chapter Eleven, or it can be covered in very light fiberglass cloth, which will virtually disappear when it is wetted out with epoxy resin, and then varnished. The first method can be satisfactory if the deckhouse-to-deck joint is very tight and you're reasonably sure it will stay that way. But in an old boat, it is more likely that the deckhouse joint is loose. In this case the thin layer of light cloth will add just enough strength to ensure the integrity of the joint and save your sleeping bag from the consequences of Murphy's Law.

DOING THE JOB

As with any other major renovation job, you should get your boat under cover if it's at all possible. Even a sheet of polypropylene stretched over a framework of 1 X 3 strapping will help substantially. Remove all the deck hardware, the toerail, hatches, stanchions, portlights, and anything else that isn't part of the deck itself. The more stuff you can remove, the easier your job will be.

Old Sealant

Typically the previous owner will have attempted to solve the leaking problem with copious amounts of polyurethane sealant or some other sticky stuff, like silicone bathtub-caulking compound. In most cases sealant has been merely smeared around the bases of the fittings and portlights where it looks awful and doesn't do any good at all, but at least it will come right off. In some cases, however, the job will have been done correctly, and the fitting will have been bedded in a small amount of polyurethane compound that will, if forced, tear a piece out of the deck before it releases. In other cases you'll find hardware that has been epoxy bonded

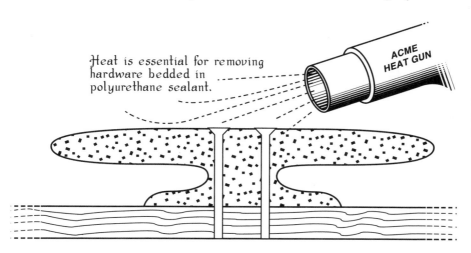

Heat is essential for removing hardware bedded in polyurethane sealant.

ACME HEAT GUN

Figure 8-1. Release bedded deck fittings with a heat gun or a *carefully* applied propane torch after the fasteners have been removed.

Figure 8-2.
Remove portlights
with a heated putty
knife. Be patent—
the sealant tends to
reseal itself after the
knife is removed.

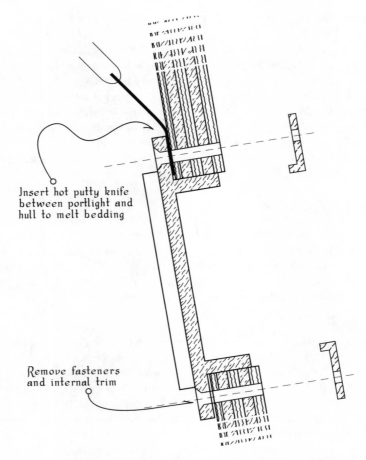

Insert hot putty knife
between portlight and
hull to melt bedding

Remove fasteners
and internal trim

to the deck. The correct response to both conditions is to apply heat to the fitting with an electric heat gun until the fitting releases. Apply the heat slowly and let it soak into the fitting. Large fittings may require 10 or 15 minutes with the heat gun, so be patient; and don't resort to a propane torch unless you absolutely must.

Portlights that have been bedded in polyurethane sealant present special problems. If you have an older boat, the portlights are likely to be bronze; newer ones are probably plastic. But in either case, unless you can remove the glass first, don't try to heat the entire fixture; you will surely crack the glass. Instead, after all the screws or bolts have been removed, use your heat gun to get the blade of a flexible 2-inch putty knife very hot, but not hot enough to burn the wood, then slide the blade under the lip of the portlight to melt the sealant. Be patient and keep working at it, and you'll eventually be able to work the portlight free.

Stripping the Old Finish

After the hardware is removed, strip all the old finish and get the deck right down to bare wood. If parts of the deck have already been fiberglassed, the chances are quite good that whoever did it used polyester resin. If so, the fiberglass may peel right off the wood once you get it started. If the fiberglass has adhered tightly to the deck, it is probably bound with epoxy resin, and removing it will require a heat gun and a large, stiff-bladed putty knife. Heat an area 6 or 8 inches square until the resin softens (about 150 degrees Fahrenheit), then scrape that area while you're heating the next; the fiberglass will come right off once you get the hang of it. Any attempt to save an old fiberglass job on part of a deck is usually false economy. It will be easier and look much better when you're done if you strip the entire deck and start from scratch.

The best tool for quickly removing paint from a deck is a 7-inch heavy-duty disc sander fitted with a foam pad that is faced with ¼-inch plywood and a 40-grit disc. Hold the disc flat on the deck with only light pressure; used properly, it's much less likely than a belt sander to gouge your boat. A good hand scraper will get into the corners and other places the sander can't reach. I shouldn't have to remind you that you'll need a face protector, a good dust mask, ear plugs, and heavy gloves when using the big sander. A pair of coveralls won't hurt either.

If your deckhouse sides are finished bright, or if there's any other brightwork you'll be fiberglassing, strip it with a chemical stripper or with a pad sander. Don't use your disc sander on your brightwork; the swirl marks will be more work to remove than you'll have saved. You can leave the decks and other areas that will be painted rough, but brightwork should be finish-sanded with 100- or 120-grit aluminum-oxide paper.

Coating

Give all areas you plan to cover with fiberglass a good saturation coat of epoxy thinned 10 percent with epoxy thinner, and top it off with another coat of unthinned epoxy to seal the wood. You can apply the epoxy with a brush or a roller, but on flat areas, a squeegee usually works best. There's no need to wait for the first coat of epoxy to set before you apply the second coat. Fill any voids with epoxy putty, but only after the saturation coats start to set so the putty will stay in the holes. You'll recall we used colloidal silica (Cabosil) as the thickening agent for the putty we used on the hull, but on the deck we don't have to worry about the planking being saturated with bilge water, and the requirement for strength is not as great. I usually use WEST System Microlight as a thickener simply because it's so much easier to sand when it cures. Never use autobody filler; I've tried it several times on decks, and it has always delaminated within a season or two.

Avoid using any filler at all in the epoxy for your brightwork—it will show through the cloth. Instead, grave in Dutchman repairs using wood for the patch that matches the original in grain and color. Make all these patches before you apply the first coat of epoxy. If you can't find matching wood and the repair is small, one neat trick is to steal wood from an area that will be painted or is hidden and use it for graving patches in brightwork. This way the patches will match the existing wood, and you can repair the spot where you stole the patch with just about anything.

Dutchman Repairs

I hope that in these days of heightened ethnic awareness and sensitivity, people of Dutch heritage don't take offense at this term. It originates with the mythical Dutch hero who saved the Netherlands from inundation by sticking his finger in a crack in a dike. A Dutchman repair is quick and easy to make once you do it a few times. The idea is to grave a sound piece of wood to replace an old piece that is damaged or rotted. For bright finishes, always select a piece of wood that matches as closely as possible the grain and color of the piece being repaired.

From sound stock, cut the plug for the patch on a bandsaw with the table set at a 10-degree angle. Most Dutchman repairs are small—2 or 3 square inches is about average—and cutting small blocks on a table saw is extremely dangerous (I have a somewhat abbreviated index finger on my left hand to prove it); trying to cut them with a Skilsaw is virtually suicidal. If you don't have a bandsaw, use a bowsaw. The plug or repair piece should be slightly larger than the area you want to repair and have a 10-degree bevel from square on all four sides. There's no need for the sides to be parallel unless you're a compulsive neatnik; some perverse individuals, like your dedicated author, actually prefer the looks of lopsided patches to square ones.

Once the plug is cut, place it over the area to be replaced with the small side down and draw a line around it with a carpenter's pencil, the kind with the broad, flat lead, sharpened to make a line about ³⁄₁₆ inch thick. (At one time I would borrow Susan's eyebrow pencils for this, but she stopped using them about the time see-through blouses went out of style—talk about your double whammies.) Also draw an arrow or some other mark on the top of the plug so you can orient the plug the same way each time you return it to the hole—the more uniform the plug, the more important this step is.

Now use a sharp chisel to carve away the damaged wood to just outside the outline you've drawn, leaving the bottom of the recess flat and the sides with a bevel of about 10 degrees from perpendicular. If the Dutchman is to be used to repair a structural member, such as a spar or a knee, the fit will be critical, and all the damaged wood must be removed, even if it means going completely through the other side. If the repair is cosmetic, however, the repair need be only ½ inch deep or so, and the fit on the bottom of the repair is not critical.

Coat the edge of the plug with carpenter's chalk and press it firmly into the recess—it will fit quite well but not perfectly. Remove the plug and pare away the chalk that has transferred to the sides of the recess. Use a sharp chisel and make very fine cuts. If it's a structural repair, keep doing this until the plug bottoms out, then chalk the bottom of the plug as well as the sides and keep going until you get a perfect fit. For cosmetic repairs, repeat the caulking and paring process only until the sides fit perfectly.

Once you have a good fit, thicken some epoxy to mayonnaise consistency and place it and the plug firmly into the recess, making sure the epoxy fills any voids that are left under the plug. The sloping sides will let excess epoxy squeeze out, and I usually give the plug a couple of good solid whacks with a hammer to make sure it's tight and to get the thinnest possible glue line. If you've done it right, about half

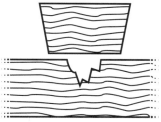

1. Make a plug slightly larger than the area you need to repair. Taper the sides of the plug about 10°. Orient the grain of the plug with the grain of the original.

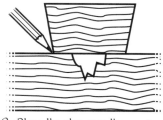

2. Place the plug over the repair area and trace around it with the thick point of a carpenter's pencil.

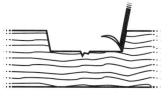

3. Chisel away the marked area to about half the depth of the plug.

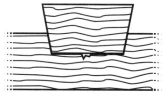

4. Glue the plug into the hole with epoxy.

5. When the epoxy sets, trim the patch fair with a hand plane and sand smooth.

Figure 8-3. Dutchman repairs are a quick and easy method of patching small areas.

the plug will still be sticking out of the hole, and the entire thing will look like hell. Don't worry about it; just go away and let the epoxy cure for awhile.

Once the epoxy has set—overnight is best—use your jack plane to remove the excess material from the plug, and sand it smooth with a sanding block. Don't try to remove the excess with a chisel unless you're an expert at reading the grain in a piece of wood; if you get it wrong, the wood can split into the repair, and you get to start all over again.

Once the repair is complete and sanded smooth, close your eyes tightly, look away, and count to 10. Now look back. If the repair has disappeared, and you can't even tell where it is, you can congratulate yourself on a perfect Dutchman repair; if, on the other hand, it jumps out at you like a hooker at a writers' convention, you probably need a little more practice.

Stealing Wood

Stealing wood, for lack of a better term, is a neat trick I learned a long time ago from a guy who made a living restoring furniture for the Smithsonian Institution in

Washington, D.C. Let's suppose, for the purposes of illustration, you're working on a 50-year-old mahogany sailboat that has bright coamings and painted cockpit seats. Let's further suppose that the coamings are perforated with holes where the previous owner had mounted his stereo speakers (I've seen it happen), and you want to repair them with Dutchman repairs that match the original wood.

The chances of finding a new piece of mahogany to match the old wood are remote at best. And even if you did find a piece of new wood that matched the old wood today, it won't match in a year or so because wood, especially acidic wood like mahogany, changes color over time, and new wood changes color much more rapidly than old wood. But since the coamings and the cockpit seats were made at the same time, it's a safe assumption that they were made from the same wood and might even be from the same tree. The answer to your dilemma is to use one of the cockpit seats for the Dutchman repairs and make a new cockpit seat from the new wood. Is it worth the extra work? Only you can be the judge.

On a smaller scale, stealing wood works very well for getting bungs to match old wood. Let's change the scenario slightly and have the cockpit seats finished bright, and let's suppose you need to reinforce the seats with a cleat that will be screwed down through the top where the bungs will show. (This is a common repair: When reinforcing old wood with cleats, always screw through the old wood into the new wood.) Simply turn the seat over and cut the bungs from the wood (careful not to cut all the way through) that will be covered by the cleat in an area that won't interfere with the screw holes, and use them on the top; fill the resulting holes in the bottom with larger bungs cut from fresh stock.

The bungs on the top will now be a perfect match in grain and color, and the unsightly bungs on the bottom will be covered by the new cleat.

Applying the Cloth

There are two general methods of applying glass cloth to wood with epoxy. The first involves rolling a coating of epoxy onto the wood and then applying the glass over the epoxy. The second involves laying the glass on the dry wood and then rolling or spreading the epoxy over it.

Neither method works particularly well in all cases, so you'll need to learn to use both. Generally, the first method works best on vertical and overhead surfaces, the second on horizontal surfaces. The weight of the cloth is also a factor—heavy cloth can be miserable stuff to hold in place on vertical surfaces, using either method. Some workers resort to temporary mechanical fasteners such as staples to hold the cloth in place until the epoxy begins to set. I frequently resort to my trusty ice picks. As you gain experience, your judgment will guide you. With either method, apply only enough epoxy to hold the cloth securely to the wood. Then, after it begins to tack, roll on another coat to fill the weave. Heavy cloth will take three or more coats.

I like to apply the second coat with a foam roller held in my right hand and smooth the cloth with my left hand as I go along. You may prefer to roll the epoxy with a serrated roller, sold by most epoxy-supply outlets for just this purpose. As I stated earlier, always wear rubber gloves when working with epoxy. I use disposable latex surgeon's gloves, which I buy by the case from a local medical-supply house for about 10 cents a pair (paint stores charge about 75¢). I always put five or six gloves on my left hand and two or three on my right before I start. Then, as the job progresses and a glove gets messy or torn, I simply strip it off and keep working.

Apply a single layer of 4- or 6-ounce cloth to all the brightwork, letting it over-lap the other areas of the hull by several inches, and wet it out very carefully. You should always use a single piece of cloth for brightwork, but if this is impossible, make careful butt joints (see Figure 8-6) and try to make them fall on a natural seam. Work in small areas and with small batches of epoxy. You won't be able to repair bubbles easily, so make sure there aren't any. This is best done by carefully smoothing the cloth with your left hand as you apply the epoxy with your right hand, as described above. If the cloth gets out of control and starts to bunch up and stick more to the roller than to the boat, it is much easier to pull off the entire piece and start over with a fresh piece than it is to try to fix the bad spots after the epoxy has cured. Don't try to use too much resin on the first coat, or you're sure to get runs and sags in the vertical areas; it will take at least two coats to fill the weave properly. The second coat should leave the surface shiny, with none of the texture of the cloth on the surface. Let the first layer of cloth cure, then sand and fair all the areas that overlap other areas of the hull so they won't telegraph through the next layer.

Working with fiberglass is an art form, like not burning toast. If you're not yet confident in your abilities, practice on some scraps of wood knocked together into an approximation of the angles you'll be dealing with. Only when you're satisfied you have the knack should you attack your lovingly prepared brightwork.

The horizontal areas of the deck and cabintop that will be painted should be covered with a single layer of heavier cloth: 8- or 10-ounce is fine. Trim and dry-fit the deck cloth around the brightwork so that it butts right up to the brightwork but

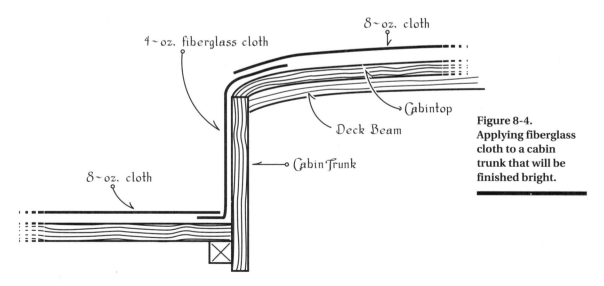

Figure 8-4. Applying fiberglass cloth to a cabin trunk that will be finished bright.

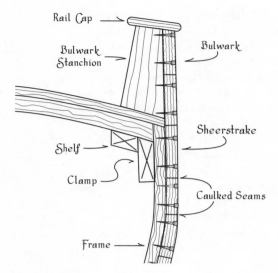

does not overlap it at all. Cut the dry cloth with a heavy pair of scissors. The cut edges of fiberglass cloth can be a real nuisance, but with practice you'll learn to deal with them. The glass on the cabintop can overlap the sides slightly, provided this seam will be covered with a trim piece; otherwise, it should be trimmed flush. Likewise, the deck cloth should lap the sheerstrake by an inch or so, and then this seam can be hidden behind a rubrail or toerail. If the boat has bulwarks (I love boats with bulwarks), you should bring the glass up the inside of the bulwark and under the caprail, which of course should be removed and finished separately.

Invisible Seams

Dry-cut as much of the cloth as you can, then, starting at the bow and working aft, wet out one piece at a time. Let the seams lap by about 2 inches. A deck is much easier to wet out than a hull, where you must work upside down. Mix small batches of resin and spread them with a plastic trowel. When the resin sets tack-free but is still pliable enough to allow you to pull the cloth off the deck (usually 1 or 2 hours), run a sharp utility knife down the middle of each lapped seam, cutting through both layers of cloth. You can use a straightedge if you like, but it isn't necessary; crooked seams will work just as well as straight ones, and they will be invisible when you're done. If the cloth drags and bunches up when you try to cut it, put a new blade in your knife and wait for the epoxy to cure a little longer. After you make the cut, remove the

**Figure 8-5.
If your boat has bulwarks, you'll have to remove the caprail and bring the fiberglass up the inside of the bulwark and under the caprail.**

**Figure 8-6.
Making a butt-joint seam.**

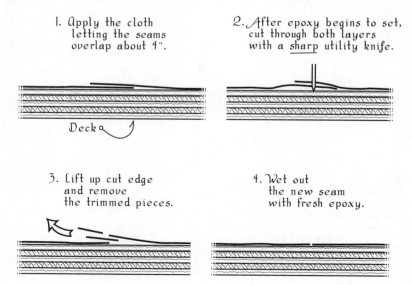

1. Apply the cloth letting the seams overlap about 4".

2. After epoxy begins to set, cut through both layers with a sharp utility knife.

Deck

3. Lift up cut edge and remove the trimmed pieces.

4. Wet out the new seam with fresh epoxy.

cut-off edge of the overlap, then peel back the cloth just far enough to remove the cut-off piece underneath. Now roll out the seam again with fresh resin.

Once the resin cures, you can fair and sand the deck, and then it's ready for paint. It's always much easier to paint the deck with the hardware, portlights, and all that other stuff that gets in the way removed. If you want applied nonskid, you can install it now—or just add a little silica to the deck paint in the heavy-traffic areas. As a final step, install all the stuff you took off (bedding it well in an appropriate sealant), put a lawn sprinkler on the deck, and go below for a well-deserved nap in a dry and comfortable bunk.

WOODEN DECKS AND OTHER FORMS OF SELF-FLAGELLATION

A lot of people have the impression that I don't like brightwork or wooden decks. This is completely untrue. I love brightwork. And I love wooden decks. I just love them a lot more on other people's boats than on my own.

It's not that I'm lazy, mind you; it's just that there are a lot of things I have to do that are more important than messing with woodwork. There are countless ponderables that need to be pondered, sunsets that need contemplating, wines that need sipping, books that need reading, kids that need to be regaled with tales of past heroic exploits, and yes, there are lots of beautiful varnished boats with teak decks that need to be admired. No, it really isn't that I don't like brightwork and teak decks; it's just that you only get old once, and I'm disinclined to do it while scrubbing teak or varnishing anything.

So you're not buying it, and now you're mad at me: You had a great-looking strip-plank teak deck, and I talked you into putting fiberglass over it. So what if it doesn't leak anymore?—it looks like a fiberglass deck, and you want your boat to look like what it is, an old wooden boat, not something you bought as a close-out at the last plastic-boat show. Well if you insist on a teak deck, you can have one—with a little work of course.

The old way of doing decks has been completely outdated by plywood and epoxy. But the old strip-planked decks did have redeeming qualities. For one thing they looked terrific on traditional boats, although teak was not used as much in the past as you might think: pine, fir, and larch were all used more than teak except on the most expensive yachts. And of course, there is the matter of traction. Natural teak decks seem to grip your feet; even a wildly pitching foredeck taking blue water will feel more secure if it's teak than any plastic deck ever will, nonskid or not. So if you really want one, and you have lots of money to spend, and you're not bothered by the rain-forest dilemma and the reprehensible politics of the exporting countries, there is some practical justification for a teak deck.

The traditional ways of decking a wooden boat are explained in detail by both Chapelle and Steward, and you should read both. But there are some very good reasons for not decking your boat in the traditional manner. For one thing, we already have a good, tight deck covered with fiberglass. You may have even fiberglassed right over a strip-planked teak deck just to make it waterproof. Weight is

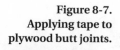

**Figure 8-7.
Applying tape to
plywood butt joints.**

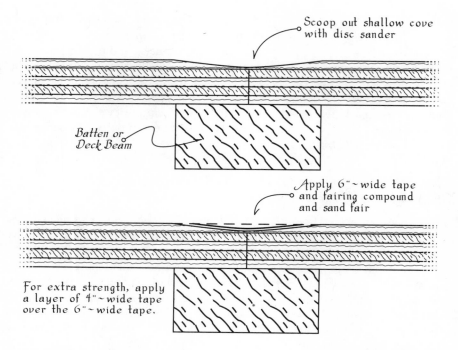

another factor. Traditional planking is anywhere from ¾ to 1½ inches thick, and teak is heavy—about 3½ pounds per board-foot. You just can't add that much bulk and weight to the top of your boat without suffering serious consequences. And then there's the expense. At the current retail of $12 to $14 per board-foot, enough teak to lay a ¾-inch-thick deck on a 30-foot sailboat would cost more than $3,000. As my daughter likes to say, "Let's get real, Dad."

The answer is to lay a thin veneer of teak over your newly applied epoxy and fiberglass deck, using more epoxy to lock the strips of very thin planking permanently into place. And even with this conservative approach, you must carefully consider the effect of the additional weight above the waterline . . . and the reduced weight of your wallet: It's still not going to be cheap.

To begin, strip the deck and fiberglass it as above. You can apply the teak veneer right over a plywood deck without the glass cloth if you wish, but this makes me a little nervous. A layer of 8- or 10-ounce glass between the old deck and the new one will add strength and stiffness and is definitely worth the effort. If you decide to do without the cloth over plywood, at least tape over all the seams with a layer of 6-inch fiberglass tape. Apply the tape with epoxy—just like cloth—but scallop the seams slightly first with your disc sander so the tape will lie flush with the deck.

Sprung Versus Straight Planking

There are two traditional methods of laying decking: sprung and straight. Sprung planking is bent to follow the outside curve of the hull while straight planking is laid (you guessed it) straight. Where the ends of sprung planking meet in the

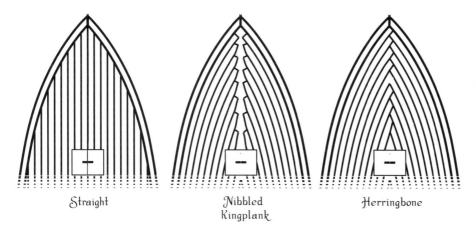

Straight

Nibbled
Kingplank

Herringbone

Figure 8-8.
Three deck-planking
plans.

center of the foredeck, they either interlock in a herringbone pattern or terminate against a *kingplank* that has been cut away or "nibbled" to accept the ends of the planks. The ends of straight planking terminate against the *covering boards* and are mitered to fit. Of the two, sprung planking looks best, to my eyes anyway, but it's significantly more difficult to do a workmanlike job on it than it is with straight planking. Sprung planking will require a higher level of woodworking skill, 10 to 15 percent more wood, and about 25 percent more time than will straight planking; and bending thin strips of teak on the bias while keeping them flat on the deck is significantly more difficult than bending thick deck planks. Neither is particularly easy. If you want sprung planking and you've never done it before, I strongly recommend that you enlist the aid of a professional boatbuilder. The following instructions are for straight planking, and even this should not be attempted without professional help except by skilled woodworkers who are confident in their abilities. If you mess up on a job like this, you can ruin your boat.

When installing straight planking, the covering boards should be installed first. These can be the same thickness as the planks, or if you want to get fancy, they can be thicker than the planking so they stand proud of the finished deck. With straight planking you install the center plank first and work out from there.

Selecting and Preparing the Wood

The stock for your planking job must be carefully selected. And although I'm describing teak decks, this installation method will work fine with almost any wood. Alternating planks of mahogany and thin strips of white pine are traditional on many runabouts and other powerboats, and many people like the looks of a teak and "holly" (usually white pine) cabin sole. The only real difference is that teak can be left raw to weather and any other wood must be epoxied and varnished.

You should order the lumber for your new deck from a hardwood lumber supplier, not your local lumberyard. (When I want teak for a deck, or anything else for that matter, I always call Mal Vatters at Zahn Lumber in Woburn, Massachusetts; Mal always knows just what is available at the best prices, and his recommendations over the years have saved me a lot of money.) You'll need rough-finished planks that are slightly thicker than the desired plank width. For example, if you want 2-inch-wide planks (a common choice) on your deck, buy stock that is nominally 2 inches thick. This is called 8/4 stock in the lumber trade, and it will actually be 2⅟₁₆ inches to 2¼ inches thick. The extra is the hedge the sawmill builds in to allow for shrinkage. You can't count on it, but it's usually there. If you buy 8/4 stock planed, it will be 1¾ inches thick, which is another reason to plane your own. If you have your own planer, as you should, run all the stock through until all the saw marks are removed from both sides. If you end up with stock that is slightly less than 2 inches, don't worry about it; just make sure all your planks are the same thickness.

Traditional boatbuilders would use the longest planks they could get for their decks to avoid troublesome butt joints, but since you won't have to worry about leaks, you'll find short lengths of 6 to 8 feet easier to work with. You may also be able to negotiate a small discount for shorter lengths of raw stock since they are generally less desirable. When installing short lengths, make sure you stagger the joints to avoid *gravestones*—adjacent planks with butt joints close together—or worse still, a line of joints across the deck.

Rip all the stock edgewise into strips ⅗₁₆ inch thick. You can rip the stock on a table saw, but the best way to rip your expensive woods is on the bandsaw, although it will take some practice before you can get a straight cut. You can't use a traditional rip fence on a bandsaw, even though most of the manufacturers make them, because a bandsaw blade almost never cuts straight. It will cut at an angle that, fortunately, is always constant for a given blade. Once the angle of cut is determined, you can simply turn the stock to compensate for it. I usually mark out the strips in pencil, then cut by eye. If you find you really need a fence, clamp a straight board to the table of the bandsaw at the correct angle and use it for a fence. Or better yet, clamp a V-shaped block parallel to the blade; the block will control the depth of the cut while still giving you the freedom to swing the stock to compensate.

Teak is unique in that its fibers contain high concentrations of silica, essentially beach sand, which will play havoc with your tools. Some old-timers swear they can see sparks flying off the saw blade when they cut teak. I've never observed this phenomenon myself because I usually use carbide-tipped blades, which don't spark, but I do know teak is tough on bandsaw blades. So if you use your bandsaw to rip your stock, you'll likely need several blades. I find that ⅜-inch 4-point skip-tooth blades cut best with thick hardwoods. And remember that the cutting angle will change with each new blade.

As you cut each thin plank off your board, run the sawn edge of the board over the jointer, if you have one, or put it in the vise and plane the edge smooth with a jointer plane. This will give you one surface finished smooth from planing and the other surface rough from the bandsaw blade. The plank will be installed with the finished surface up, and the rough texture on the back will give the epoxy a better grip. If you don't have the heavy shop tools required for cutting the stock into planks, don't worry; any good cabinet shop or boatshop will be happy to mill it for you for a nominal fee.

Clamps

The next thing you'll need is about a dozen pieces of ¾-inch aluminum bar stock about 12 inches long—8 inches if your deck is cambered. The width isn't that important as long as it's over ¾ inch and under 1½ inches. You can get suitable stock from any scrap-metal dealer for a few bucks. These straps will be drilled with holes spaced exactly the width of your planks and will be screwed into the deck to hold the planking in place at the proper spacing while the epoxy sets.

Some craftsmen who do laminated decks use screws and fender washers to hold the planking, and this is the best choice for dealing with the curved surface of a deck with a radical camber, but on a fairly flat deck, the aluminum straps have the considerable advantage of leveling the decking as it is installed. Straps also do a better job of holding the decking flat; when you use screws with washers, the deck

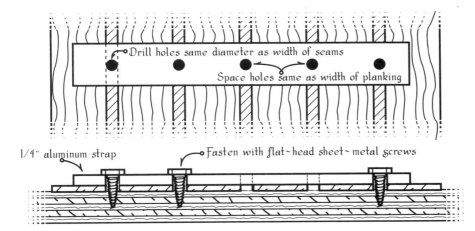

Figure 8-9. Aluminum hold-down straps.

will be quite uneven when the epoxy cures and will require a lot of tedious sanding to get all the planks level. And let me tell you—sanding a deck is a real back-breaker. The aluminum straps hold the deck planks in a plane relative to each other, so the deck is quite level when the epoxy cures, and only surface sanding is required.

Before you drill the holes in your aluminum straps, you'll need to decide how wide you want to make the seams in your deck. Usually something between ⅛ and ³⁄₁₆ inch looks best. Select a screw size that corresponds to the desired thickness of the seam and drill corresponding holes. Use a #8 machinist's drill bit for thin seams, #10 for medium seams, and #12 for wide ones. Make all your seams consistent: Don't put wide seams in one section and narrow ones in another. If you drill a hole in the wrong place in a strap, just fill it with epoxy putty so you'll know not to use it and drill another next to it.

Laying Out the Deck

Before you proceed with the actual installation of your planking, you should lay out your planking scheme on the deck with a felt-tip pen such as a Magic

**Figure 8-10.
Laying out the
decking.**

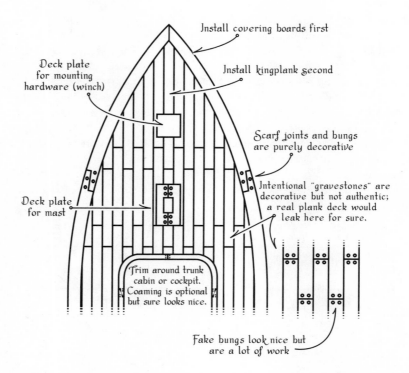

Install covering boards first

Install kingplank second

Deck plate
for mounting
hardware (winch)

Scarf joints and bungs
are purely decorative

Intentional "gravestones" are
decorative but not authentic;
a real plank deck would
leak here for sure.

Deck plate
for mast

Trim around trunk
cabin or cockpit.
Coaming is optional
but sure looks nice.

Fake bungs look nice but
are a lot of work

Marker or a Sharpie. Lay out the covering boards first. Mark the location of the kingplank, which will run down the center of the boat. Mark the location of any blocking that will define deck fittings and the mast. If you plan to outline the trunk cabin and/or cockpit coaming with trim, mark this. Now mark the location of the individual planks. You needn't draw the entire planks, just short lines at the correct intervals across the widest section of the hull that will be planked, usually on the foredeck just forward of the cabin trunk or cockpit. This marking sequence is the same sequence that you should use in installing your planking.

As you lay out your deck, try to visualize where the butt joints will fall. If you use short planks, there will necessarily be a lot of them and you want to avoid *gravestones* or lines of joints. Some modern builders of plastic boats, notably Henri Wauquiez, alternate the butt joints of their decking by only a few inches for dramatic effect. This is not authentic, and no shipwright of the past would have ever laid a deck this way, but since you don't have to worry about leaks, there's no reason not to do it like this if you like the way it looks.

Authentic strip-planked decks had rows of bungs where the decking was screwed or bolted to the deck beams. You can duplicate this look easily by simply drilling rows of holes transversely across the deck at regular intervals and filling them with bungs. With epoxy, there is no need to actually install screws. If you want fake bungs, install them after the decking is installed but before the deck is sanded.

Covering Boards

To install the covering boards, cut the stock to shape first, as shown in Figure 8-10. The outer edge can run a little wild and be trimmed later, but the inside edge must be perfect. Make the covering boards about 4 inches wide, and join pieces with scarf joints (for fancy joints, see the Scarf Joint section later in this chapter); the number of pieces you use really isn't important. Clean the back of the plank and the deck with acetone or epoxy thinner. Then apply epoxy thickened to the consistency of mayonnaise to the deck and to the rough side of the deck plank. If you're using WEST System products, thicken the epoxy with colloidal silica (#406) and add about 10 percent, by volume, of their graphite powder (#423), which will turn the epoxy jet-black.

Hold the covering boards in place using the aluminum straps for light clamping pressure. First coat each strap liberally with mold release or Butcher's wax, then place one end of a strap on the covering board and the other end on a scrap that's the same thickness as the covering board. Now simply drive a screw through one of the holes that fall between them and into the deck. Tighten the screw just enough to hold the board in place.

Space the straps about 6 inches apart and use 1-inch self-tapping hex-head sheet-metal screws to fasten the straps. The screws should be the same diameter as the holes in the aluminum strap (#8, #10, or #12, according to your choice), which is also the width of your seams. One-inch screws are long enough to pass through the bar, past the strip of new decking, and halfway or so through the existing deck. The self-tapping screws will save you a lot of work, cutting through the fiberglass and avoiding the need to drill pilot holes.

You can caulk your planking in two ways. The easier one is to slather on enough of the blackened epoxy so that it oozes through the seams between the

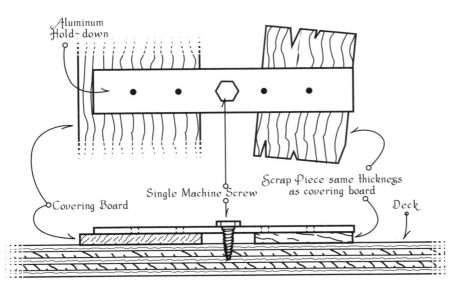

**Figure 8-11.
Holding the covering
board in place.**

planks as they're installed, then smooth off the top of each seam with a putty knife. This results in a solid epoxy base for the wood planks, and the whole thing can be done in one operation. If you use this method, the epoxy must be blackened with graphite powder. The other way is to apply less epoxy so that the planks bed solidly but epoxy doesn't ooze up through the seams. After the epoxy is set, the seams are payed with polysulfide seam sealant, a two-part concoction that dries to a tough rubbery consistency. This second method is substantially more work than the first, but the polysulfide will add to the traction on the deck, and it will result in a deck that looks a lot more like the real thing.

Laying the Deck

Dry-fit three or four planks at a time, making sure the spacing at the tapered ends where they meet the covering boards is even; make any necessary adjustments with a block plane. Don't forget to leave a space at the butt joints equal to the width of the seams, and double-check for gravestones. Apply the epoxy to the deck with a disposable notched plastic trowel. The ones made for wall-tile adhesives and available in hardware stores for about 50 cents apiece work just fine. Secure the planks to the deck using aluminum straps spaced about 12 inches apart. Tighten the screws only enough to set the planks firmly into the epoxy without depressing the planks. Remember, epoxy doesn't need a lot of clamping pressure; tighten the screws just enough to get the planks level. Your straps will accommodate five or six planks at a time, but as you progress across the deck, move the straps so that they cover three or four new planks and rest on two or three planks of the previously laid section.

Anywhere there is a deck fitting, shape a solid piece of stock to serve as a base so there will be no seams under the fitting. Do the same around the mast step and anywhere else it will look good. There's no structural requirement for these base blocks, but they really dress up the deck for a modest investment of time and trouble.

**Figure 8-12.
Holding the deck
planks in place.**

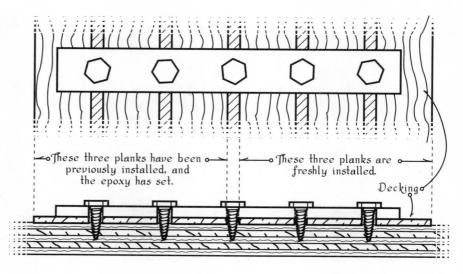

←∘These three planks have been ∘→   ←∘These three planks are ∘→
previously installed, and   freshly installed.
the epoxy has set.

Decking∘

Once the entire deck is laid, there will be rows of holes between the planks where the screws were removed from the aluminum straps. Fill these with more epoxy. If you're using polysulfide in your seams, apply it at this time. Polysulfide seam sealant is available in liquid form designed to be dispensed from tubes or in knife grade for application with a putty knife. Either way it's difficult and nasty stuff to use, but the knife grade is what you want for this type of application. Use a stiff-bladed putty knife to fill all the seams level with the surface of the planking. Now go away for a few days and let everything cure hard enough to sand.

Finishing

Rough-sand the entire deck with your disc sander fitted with a foam pad and 80-grit paper until all the irregularities are removed and the deck is perfectly smooth and level. Then finish sanding with 100-grit paper on your half-sheet pad sander. If your deck is teak, you're all done and can begin reinstalling fittings and hardware. If it's any other kind of wood, continue with the finishing as explained in Chapter Eleven.

Bedding Deck Fittings

All deck fittings, winches, portlights, and anything else screwed or bolted to the deck should be bedded securely to keep out water. The original way of bedding deck fittings on wood decks was to cut a felt gasket that would profile the fitting and soak it in tar before installing it under the fitting. This undoubtedly worked first-rate, but it must have been pretty messy on a hot day in the tropics. Although you'll hear recommendations to the contrary, the best beddings for use today are the one-part polyurethanes like 3M-5200. The adhesion and the elastomeric properties of these products combine to form a leak-proof seal that will last for years. The only real argument against their use is that they may damage the decking if you need to remove them, but this is easy to avoid by heating the bedded fitting with a heat gun as explained at the beginning of this chapter.

The dynamics of wooden decks are quite different from those of fiberglass decks. When a deck fitting is installed in a wooden boat, the through-bolts are installed very tightly. When the wood expands with an increase in moisture content, the wood fibers under the washers on the underside of the backing block are crushed, and when the wood contracts with a reduction of moisture content, these crushed fibers contract with the block, making a previously tight bolt slightly loose. A strong vertical force on a fitting with even slightly loose mounting bolts, such as a dock line might impart on a deck cleat, will be enough to break the seal of weaker sealants, but the polyurethanes are usually strong enough to retain the bond between deck and fitting.

To install deck fittings with polyurethane, tighten the bolts just tight enough so that they are snug and the sealant starts to ooze out around the edges of the fitting. Let the sealant set for a few days, then tighten the bolts as much as you like.

All through-bolted fixtures should have backing plates, of course, and I've seen many people put sealant on these plates. This is a serious mistake even though it may be recommended in the installation instructions that come with many pieces

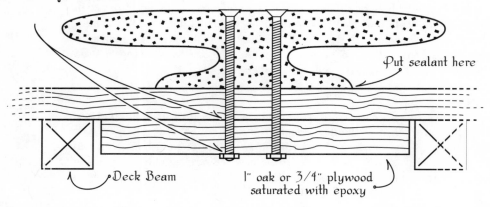

Do not put sealant under washers or between deck and backing plate.

Put sealant here

Deck Beam

1" oak or 3/4" plywood saturated with epoxy

Figure 8-13. All deck fittings should have backing plates.

of equipment. The primary purpose of the sealant is to stop water from penetrating the deck. But if water does penetrate the seal, you want to know about it right away. Without sealant on the backing plate, water will leak right through where you can spot it instantly. If you put sealant on the backing plate, the water will be trapped where it can slowly saturate your decking and cause damage that you may not notice until major problems develop.

Now that you have everything put back together, you can once again stand back and admire the results of your considerable efforts. Doesn't that look just fine? In fact you did such a beautiful job that you may have convinced me to change my mind. Maybe I should give the old *Duchess* a teak deck after all—if only I could find the time. Let's see, there are some guitar chords that need learning, the kids need to be shown how to get the dinghy out of irons, there's a collection of Rossini recordings that need to be transferred to tape for the next cruise, and . . . well, maybe next year.

CABIN TRUNK AND DECKHOUSE

Repairs to a trunk cabin or deckhouse, usually necessitated by rot—caused by water penetration at the corner post or deck seam—are often repairable by removing the affected piece, making a duplicate of sound stock, and replacing it. In fact, the entire trunk cabin on some boats can be replaced by carefully disassembling the old one, making duplicate parts, and reassembling the new one.

The cabin trunk is usually constructed just like a hull (plywood, strip planked, carvel planked, etc.), and smaller repairs can be made to the cabin trunk in exactly the same manner as they are made to the hull. The cabintop can be fiberglassed just like the deck, and deck beams can be repaired or replaced in the manner of frames.

SPARS AND RIGGING

There's not a lot to say about spars and rigging here, not because they aren't important but because there are few differences between the rigging of a wooden boat and that of a boat made of any other material. And the subject is covered thoroughly and well by any number of other current publications listed in Appendix A. I would, however, like to go into detail on several subjects about which I think I may be able to add something rather than just repeat what others have already said.

Rigging is found on all sailboats, of course, but it's not uncommon to find a rudimentary mast on old wooden powerboats. Indeed, with the increasing popularity of so-called trawler designs, masts may become even more popular than ever as the benefits of a steadying sail and a boom strong enough to do duty as a derrick are rediscovered. If properly installed by someone with an eye for proportion, these masts give a boat a shippy look, and they're the perfect place for modern accouterments such as a forest of special-purpose antennas and the increasingly common radar dome.

Most modern spars are made of extruded aluminum, but the use of space-age materials—notably carbon fiber—in spar construction is allowing incredibly strong and light (and expensive) spars to be built that need no external bracing. Such spars are of little practical interest to us. If your old wooden boat is a sailboat, it probably has a wooden mast and boom. But if, due to deterioration or failure, the original spar has been replaced, you could very well have an aluminum mast. Whatever your spars are made from, you're better off sticking with what you have than making new ones that aren't needed.

Building a Box Spar

Building new wooden spars is a highly intricate and demanding piece of woodwork, but if you're faced with the necessity of replacing a mast, it's definitely worth the effort to learn the skills. Wooden masts are constructed in several ways, the simplest being the solid mast hewn from a single log—as might be found on a large schooner, a catboat, or a skipjack. Today most solid spars are made from laminated wood because logs suitable for spars just aren't available unless you live in the Northwestern woods. Laminated spars are also stronger for their weight than single-log spars because the builder can reject boards with defects and can orient the grain to best advantage. Solid spars are heavy, and they're not an efficient way to use scarce and expensive wood, but they are comparatively easy to build.

Another way to build wood spars is by constructing a hollow shaft with six, eight or more sides. Some large spars are strip planked in female molds in halves that are then glued together. Others are constructed from solid halves hollowed out like dugout canoes before being joined. But the only type of wooden spar construction really suitable for consideration by amateur builders (except for the solid spar) is the hollow box spar. Box spars are light in weight, comparatively easy to build, quite strong, and make efficient use of materials.

Before working on any spar, you'll need a spar bench, the simplest of which is

**Figure 8-14.
Six different kinds
of wooden mast
construction.**

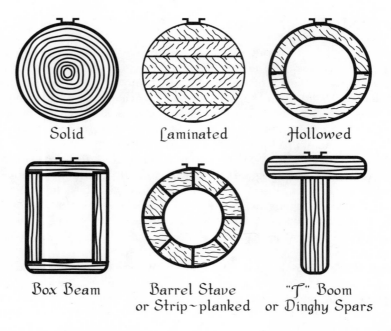

Solid   Laminated   Hollowed

Box Beam   Barrel Stave
or Strip~planked   "T" Boom
or Dinghy Spars

made from a bunch of sawhorses spaced about 4 feet apart, held together with strapping, and trimmed dead-level with shims under the legs. This presupposes a room with clear space long enough to accommodate your spar. In a pinch the backyard will do, as long as you have plastic sheeting standing by to take care of bad weather. The primary requirements of a spar bench are that it supports the entire length of the spar and allows free space all around the circumference for clamping. Use your imagination and you are sure to come up with an acceptable arrangement.

A box spar in the classic pattern is a simple, hollow rectangular box made with four boards glued together with rabbet joints. When stepped, the spar is oriented fore and aft, so the short sides overlap the long sides and are rabbeted to receive them, which increases fore-and-aft compression strength. This also reduces the width of the widest piece of lumber you'll need.

Box spars are frequently tapered at their upper or lower ends and sometimes at both. The result is called *entasis* by students of classical architecture, and it gives the spar a very pleasing shape unobtainable in extruded aluminum. When spars are tapered, the luff and foot tracks must be straight so the sail will set properly.

Any hollow spar will have solid sections at the masthead, spreaders, shroud tangs (hounds), gooseneck, partners or deck thimble, at the heel, and anywhere else they're needed. The block at the head seals the spar from the weather, and the others provide for added strength and through-bolting at the tangs and spreaders. Most traditional boats have external halyards, but if internal halyards and wiring are to be used, the blocks must be drilled for fairleads, and it will save a lot of frustration with fish wires if the spar is constructed with messenger lines preinstalled.

If you use polypropylene messengers, you'll be less likely to epoxy them to the inside surfaces of the spar as you assemble it because polypropylene is one of the few things epoxy won't stick to.

Box spars are constructed from four boards, but since the maximum available length of rough spar-grade Sitka spruce lumber is about 13 feet at this writing, it's obvious that unless you have a very short rig, you'll be doing some scarf joints. It's much easier to scarf the boards together before assembling the mast and even before trimming the stock to size. And while a straight tapered scarf glued with epoxy will be plenty strong enough, a double-taper scarf joint will allow the mast to flex more uniformly. What's a double-taper scarf joint? Let's take a closer look at the whole matter of scarf joints.

Making Scarf Joints

Scarf joints are one of those things that make woodworking skills worth acquiring. Properly made, they're lovely to look at, they're functional, and they're fun and challenging to construct. A good scarf joint in a box spar will render the joined area stronger than the rest of the wood.

Scarf joints are usually used where it's necessary to join two pieces of wood end-to-end in places where a butt block would be unsightly or impractical, or anywhere a long straight piece of wood is needed that exceeds the length of the stock available at the lumberyard. Plywood in lengths of more than 10 feet used for hull planking is made from 8-foot panels joined by scarf joints; the covering boards of a proper yacht will often have intricately fitted, decorative stepped (or haunched) scarf joints; and wooden masts nearly always have numerous straight or double-taper scarf joints that are practically invisible.

The general use of epoxy in boatbuilding has made scarf joints even more useful than they were in the past. Previously, scarf joints made with resorcinol glues had to have perfectly matching contact surfaces with a very thin glue line, a run—the joint's length compared to its width—as long as possible to maximize the contact surface, and for structural applications such as solid spars, mechanical fasteners such as bolts, drift pins, or rivets to reinforce the joint. Epoxy, however, has excellent gap-filling qualities, especially when thickened with a little colloidal silica, so today joints don't need to fit as tightly as they did in the past. (In fact a slight gap between the mating surfaces will usually make a stronger joint.) The extra strength of epoxy allows for a shorter run, and it's frequently OK to forego mechanical reinforcement.

There are many ways to make scarf joints. When joining two boards that will be used flat, such as in a covering board, the look of triple-stepped joints is hard to beat. And while they look intricate and difficult, they are easy to make.

On any kind of stepped joint where the wood is cut across the grain, start by drawing the joint freehand on one of the two pieces of stock that you want to join. When it looks right, cut it out with your bowsaw. (A jigsaw will work, if you insist, but the bowsaw will be quicker, it will do a better job, and it won't make an offensive racket while it's doing it.) Clean up the joint with a block plane and a chisel until all the saw marks are removed. Once you get the surface of the joint perfect on

**Figure 8-15.
Scarf joints.**

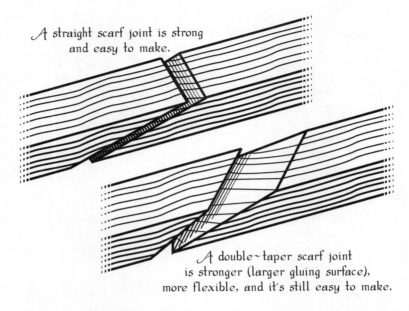

*A straight scarf joint is strong
and easy to make.*

*A double~taper scarf joint
is stronger (larger gluing surface),
more flexible, and it's still easy to make.*

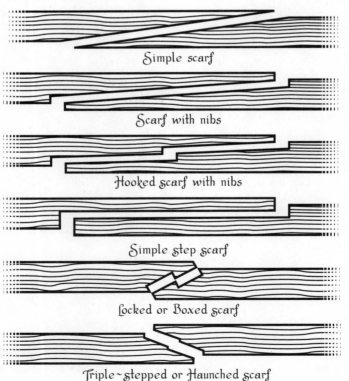

Simple scarf

Scarf with nibs

Hooked scarf with nibs

Simple step scarf

Locked or Boxed scarf

Triple~stepped or Haunched scarf

the first board, lay it in position on top of the second board and trace its outline with a very sharp pencil. Now simply cut out the second piece as you did the first, and fit them together with the cut-and-try method described earlier under Dutchman repairs. Glue the joint together with epoxy thickened to catsup consistency (mayonnaise if your joint was a little sloppy), with just enough clamping pressure to hold the pieces together. Once the glue cures, plane the joint fair and take it around to show some friends. They're going to be very impressed.

But we digress. For your box spar, the kind of scarf joints you will use are made on the flat and require an entirely different approach. For these long, flat scarfs you'll need a jig, but don't let that bother you; they're still simple to make. Construct your jig out of three pieces of lumber (practically anything will do as long as it's straight and fairly robust—¾-inch plywood is just dandy), 3 feet long or more, nailed together in a U shape with the bottom of the U slightly wider than the stock you're scarfing, and the sides four or five times as high as the stock is thick. Now with a sharp handsaw, cut one end of the U into a taper that corresponds to the taper you want in your scarf joint—8 or 10 to 1 is about right for spar stock. If you want a double-taper scarf joint, cut a 4-to-1 taper across the jig in addition to the lengthwise taper.

Since any angle added to its complement equals 180 degrees, you will only need one jig regardless of the taper you select—remember your high-school math?

To use your jig, simply clamp the stock into the jig so that the stock protrudes past the tapered end of the jig. Place the first piece in the jig with the surface that

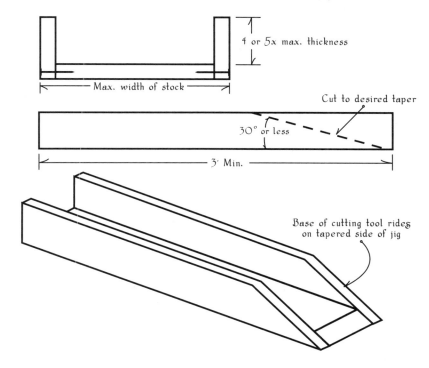

Figure 8-16.
A scarfing jig.

will eventually be the finish surface *facing up*. Now cut away the part that is sticking out by letting your cutting tool ride on the tapered sides of the jig. Your router, hand plane, or power plane will all work very well on this type of jig, but the base of the tool you use must be long enough to span the gap between the two sideboards of your jig. Because the base of most routers can be removed and replaced by a rectangular piece of ¼-inch aluminum that can be any length you like, the router should be your first choice for wide stock. A jointer plane with its 24-inch-long base also works well for wide stock. Be sure to plane at a slight angle to avoid planing the jig, too.

Once the joint is cut in one piece of the stock you want to scarf, place the second piece in the jig with the finish surface *facing down* and complete the cut as you did on the first piece. Now glue the two pieces together with epoxy as above, plane the joint fair, and you're done. This joint won't be as pretty as a haunched joint, but it won't look bad, and it'll be as strong as new wood.

Preparing the Mast Parts

When laying out the mast, the scarf joints should be staggered as much as possible. After the rough boards are scarfed together, you're ready to run them through the planer. Windows at opposite ends of my shop make planing long pieces easy. I set up the portable planer in the middle of the shop and run the stock in through one window, through the planer, then out the opposite window. Were it not for this fortuitous accident of architecture, I would simply move everything out onto the driveway and do the planing outside. In either case you'll need lots of helpers to support the long stock as it's fed through the planer.

The rest of the trimming is best done on the spar bench. If the spar is tapered, mark off the lines corresponding to your old spar using a long fairing batten and a few ice picks. Do this marking very carefully. Nothing is quite as discouraging as messing up a 30- or 40-foot piece of very expensive wood. Cut slightly outside the lines with a bowsaw, then plane down to the lines with a jack plane.

The rabbets can be cut with a router, but it's actually easier and much safer to cut them by hand with a rabbet plane. They need not be deep: ¼ inch or so is fine. Give all the inner surfaces of the spar planks two good saturation coats of epoxy and let it set. This will seal the inside of the spar from moisture penetration.

Fashion the internal blocks from Sitka spruce or from white pine, using the blocking in the original mast as a guide. If you don't have the original spar to copy, put blocking anywhere fixtures will be through-bolted. Use your judgment as to the length; I usually make blocks about a foot long. You can cut them from solid stock, but it's better to laminate them out of 4/4 (1-inch) boards to minimize the tendency of the wood to expand and contract, which you will further reduce by saturating each entire block with epoxy before it's installed. The blocks should be a loose fit inside the mast so that the thickened (mayonnaise consistency) epoxy will form a heavy joint. Drill any holes for wiring or halyards using an electrician's extension bit before the blocks are installed, bearing in mind the location of the through-bolts. I like for these holes to be at least ¾ inch in diameter, and I radius the edges with a router after the holes are drilled.

Assembly

Assembling a long box spar is a trick worthy of Houdini. The entire thing must be glued up at once to ensure good joints, so you'll need several helpers and all the clamps you can get your hands on—dozens and dozens of them. In a pinch you can alternate Spanish windlasses on blocks between clamps (see Figure 8-17).

You should always assemble the entire spar dry just to get the procedure down and to make sure everything fits. While it's assembled dry, mark the location of the sheaves, spreaders, and the rest of the fittings and hardware, and try to anticipate any problems you'll have after assembly. If everything is OK, take it apart and do it again with the glue.

Before you do any gluing, however, give all the cross pieces of your spar bench a heavy coat of Butcher's wax, or staple a piece of polypropylene plastic to each one; you really don't need all those sawhorses permanently bonded to your new mast. While you're at it, put a good coat of wax on your clamps for the same reason. Use epoxy, naturally, and thicken it to the consistency of ketchup. Make sure you use the hardener that gives you the longest working time, which if you're using WEST System products will be #209 tropical hardener. This will give you about one

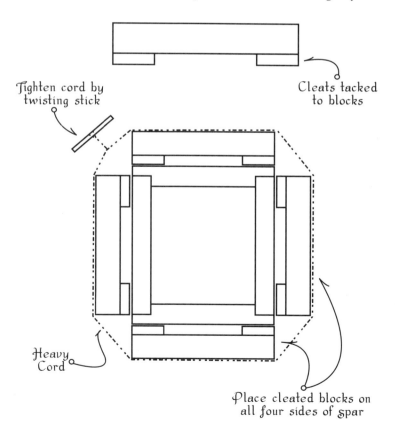

Tighten cord by twisting stick

Cleats tacked to blocks

Heavy Cord

Place cleated blocks on all four sides of spar

Figure 8-17. A Spanish windlass can work as well on a spar section as conventional clamps. The cleats at the edges of the blocks put all the pressure from the clamp on the joints where it is needed. When using epoxy, remember that light, even clamp pressure is much better than the heavy, uneven pressure that results from trying to do the job with too few clamps.

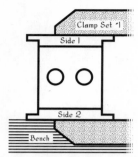

A. Start your clamping procedure by clamping side 1 (the aft side which will eventually get the sail track) and side 2 to the solid blocking with clamp set #1.

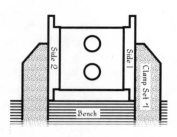

B. Rotate the spar by 90° so that clamp set #1 is hanging below the spar bench.

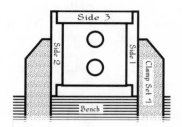

C. Install side 3. You may have to loosen clamp set #1 slightly.

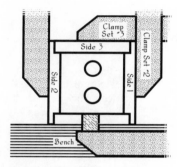

D. Install clamp set #2 on the top of the spar and remove clamp set #1. Install clamp set #3 with a temporary block opposite side 3 to prevent damaging the rabbets.

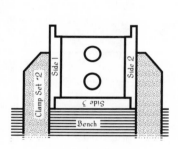

E. Rotate the spar 180° so that clamp set #2 hangs below the spar bench. Remove clamp set #3.

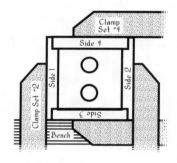

F. Install side #4 and clamp set #4.

**Figure 8-18.
Spar-gluing
sequence.**

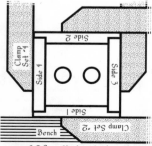

G. Rotate the spar 90° so that side 1 is down and resting on the bench. Straighten the spar by stretching a piece of string along one edge and clamp the spar to the bench.

H. Now that you see how easy it is, take the entire spar apart and do it again, only this time use epoxy.

hour to do the job at 70 degrees Fahrenheit—not an excessive amount of time by any means.

Start by gluing and clamping the narrow sides (the ones with the rabbets) to the solid blocking, applying all the clamps from one side of the spar and leaving the other side open. Now rotate the spar so that the clamps hang below and the side clear of clamps is up. Fit this side carefully into the rabbets and clamp it temporarily to the solid blocking. Place a third set of clamps opposite the first clamps, rotate the spar 180 degrees, and remove the first and second sets of clamps. This is where it gets tricky because all the parts are slippery with epoxy and you're relying on the weight of the spar to hold the side that's now on the bottom in place while you fit the last side into the top. If you mess up, the whole thing will disassemble like Clementine's bridge in the Johnny Mathis song, and you'll have to start all over again.

Make sure your messenger lines are installed before you glue and clamp the fourth side in place. Turn the spar so the aft side, where the sail track will be installed, is on the bottom, and lightly clamp the spar to the bench for its entire length. Sight along the spar to make sure it is die straight in the fore-and-aft plane, and make any necessary adjustments to straighten it. Place wedges (cedar shingles work best) under the spar to accommodate any taper at the ends. Place clamps on alternate sides of the spar for its entire length. If you have enough, put them every few inches: It's really impossible to have too many. Tighten the clamps only enough to squeeze out the excess epoxy. Excessive clamping pressure isn't necessary with epoxy and can actually weaken the joint. Give the messenger lines a tug to make sure they're not embedded in epoxy, then go out and buy your helpers a brew or two. You might need them again someday.

Finish

After the epoxy sets, remove the clamps and start cleaning up the mess on the outside of the spar. It looks terrible right now, but a few days' work with planes, scrapers, and pad sanders will turn it into a thing of beauty. Please leave your power plane, belt sander, and disc grinder in the box for the finishing operations. Power tools go through Sitka spruce like Democrats go through taxes, and you have way too much invested in your new stick to risk ruining it by trying to rush things.

Finish the mast by painting or, if you insist, varnishing it as described in Chapter Eleven. Now install the sheaves and other hardware just like on the original, step the mast on the boat, hank on the sails, and cruise off into the sunset, knowing your new spar will last for years and years with only periodic touch-up and inspection. In fact if you care for it properly, it will require no more attention than those clangy-bangy aluminum things on all those other boats. And you'll have the considerable satisfaction of knowing you did the job yourself and saved from 60 to 75 percent of the cost of a new mast—even when you count what you spent on beer.

Repairing Wooden Spars

Not too long ago, on one of those rare days in the Caribbean winter when the trades don't blow and the temperature rises, I was whiling away some vacant hours in a large open-air bar that looks down over the docks in Charlotte Amalie Harbor in the U.S. Virgin Islands, sharing a drink with a particularly salty individual I'd met an hour or so before. He was a slightly built little man with bad teeth and of indeterminable age who claimed to have spent a good part of the past 10 years sailing wherever he felt like sailing and the rest of his time talking about it to strangers in bars along the way.

It turned out my new-found friend was on the last leg of a circumnavigation with his girlfriend. They had just crossed the Atlantic from the Azores and were on their way to Panama when the girlfriend jumped ship and ran off with a West Indian diesel mechanic named George. My heartbroken friend was hanging around Charlotte Amalie until he could fill out his crew roster with a suitable replacement. He wasn't fussy—any attractive lady who could cook and clean and pay half the expenses would do.

My friend's boat was anchored off to one side of the harbor. It was a Garden-designed ketch of traditional lines and ample dimensions but sporting a noticeably short mainmast. I couldn't help but comment on this curious arrangement, and that led to a most interesting tale.

They were in the South Pacific, somewhere south of Fiji, when they were dismasted by a rogue wave. "That sumnabitch just picked us up like we was Tinkertoys and plopped us back into the trough, clean upside down." His voice quivered with emotion, and the setting sun reflecting in his watery eyes gave him a look of demonic intensity.

"We was both below catchin' a little nap—if you know what I mean." He gave me a licentious squint that might've been a wink, and a little punch in the arm, like macho guys do when they know you know what they mean.

"When all of a sudden there we was flat on our backs on the cabin roof with everythin' we had aboard raining down on us. I thought the gates of hell was opened up and the Devil himself was dumpin' cases of Dinty Moore Beef Stew and Campbell's Pork and Beans on our heads—like some kind of retribution or somethin'.

"I looked out the portlights and there's a great white shark about as long as the boat lookin' in to starboard. And off to port, why there's Saint Pete hisself starin' in with a big grin on his face, as if to say `take yor time folks; I ain't in no hurry.'

"Anyway, we stayed upside down for what seemed like about nine hours but was really probably only about a couple of minutes or somethin' like that. It wasn't really very long, but it was plenty long enough to get me to worryin' cause that old tub is some kinda beamy and she ain't got but 8,000 pounds of iron in her keel. I always figured if she ever got herself upside down, there wasn't enough iron in her to get her back up again. And there we was floatin' around, about to prove my theory by dyin' or somethin'.

"Well, I'd took a good hit upside the head from a fryin' pan that come loose from the galley, and I weren't thinkin' too fast. Course thinkin' wouldn'a done no good anyhow cause there wasn't a whole lot we could do about it by thinkin'. Then all a sudden another of them big suckers comes a-roarin' in and lifts us clean outta the water. It holds us there for a while, like a cat playin' with a half-dead mouse, then . . . BAM . . ."

He gestured wildly, making wave actions with his arms, then slammed his palm flat, splashing Black Dog out of the glasses onto the table.

". . . it plops us back down right side up again.

"Well that was like a miracle or somethin', but that weren't the weirdest part. You know when we landed, all them cans of beans and stuff like that bounced right back into the lockers they'd bounced out of, the fryin' pan bounced right back to the galley, I landed on my back on the bunk, and that old gal come off the roof and landed on me like Sherman landed on Georgia."

My friend went on to describe how the encounter with the rogue wave had washed away their dinghy, knocked out their steering vane, and snapped their mainmast right above the spreaders. They managed to get the motor started, and with a jury-rigged jib and the mizzen, they limped on to New Zealand. Once ashore he discovered, to his dismay, that a new wood or aluminum mast would set him back enough money to go cruising for an entire year. In sheer desperation he considered the possibility of making one himself, but he had neither the skill nor the tools, and even the cost of the wood was prohibitive.

A few days later, while recounting the tale of the rogue wave to the patrons of a bar in Whangarei, he met a young carpenter who offered to repair the mast and help my friend re-rig his boat in exchange for passage to Australia. They set about the repair the very next day.

The carpenter began by setting up a spar bench. And after stripping the mast of the sail tracks and all the other hardware, he proceeded to plane a long shallow scarf joint in the two broken sections of the mast. When he finally got the mast perfectly straight, he glued the joint with epoxy, and they went back to the bar to celebrate.

The next morning when the mast was stepped on the boat, they discovered that, because of the wood used by the overlap of the scarf joint, the mast was about 5 feet shorter than before. This was not something my friend or the carpenter had anticipated, so back they went to the bar to do a little more planning. The next day they shortened all the standing rigging enough to compensate for the abbreviated mast, tied a deep reef in the main, cut 6 feet off the foot of the jib, located the girl-friend, and the three of them took off for Australia—just one jump ahead of an angry constable waiving a rather substantial unpaid bar bill.

The only reason I'm relating this admittedly long-winded tale to you is that it illustrates a good point about wooden masts. Sitka spruce makes a tough and flexible stick. It's not as durable as aluminum, but if you do break one, you can repair it with basic tools just about anywhere in the world. If my friend and the carpenter had had a little foresight and a few pieces of spruce, they could've scarfed in a new section of mast between the old ones and not had to worry about shortening the rig.

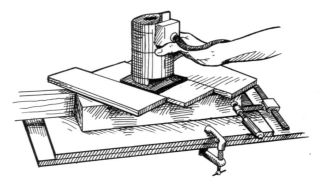

CHAPTER NINE

Internal Spaces

One of the true abominations of the modern fiberglass boat is the molded hull liner—an invention of misanthropic designers and builders who were trying to save the same amount of money inside their boats as the molded plastic hull saved them on the outside. Hull and cabin liners make the inside surfaces of plastic boats neat and tidy, but they hide the mounting bolts of critical components such as chainplates, deck-to-hull fasteners, and winch bases. Locating the source of a leaking deck fitting on these boats is practically impossible. And even if you do find the leak, you can't fix it because you can't get at the mounting bolts.

You can, of course, make a valid argument in favor of production expedients such as hull and cabin liners. They do save the manufacturer a lot of money that would have to be spent on interior cabinetry, and at least a portion of this savings is passed on to the buyer. Even so, I can't help but find it amusing when things stowed in boats costing a quarter of a million dollars or more end up rolling around in the bilge because there are no dividers or bottoms in the lockers. There I go, knocking fiberglass again. Some will say I'm just bitter because I can't afford a plastic boat, but that can't be it; I can't afford a wooden boat either, but I'm not critical of them.

Wooden-boat owners, of course, don't have to worry about hull liners. I mentioned them only to point out that the interior is one area where wooden boats really display their superiority. Sure, a well-maintained wooden boat looks great on the outside, but so does a well-maintained fiberglass, steel, or welded aluminum boat. In fact, from 100 yards away you probably can't tell the difference. Once

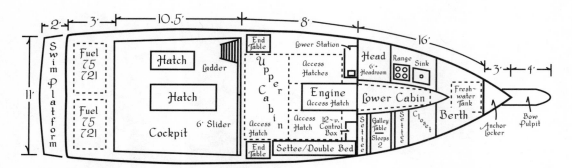

Figure 9-1.
A sketch of *Duchess'*
interior.

you're inside, though, wood reigns supreme. Very few people prefer a steel, welded aluminum, or fiberglass interior over wood. This is why the makers of the million-dollar yachts like Hinckley, Little Harbor, and Deerfoot all take great pains to point out the quality of the joinery of their solid-wood interiors. At the end of a long, wet watch in a cold cockpit, nothing can equal the welcoming warmth and cozy security of a wood cabin. Let's see what can be done to make it even warmer and cozier.

The best way to begin an analysis of your interior is with a scaled sketch. It doesn't have to be anything fancy, but it should show everything in proper perspective so you can visualize any changes you might want to make. If the interior is well laid out and in reasonably good condition, you'll want to minimize any changes. Perhaps some paint and varnish and a lot of elbow grease are all that's required. Cover the cushions with a bright and lively fabric, make some matching curtains, and your living space is as comfortable as any at home. It might even *be* your home.

If, however, your old wooden boat project involves major structural work on ribs and planking, you probably removed a lot of the interior in order to gain access and work space. If so, there's no reason not to make a few well-thought-out changes in the layout and design as the interior is reinstalled. Just make sure the changes actually will increase the enjoyment and utility of your boat.

Structural bulkheads must, of course, be reinstalled where the designer intended them to be, and you should give careful consideration to the consequences of relocating major components such as the galley and the head. In one nicely renovated boat I looked at recently, the owner had moved the head into the forepeak and constructed a sumptuous master cabin aft of it. It was beautiful, but since the boat had only one head, everyone had to traipse through the owner's cabin every time they needed to use it. Such a compromise is frequently necessary, and you just have to put up with the inconvenience. But also carefully consider how any radical departure from standard layouts and designs will affect the utility and resale of your boat before you plunge ahead.

I've listed several good books on interior carpentry in Appendix A, and I don't want to repeat a lot of instructions that have been well covered by others. However, there are a few areas where I've developed a way of doing things on the insides of boats that I like better than the standard practice, and I'd like to share these with you.

THE TICK-STICK TRICK

I first saw a tick stick used in Lincoln, Nebraska, and it had nothing to do with boats or boatyards. I was working as a part-time helper to a finish carpenter named Charlie, installing custom-built kitchens in expensive new houses. One bright summer morning we were faced with making an unusually complex piece of plywood countertop for an odd-shaped corner of the kitchen. The top had to accommodate a concave section of curved wall with several protrusions and numerous odd angles, and I was at a complete loss as to how to proceed. Without batting an eye, Charlie cut a piece of a large cardboard carton into the rough shape of the top and took a standard flat, wooden paint stirrer from his tool box. He tacked the cardboard securely to the cabinets, and after sharpening one end of the paint stirrer to a point with his pocket knife, he laid the pointed stick on the cardboard. He then slid the pointed end of the paint stick against the wall at each strategic spot and quickly but carefully outlined the shape of the stirrer on the cardboard. At the curved sections of the wall the lines were no more than ¼ inch apart, and on the straight sections they were a foot apart. In short order he had the entire surface of the cardboard covered with hatch marks that were totally incomprehensible to me.

We took the cardboard into the backyard where the lumber was stacked and the sawhorses were set up. Charlie laid a fresh panel of ¾-inch plywood on the horses and placed his cardboard pattern on top of the plywood, holding it in place with an empty nail keg. Placing the paint stick on each and every mark he'd made on the cardboard, Charlie made a small tick mark on the plywood right at the point of the stick. When he was finished, an erratic line of tick marks a few inches apart ran all around a large section of the panel. Then, using the side of the stick as a straightedge and drawing free-hand around the curves, he connected the tick marks with a solid line and cut to the line with a sabersaw. I'll never forget my amazement when we carried the countertop back into the kitchen and it fit perfectly on the very first try.

Later, during lunch when no one would notice, I dragged the paint stick and the cardboard from the scrap pile and studied them until my young, inexperienced, and somewhat befuddled mind finally grasped how the thing worked. Several weeks later, in the same house, we needed to make a large, intricately shaped cover for a window seat, and I was ready. I got a large scrap of cardboard and a fresh paint stirrer, and, working slowly and carefully, I repeated each step Charlie had used to make the countertop. When the old

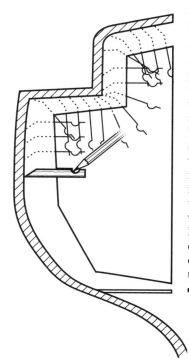

Figure 9-2a.
To make a tick-stick pattern, tack or clamp a piece of pattern stock (¼-inch plywood works well) that is rough-cut to the bulkhead. Place the stick on the pattern with the point touching the hull and mark one edge and the end of the stick with a heavy pencil. Repeat this procedure around the entire periphery of the pattern.

Figure 9-2b.
Place the pattern
on the bulkhead
stock and secure it
with clamps. Place
the stick on each
mark on the pattern
and make a small
tick right at the
pointed end.

Figure 9-2c.
Remove the pattern
and connect the ticks
using a fairing
batten or straight-
edge as appropriate.
Cut the bulkhead
with a sabersaw or
bowsaw.

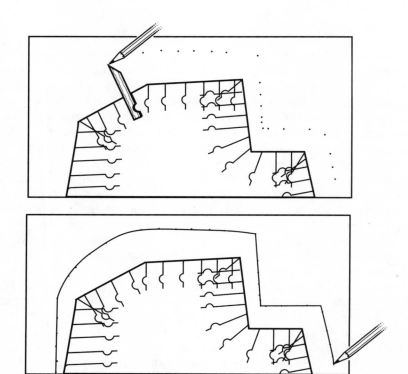

master came by just in time to see the new window sill plop into place without a hitch, he never said a word—just grunted approvingly and went on about his business—but that Friday there was an extra 10 cents an hour in my pay envelope, and I knew old Charlie had been pleased.

Since that time, well over 30 years ago, I've made thousands of tick-stick patterns. I usually use a piece of cardboard or thin plywood for the pattern and any short piece of scrap wood that's lying around for the stick, but when an important piece or a critical component must be a perfect fit, I always feel most comfortable when the stick is a paint stirrer.

Old Charlie was the only dry-land carpenter I ever met who regularly used a tick stick. That's because in most residential construction everything is straight, square, plumb, and level. In boat work, however, the tick stick is the only practical way to make quick and accurate patterns of such things as bulkheads, cabinet sides, locker bottoms, and any other pieces of wood that do not have straight sides and square corners. Come to think of it, that's just about every piece of wood in a boat.

THE BUILT-UP BULKHEAD

Writing books and fixing up old boats have a number of things in common. Both are ways of expressing an artistic temperament, and the results of that expression can be either rewarding or cruelly disappointing. Each requires practice, and you must always be ready to redo things that aren't just right the first time. Neither forgives ineptitude, and the results of attempted shortcuts are always glaringly obvious in the finished products. And in pursuing originality, it is easy to unconsciously pick up on the way others do certain things and to embrace them as your own, completely forgetting where the original inspiration came from. Writers will, for example, frequently come up with some devilishly clever bit of verbiage to make a point, only to discover that some upstart like Descartes or Johnny Carson said exactly the same thing in exactly the same way—but they said it first.

It's the same in boat work. I once worked for a well-known designer and boatbuilder (I won't say whom) who claimed to have developed a way to bend brittle and inflexible woods, such as teak, into intricate shapes for interior trim. He was so concerned his competition would learn the process that before I was allowed to work in the shop I had to swear I wouldn't reveal it to anyone outside the company. The "secret" turned out to be a well-known procedure furniture makers have used to bend wood since well before the Civil War.

In this way, I *think* I may be the first discoverer of the advantages of the built-up plywood panel, since I don't really remember ever seeing anyone else do it just the way I do, but I'm a bit leery of laying claim to it: If I do, some nautical historian will point out that Captain Nat himself—or maybe even Donald McKay—always did it just the same way. (A cored bulkhead is described in *The Gougeon Brothers on Boat Construction*, but it isn't the same thing.) Not that the built-up panel is all that profound an invention, mind you. It certainly won't revolutionize boatbuilding, but it does serve a purpose, it's easy to do, and it works.

Advantages

The first built-up panel I made was a matter of expediency. While making a structural bulkhead for a friend's boat, I discovered I didn't have a piece of ¾-inch plywood large enough to do the job. I did have several sheets of ¼-inch lauan that I primarily used for spiling stock, however, and I had plenty of epoxy. It seemed a lot easier to make up the bulkhead with three layers of the lauan epoxied together than to drive to the lumberyard for another piece of plywood. As I worked on that first bulkhead, it became apparent that a built-up bulkhead had several advantages over and above saving a trip to the lumberyard.

The first thing I noticed was how much easier it was to handle the ¼-inch stock than to horse around with something ¾ inch thick. Getting a good fit on the first layer was quick and simple because the thin lauan was easy to cut. Once the first layer fit perfectly, it served as a template for the other two layers, and the only tricky part was allowing for the slight bevels to compensate for the shape of the hull. It also occurred to me that I now had six surfaces from which to pick the ones I wanted to show. And since the quality of the veneers in the stock I was using happened to be unusually high, I ended up with the equivalent of AA mahogany plywood for less than a quarter of the price.

As I thought it over, other advantages of built-up panels came to mind. If I want additional strength, it's a simple matter to laminate a layer or two of fiberglass, or even aluminum or steel, between the layers of plywood. If weight is a problem, I can make the core from lightweight foam (called Foamcore) available in art-supply houses. The plywood can be built up to any thickness needed, from ½ inch on up. Since underlayment-grade lauan is made with all the defects plugged, the built-up panels have no voids. For the core pieces, I can make use of scraps of plywood that would otherwise be wasted. And because the thin pieces bend easily, curved bulkheads are nearly as easy to make as flat ones.

The second time I made a built-up bulkhead, I was replacing a nonstructural divider between the galley and head of an old powerboat. There was to be a mirror with a light over it on the head side of the partition and a propane shut-off switch on the galley side. Normally the wires for these two items would have been exposed for at least a short distance, or perhaps hidden in wire mold, which is some improvement but not much. With a built-up bulkhead, it was an easy matter to make up the core layers in pieces, leaving ½-inch-wide spaces between them as wire chases. The wires were routed directly to the back of the fixtures through the interior chases, hidden from view and protected from damage.

Gluing

Gluing a built-up panel is simple enough, but there are a few tricks to it. If you simply slather on the glue and clamp the pieces together (their number will depend on how thick you want the panel), they will continually slip and slide around and be impossible to keep lined up. To beat this frustrating problem, clamp all the pieces together just the way you want them, but without the glue, and drill several ¼-inch holes in strategic spots around the periphery where they'll be out of sight. Two holes are usually enough, unless the core layers are more than one piece, but put in as many as you like—a few extras won't hurt a thing. As you glue up the panels, insert short pieces of ¼-inch dowel into the holes to serve as register pins, locking the various layers into perfect alignment. After the glue dries, it's a simple matter to trim the dowels and sand them flush.

The best glue to use is lightly thickened epoxy (catsup). But where *nonstructural* bulkheads or partitions are involved, plain old yellow carpenter's glue works fine. True, it isn't waterproof, but it takes a lot of soaking to get it to break down. Make sure the wood is completely sealed with paint or varnish—especially around the edges—*before* you install the bulkhead, and you won't have any problems. Clamp the layers together by laying them on a flat surface and weighting them with a few bags of sand or birdshot.

I don't use built-up plywood for everything. Frequently it's easier to buy a sheet of whatever thickness is needed. But it's much easier to build a built-up panel than it is to describe how to do it, and I use built-up plywood for a lot of things other than bulkheads, particularly shelves and locker bottoms. Try it yourself; I know you'll like it.

INTERIOR CABINETRY

I don't think there has ever been a boat with enough internal storage, not a cruising boat anyway. And while the most convenient and handy storage is in drawers, the irony is that drawers waste a substantial portion of the already scarce storage space because of the way they're usually constructed. Another problem with conventional drawers is keeping stuff in them. About once a season we seem to get the old *Duchess* stood on her beam-ends either by getting beam-to in a rough sea or, as on one occasion, from a close encounter with an outrageously aggressive whale-watch boat. When this happens with conventional drawers (even those with stops that keep them from flying open), everything ends up out of the drawer and strewn around in the dead space that surrounds it.

Building quality cabinets aboard wooden boats traditionally has been a complicated and time-consuming affair. A framework of light lumber is constructed and covered with a plywood skin, and the front of the cabinet is given a face frame (one piece or assembled) on which the locker doors are mounted and into which the drawers slide. An excellent description of this technique, along with clear illustrations, is contained in *Practical Yacht Joinery* by Fred P. Bingham (see Appendix A).

Frameless Construction

There is another way to build cabinets that's much easier for amateurs, stronger, uses space more efficiently, and actually provides drawers that retain their contents in a rough sea. Called frameless construction, it was developed in Europe for fancy continental-style kitchens—and what is a galley but a small kitchen? The front of the cabinet, the part you see, can be made from any wood to match the other woodwork, but the rest of the cabinet uses nothing but plywood.

Customizing frameless cabinets is easy, and limited only by your imagination. Many people prefer a toe space under the front of a galley cabinet, probably because they have one in their kitchens at home. I prefer a straight front because I think it looks better, and because the cabinet is a little easier to build and will have a little more room in it. If you do want a toe space, it should be at least 3½ inches high and at least 3 inches deep. Your kitchen counter at home is probably about 36 inches high, so this might be the best height for your galley cabinets since it's what you're used to.

One problem on almost all boats is where to put the trash bin. It always seems to get stuck in some inconvenient spot where it's unsightly, difficult to get at, or always underfoot. If you have the space in your new cabinet, consider installing a built-in trash bin. The best are located right under the countertop.

Constructing Frameless Cabinets
Instructions on following pages

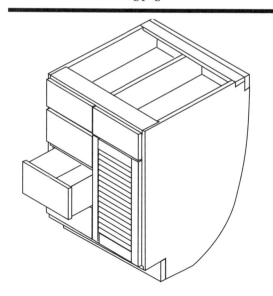

Text continues on page 178

Figure 9-3a. (1) Determine the exact width you want your cabinet to be; we'll call this *"dimension W."* (2) Determine the exact height of your cabinet *without the top;* call this *"dimension H."* (3) Determine the exact depth of your cabinet at the longest dimension of the top (they won't be the same because of the curvature of the hull); call this *"dimension D."* (4) Construct the sides of the carcase, parts A and B, from ¾-inch plywood cut to fit the contour of your hull using the tick-stick procedure described in the text. Due to changes in the curvature of the hull, these side pieces will most likely have different curves and bevels where they meet the hull. Fit them individually on a cut-and-try basis.

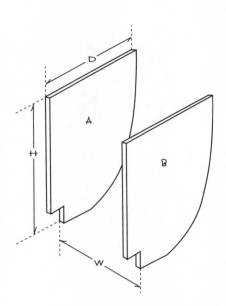

Figure 9-3b. (1) Cut dadoes ¾ inch wide by ¼ inch deep in the sides of the carcase, parts A and B, to receive the bottom, part E. (2) Cut rabbets 3 inches long by ¾ inch wide by ¼ inch deep in the top front corners of the sides to receive the front top cleat. (3) Cut a notch in the upper rear of the sides to receive the mounting bracket. Make the notch ¾ inch deep and 3¾ inches long on the top and 3 inches long on the back. (A dado is a groove or rectangular-shaped channel cut into a board to receive the butt end or edge of another board to make a dado joint. A rabbet is a dado cut into the edge of a board to make a rabbet joint.)

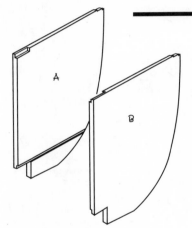

Figure 9-3c. (1) Cut two pieces of ¾-inch plywood 3 inches wide and the exact length of *dimension W.* (2) Screw and glue these two pieces together into an L-shaped mounting bracket to make part C. (3) To make the top cleat, part D, cut a second piece of ¾-inch plywood 3 inches wide and exactly 1 inch shorter than *dimension W.* (4) To make the bottom, part E, cut a piece of plywood that is in length exactly 1 inch shorter than *dimension W* and as wide as the longest dado is long. (5) To make the toe kick, part F, cut a piece of plywood that is 3½ inches wide and exactly as long as *dimension W.*

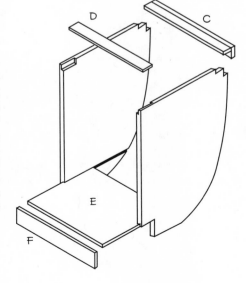

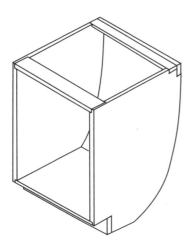

Figure 9-3d. (1) Temporarily assemble the carcase using small nails, screws, or clamps to hold parts C, D, and F in place with parts A and B, and slide the bottom, part E, into its dadoes as far as it will go. (2) Scribe the back edge of the bottom using a tick stick. (3) Trim and cut the bevels so that the bottom is a perfect fit against the hull and the front edge is flush with the sides. A good trick is to leave the bottom piece a bit wide until the back edge is scribed to the hull, then trim the front edge to fit flush; this is *"trick #1."*

Figure 9-3e. (1) Once the bottom fits just right, determine the location of any vertical partitions that will define drawers or other internal structures. In this illustration, half of the cabinet is devoted to drawers and the other half to open space under a single drawer. (2) Cut a dado ¾ inch wide by ¼ inch deep at the location of the vertical partition. (It would seem that you need a corresponding dado on the top cleat at the mounting bracket, but you don't—trust me.)

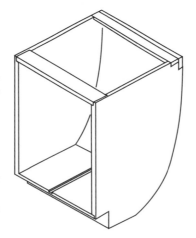

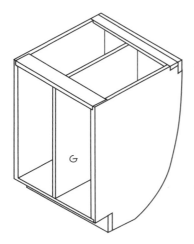

Figure 9-3f. (1) To make the partition, part G, cut a piece of plywood that is 4¾ inches shorter than *dimension H* and as deep as *dimension D* and slide it into position in the dado, keeping it parallel to the sides, parts A and B. (2) Scribe the back edge of the partition using a tick stick. Note that you will have to notch the back edge to accommodate the back piece of part C. Use *trick #1* to save a little time.

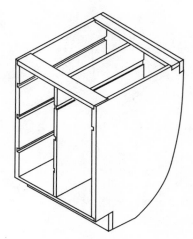

Figure 9-3g. (1) Mark the locations of the drawers on parts A, B, and G. (2) Disassemble the carcase and cut ¾-inch-wide and ¼-inch-deep dadoes corresponding to the locations of the drawers. (3) Reassemble the carcase using the temporary fasteners as before.

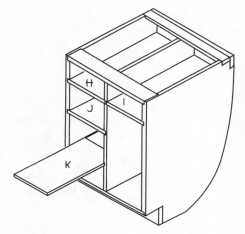

Figure 9-3h. (1) Carefully measure and cut the horizontal drawer dividers, parts H, I, J, and K, using trick #1. You should be getting good at it by now. (2) At this point, it's an excellent idea to disassemble the entire carcase and apply your desired finish. It's much easier to paint or varnish the interior surfaces while the parts are separated and lying flat than to winkle a paint brush into all those little cubbyholes. Just remember to tape off the dadoes and rabbets and any edges that will be glued, or your glue won't. (3) Now assemble the carcase for the final time, using glue and clamps and a few stainless screws. You won't need screws on any part other than the mounting bracket, part C. Plain old yellow carpenter's glue is plenty strong enough to hold everything together, but I usually use screws with bungs on parts D and F as well—just for peace of mind.

Text continued from page 175

Dividing the Space

If the cabinet you're building is for the galley, you can add a built-in icebox. Make an outside liner of ½-inch stock large enough to hold at least 4 inches of foam insulation and a ¼-inch-thick inner liner. Leave room for a drain and, if you plan to install refrigeration, access for plumbing lines.

When designing galley cabinetry, it's important to keep heavy objects such as pots and pans and canned goods as low as possible, so the deeper drawers are usually at the bottom, with the shallower ones above. This, of course, is not a hard-and-fast rule, and if you want shallow drawers at the bottom and deep ones at the top, then that's the way they should be.

With your basic cabinet completed and ready to install in the boat, first give it at least two coats of epoxy sealer or primer on all surfaces. Take special care with the edges and with those surfaces that will be hidden once the cabinet is installed.

One word of advice: Later on in this chapter, you'll learn how to make and install a plastic laminate countertop for your cabinet. If you plan to do this, *install the countertop first*, then the cabinet. If you must install the countertop after the cabinet is in place, you may find access to the underside restricted, to the point where you can't drive screws. In this case, it's perfectly OK to glue the countertop in place with a heavy bead of 3M-5200, or a similar sealant. Just be aware that if you do this, the installation is permanent.

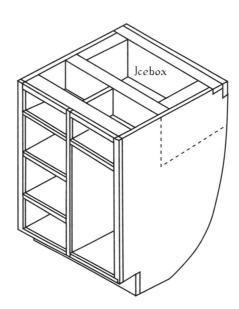

Figure 9-4.
A cabinet with icebox partitions.

Assembly

The cabinet is best secured to a stringer attached to the frames with pan-head screws through fender washers and oversize holes. Use only two screws to hold the cabinet securely in place against the hull. The screws should go through the ceiling and into the frames. If the cabinet is installed against a bulkhead, one or two screws installed along the front edge of the cabinet side adjacent to the bulkhead should be plenty. Also put two screws through the toe kick into a block screwed to the

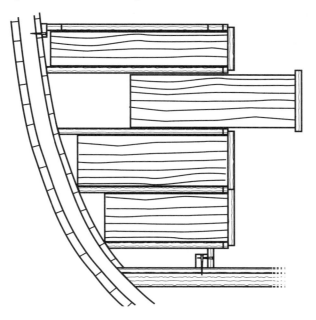

Figure 9-5.
Secure the cabinet to the hull with a minimum of mounting screws. Where possible, use pan-head screws with fender washers and oversize holes in the cabinet; this prevents the interior cabinetry from being distorted by a working hull and will ensure that drawers won't stick and doors will open and close only when wanted.

cabin sole. Use a minimum number of screws to hold the cabinet securely; that way, if the hull wants to move around a bit, the cabinet won't get in the way, and the working hull won't loosen the joints in the cabinet.

Now that you have the open framework of the cabinet in place, you can see that the structure is quite strong and every compartment is isolated from all the other compartments. You can also see that we have a lot of work left to do. The next step is to take care of the ugly raw edges of the plywood now facing the living areas.

Finish and Trim

First decide how you want to finish your completed cabinet. I strongly suggest you paint the interior white—for purely practical reasons: White paint helps visibility by reflecting what light there is in the dark recesses of the cabinet, and it's easy to keep clean. The outside of the cabinet can be anything you like—paint, natural wood, or a combination of finishes. Since the interior surfaces are more or less protected from the intense ultraviolet radiation that so severely limits our choices of exterior finishes, your only interior limitations are your imagination and your own good taste. Natural wood can either be varnished or oiled.

If you've settled on a natural finish for your cabinet, you'll need ¾ X ½-inch strips of the wood you've selected, in lengths that correspond to each visible unfinished edge of plywood. If you plan to paint your cabinets, cut the strips from any available wood—pine works fine. Starting with the longest vertical edges, glue the strips in place with carpenter's glue. Run the strips from the very top to the very bottom and let the ends run a little long. It's easier to trim them after the glue has dried. You don't need to clamp the strips; just hold them in place with masking tape. Be conservative with the glue—you don't want a lot of it to squeeze out of the joints because cleanup is difficult.

Once the glue is dry on the vertical strips, install the horizontal pieces. Since the vertical pieces fit between the horizontal pieces, they must be trimmed to the exact length. Cut and fit the longest pieces first. That way when you goof up and cut one too short you can use it later for a shorter section. If you feel like getting fancy, miter the corners and make decorative false dovetails where appropriate. It's easier to miter the corners of the vertical strips after they're glued in place and miter the cross pieces to fit as they're installed. But plain old butt joints are the easiest, and they look just fine.

Now that you have the front edges squared away and your handiwork is starting to look half decent, it's time to build some drawers.

Figure 9-6. After you've assembled the carcase and the glue has dried, it's time to trim out the rough edges visible on the front surface of the cabinet. You can use any decorative wood you like (I'm partial to cherry trim on a white-painted carcase), or you can use pine and paint it to match the rest of the cabinet.

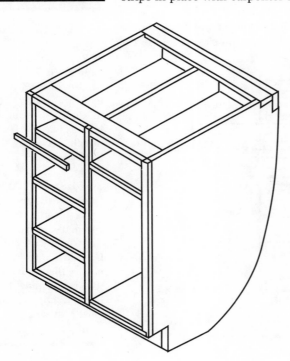

DRAWERS

Drawers are essentially boxes without tops, and if you want an example of the traditional ways they've been built in boats, simply take a look at the drawers from your furniture at home. Better-made drawers are constructed from hardwood, with dovetails at the corners. Less expensive furniture or cabinets will have drawers built from plywood, with rabbets and dado joints holding them together. The really cheap ones are made from particle board covered with wood-grain contact paper and held together with staples and glue. All these types of drawers, including the last, are found in modern boat interiors. And all except the last are appropriate, with a few modifications, for use in your new cabinet.

One of the things all these drawers have in common is that the bottoms are held in place by dadoes cut into the sides and fronts of the drawers. Drawers have been built this way for as long as drawers have been built, because the method is strong and easy. But it necessarily leaves a dead space under the drawer that is wasted. At home it doesn't matter, but on a boat with a lot of drawers that wasted space can add up to several cubic feet—the equivalent of an extra small locker.

Another thing you'll notice about the drawers at home, especially the ones in your kitchen cabinets, is that many of them are only half as deep as the opening they fill, and they're supported on the sides with some type of suspension system that takes a minimum of ½ inch of space on each side of the drawer. When this type of drawer is used in a boat, every time you get bounced around in a seaway small items that were in the drawers get bounced out into the dead spaces. And if there are no partitions between the drawers, which there probably aren't, these small items may bounce right on down into the bilge. Now you know why you put full-length partitions between the drawers in your new cabinet.

Construction

You can build your drawers from hardwood with dovetailed corners or of ⅜-inch or ½-inch plywood with rabbeted corners. Both methods yield drawers that are strong and utilitarian. I prefer to build dovetailed drawers because they look better, but dovetail joints are admittedly tricky to make by hand, and a decent jig will cost $100 or more. Don't waste your money on a cheap jig; there are some on the market (Sears makes one, and there's a Chinese import) that sell for $30 to $50, but by the time you get them set up you could have cut the dovetails by hand. I won't go into the details of constructing these joints simply because there are so many good books available with detailed instructions. *Fine WoodWorking on Boxes, Carcases, and Drawers* (see Appendix A) is just one.

As you lay out your drawers, there may be several that are unusually long. For example, if your cabinet is more than 18 inches or so from front to back, the shallow top drawers might be awkward if they're made long enough to use the entire space. A neat trick is to divide the drawer into two parts—a front section and a smaller back section—and install them one in front of the other in the same compartment. Put a simple twist catch to hold the short one in place in the extreme rear of the drawer compartment, and tack a small leather tab to the top edge of the front

Drawer Assembly

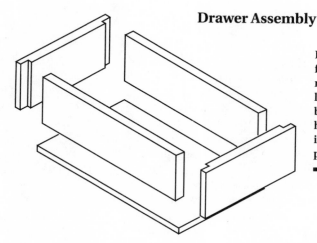

Figure 9-7a. Construct the sides of your drawers from ½- or ⅜-inch plywood or hardwood (oak, maple, and birch are excellent choices) with the long sides rabbeted into the front and back. Cut the bottom from ⅜-inch plywood for any drawer that has a bottom area larger than 1 square foot (12 inches by 12 inches). For smaller drawers, ¼-inch plywood is fine.

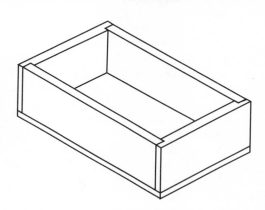

Figure 9-7b. Assemble the drawers using yellow carpenter's glue and 1-inch brads in the corners. The bottom should be secured with #6 X 1-inch screws.

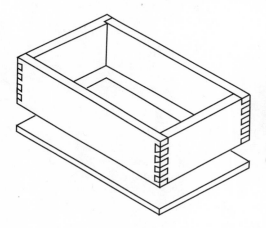

Figure 9-7c. If you feel like challenging your woodworking skills, make dovetail joints in the corners of your drawers. These can be cut by hand with a dovetail saw and a chisel, or they can be cut with a router, using a special jig. I always cut the tails in the side pieces first, then use that piece as a template to mark the doves in the front and back pieces.

Figure 9-7d. Mount the drawer front on the front of the drawer (phrases like that drive editors crazy—it's one of the fun parts of writing a book) with two #8 X ⅞-inch pan-head screws and fender washers located more or less on the horizontal centerline of the front. Use a ⅜-inch drill to drill the holes, and you'll be able to move the drawer front around a bit to adjust it before you tighten the screws all the way.

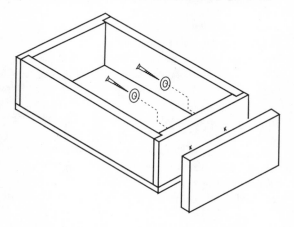

so it will be easy to remove when you need to retrieve something. These little "secret drawers" are great for small, infrequently used items, but they're even better as a place to hide the ship's papers, extra cash, or anything else you might feel uncomfortable leaving lying around. Just be sure you tell the Coast Guard, should they board you, that you have a secret drawer. They won't be amused if they find it themselves.

Once you've decided how you're going to construct your drawers, make the width exactly ⅛ inch shorter than the width of the opening, the height including the bottom, exactly ¼ inch shorter than the height of the opening, and the length approximately ¼ inch shorter than the shortest side. (The length of the sides will vary because of the curvature of the hull.)

For the bottoms of your drawers, cut a ⅜-inch piece of plywood (¼-inch plywood is OK for small drawers) to the exact outside dimensions of the drawer. Assemble the sides of the box using carpenter's glue. If the corners are dovetailed, you won't need anything but the glue, but if you used rabbet joints, put three 1-inch brads in each corner. Use the bottom to square up the drawer before the glue dries, and secure it in place with glue and #6 X 1-inch flathead screws spaced about every 4 inches around the entire perimeter. Make sure these screws are well countersunk so they won't interfere with the operation of the drawer.

Insert each drawer into its space in the cabinet for a test fit. When pushed all the way in, it should fit ¼ inch into the cabinet, it should have ⅟₁₆ inch clearance on each side, and it should have ¼ inch clearance at the top. It's easy to see that this is a significant improvement over the old way of installing drawers. For one thing, there's very little wasted space; for another, you could turn the boat upside down and nothing would fall out of the drawers.

**Figure 9-8.
Apply Teflon tape to the inside surfaces of the drawer compartments.**

Finish

Once you get the fit just right, sand the entire drawer with 100-grit aluminum-oxide paper and give it two coats of whatever finish you like. When I paint the inside of a cabinet white, I usually use clear finish on the drawer. I do this for no other reason than that's the way I like it. The clear finish looks great, especially with dovetailed corners. You may have noticed that many of the drawers in your fine furniture are left unfinished. This works fine at home, but don't leave the drawers on your boat unfinished. You've built your drawers to close tolerances that don't allow for expansion of the wood due to changes in moisture content, and a good coat of epoxy sealer or paint will help keep them stable.

We could leave the drawers just the way they

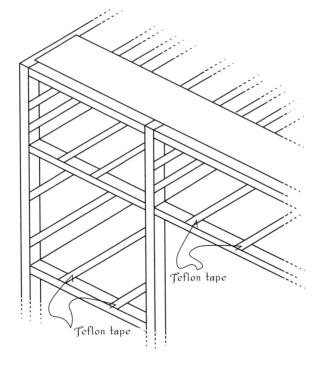

Teflon tape

Teflon tape

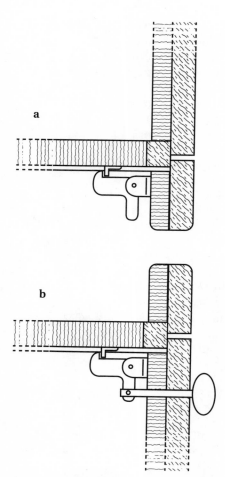

Figure 9-9. Two types of drawer latches. (a) The standard finger-actuated spring latch for drawers works OK
and is easy to install. (b) A slick modification: Glue a
wooden knob on the end of a ½-inch hardwood dowel
that is just long enough to extend from the front surface of the drawer to slightly past the finger catch
mounted on the inside of the drawer. Cut a 1-inch-long
by ⅛-inch-wide slot in the opposite end of the dowel so
it will slip over the finger lever. It may be necessary to
relieve the sides of the latch so that it will fit into a slot
in the dowel, but you can do this easily on a bench
grinder. Drill both the dowel and the latch with a ⅛-
inch drill. Now drill a ⁹⁄₁₆-inch hole through the drawer
front, insert the dowel, and secure it to the latch with a
clevis or cotter pin.

are, but the friction of the painted surfaces rub-
bing together will soon wear through the finish.
One way to prevent this is with a periodic coat of
Butcher's wax on the outside of the drawer and
the inside of the cabinet. The wax makes the
drawer easy to open and protects the finish, but it
must be renewed periodically to remain effective.
A more permanent way to do the same thing is
with peel-and-stick Teflon tape. Simply put two
strips of tape on the bottom of each drawer opening and two strips on each side. The drawer will
slide on the slippery tape, and the finished surfaces will not contact each other. One brand is
called *Nylo-Tape*, and it's available from The
Woodworker's Store in Rogers, Minnesota (see
Appendix B). Any good hardware store might
carry something similar. Get an extra roll or two
because it will eventually wear out and need
replacing.

Take the dimensions of the doors and drawer
fronts off the openings in the cabinet by measuring each opening exactly and adding ½ inch to
each dimension. This will give you the finished
trim size for each door and drawer front and
allows for a ¼-inch overlap on all edges. Drawer
fronts are usually plain pieces of lumber trimmed
to size, then sanded and finished to match the
doors. Mount them on the fronts of the drawers
by screwing from the inside. Use two screws (just
a bit shorter than the combined thicknesses of the
drawer front and face) located on the long centerline and evenly spaced from the ends, and don't
use glue. Drill the holes in the drawer slightly
oversized and use a fender washer so the position
of the drawer fronts can be adjusted straight and
level.

Latches

The drawers may be held in place by spring-
actuated finger catches—you know, the kind that
are released by inserting your finger through a
hole in the front of the drawer. I must admit I'm
not crazy about these latches, having nearly broken a finger with them on more than one occasion, but they do work, and they do hold the

drawer securely closed. And the part of the catch inside the cabinet also acts as a drawer stop that will keep you from pulling the drawer all the way out and dumping its contents on the cabin sole.

To install the catch, cut a 1¼-inch hole through the drawer front with a Forstner bit so that the top edge of the hole is even with the bottom end of the actuating lever. Radius the inside and outside edges of the hole with your router and a ⅜-inch rounding-over bit with pilot bearing (see Figure 9-9a).

A simple modification to these finger catches, shown in Figure 9-9b, makes them much more finger-friendly. Simply drill a ⁹⁄₁₆-inch hole through the front of the drawer so that the latch can be activated by a ½-inch dowel with a wooden knob glued on the end of it. Secure the dowel to the latch by drilling a ⅛-inch hole through both and inserting a clevis or cotter pin.

With the drawers and the cabinet case complete, the next item is the doors. Here the depth of your imagination and the breadth of your woodworking skills are your only limits. The easiest type of door to make is simply a flat panel of ¾-inch plywood edged with wood strips—the same way you edged the front of the cabinet case. You can use fancy hardwood plywood or combine painted plywood and natural wood trim, which always looks good. I made mahogany raised-panel doors for the *Duchess*, and they look fine. There are about a dozen different ways to make good raised-panel doors, and about half of them easily fall within the realm of the home craftsman. Just about any good book on woodworking will have at least one acceptable method.

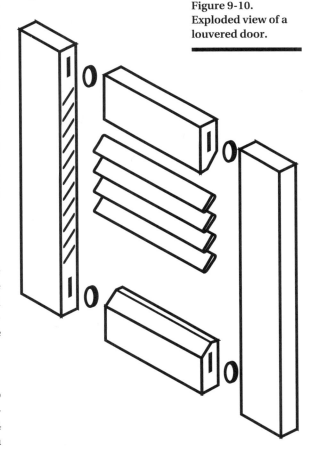

Figure 9-10.
Exploded view of a
louvered door.

One practical and attractive type of door that isn't easy to make is a traditional louvered door. But I know a way of making them that's easier than most, and since I've never seen it in print, I'll take a few pages to share it with you.

LOUVERED DOORS

To make a louvered door you'll first need to make two jigs. The vertical side pieces of the door are called *stiles* and the horizontal pieces are called *rails*. You'll need one jig for each side—a right-hand jig and a left-hand jig—as shown in Figure 9-11a.

Jig Construction

The jigs are simple to make from your scrap pile. For each you'll need 2 pieces of ¾-inch plywood at least 12 inches square for the bases; 4 blocks of wood that are just a whisker thicker than

Making the Jigs

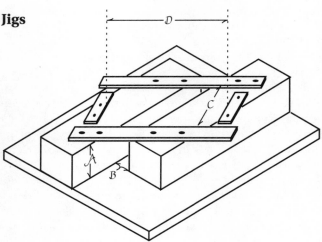

Figure 9-11a. *Dimension A* is the width of your door stile; *dimension B* is the thickness of your door stile; *dimension C* is the diameter of your router base, and *dimension D* is the diameter of your router base plus the length of the slot you want to cut minus ⅛ inch (the radius of the ¼-inch bit you will use to cut the slot). *Angle A* (in Figure 9-11c) is the angle of the slant of the louvers. I find a 45-degree slant works fine for indoor use with a louver that is ¼ X 1 inch. If you make doors for outdoor use, a ¼ X 1¼-inch louver on a 60-degree slant works better.

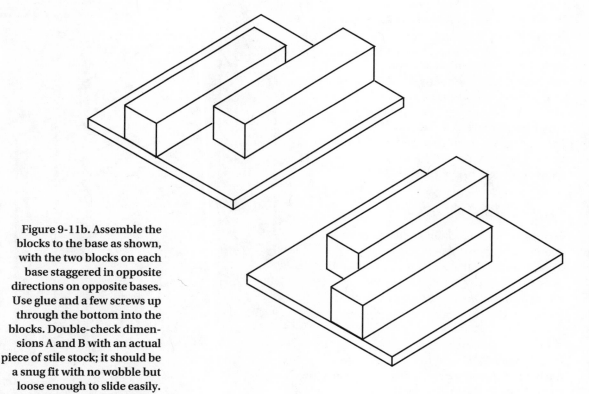

Figure 9-11b. Assemble the blocks to the base as shown, with the two blocks on each base staggered in opposite directions on opposite bases. Use glue and a few screws up through the bottom into the blocks. Double-check dimensions A and B with an actual piece of stile stock; it should be a snug fit with no wobble but loose enough to slide easily.

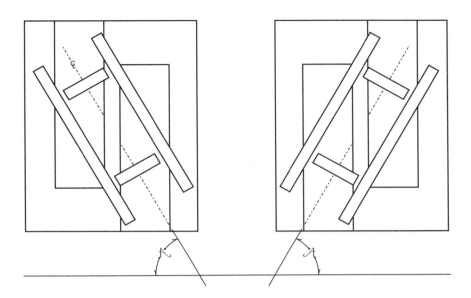

Figure 9-11c.
This shows a bird's-eye view of the two jigs as they should look when completed. Carefully mark the exact centerline between the two router guide rails on each jig as shown.

the stiles of your doors are wide and about 10 inches long for the guide blocks; 4 strips of ¼ X 1-inch hardwood about 10 inches long for router guides; and 4 strips of the same hardwood about 4 inches long for the router stops. The width of the guide blocks doesn't matter, but they must be wide enough to mount securely on the base. If you don't have stock that's thick enough, glue some up from plywood or pine scraps. When assembled, the jigs will look like the one shown in Figure 9-11a.

Mount the blocks on the plywood base with screws and glue so they are parallel, leaving a space between them the same thickness as your door stock. One end of one block should be flush with one edge of the baseboard, and the opposite end of the other block should be flush with the opposite edge. The blocks are staggered to provide a clamping surface for the door stock.

Since I like heavy stiles, I usually make mine 3 inches wide and ⅞ inch thick. For these dimensions, my jigs would have guide blocks 3 inches thick, spaced ⅞ inch apart. When you're finished, a sample piece of your door stock should fit between the guide blocks just snug enough not to wiggle port and starboard but loose enough to slide fore and aft, and it should be flush with the tops of the blocks.

I usually make the louvers ¾ inch wide and ¼ inch thick, with a ⅛-inch radius on each edge. Setting the louvers at a 45-degree angle works OK for interior doors. Exterior doors need a steeper angle and wider louvers to provide protection from the weather.

Since we're doing interior doors, scribe a line representing the centerline of your jig at 45 degrees across the center of your guide blocks. Divide the diameter of the base of your router in half to determine the radius. Scribe a line parallel to the centerline at a distance equal to the radius of the router base, then do the same thing on the other side of the centerline; the two outside lines should be parallel and the same distance apart as the diameter of the router base. Tack straight pieces of ¼ X 1-inch hardwood along each line and check to see that the base of your router fits securely between these two guide strips but is free enough to slide back and forth without effort.

Next, measure along the centerline from the inside edge of each guide block a distance equal to the radius of your router base minus ¼ inch, and tack a small stop block on each side. Mount a ¼-inch straight-cut bit in your router, adjust it to extend ¼ inch below the base, and place the router into the jig. As you move the router back and forth, the bit should stop ⅛ inch from the inside edge of each guide block. If it doesn't, adjust the position of the stop blocks until it does.

The first jig is now complete. Make the second jig in exactly the same way as you made the first, but scribe the centerline at a 45-degree angle that is opposite from the first, and attach the router guides accordingly. This procedure for making jigs may sound dreadfully complicated the first time you read through it, but it's actually quite simple. Read the instructions and study the drawings, and after you make your first set you'll be able to throw the jigs together in just a few minutes.

Now trim and mill the stock for the frames of your doors. The stiles run from top to bottom and the rails fit between the stiles. If you are using a biscuit joiner (described below), you can leave the stiles a little long and trim them after the glue dries, but the rails must be cut to the exact length from the start. If you're not using a biscuit joiner, make half-lap joints, or one of the other joints illustrated in Figure 9-13. Make the slats or louvers as described above and leave them ½ inch longer than the rails. Sanding and finishing all the pieces before the door is assembled will save you a lot of work later on.

Cutting the Slots

You're ready to make a few test cuts with the router. Trim a foot-long scrap of stock to the exact width and thickness of your rail stock. Scribe a series of parallel lines at 45 degrees and ⅜ inch apart along one edge of the test piece—half a dozen should be enough. Slide the test piece into the jig and clamp it in place so that the first diagonal line on the test piece lines up with the centerline of the jig. Start the router with the edge of the base resting against one of the stop blocks and slowly lower the cutter into the test piece. Now simply slide the router forward until it is stopped by the opposite stop block. This operation is easier with a plunge router, but an ordinary router works fine. I usually use one of my little laminate trimmers because they're so easy to control.

After you make the first cut, slip one end of one of the louvers into the resulting slot. It should insert easily with no force required, but it should be tight enough so that the louvers won't rattle in the finished door. If the louver doesn't fit perfectly, make any required adjustments to the jig and try again. You may have to make two or three test cuts to get it perfect.

Once the jig is squared away, simply advance the stock to the next line and make another cut. Repeat the process for all six lines, then make another test piece and do the same thing with the other jig. Assemble the test pieces using six louvers, stand back, and take a look. The louvers should have a ⅛-inch space between them

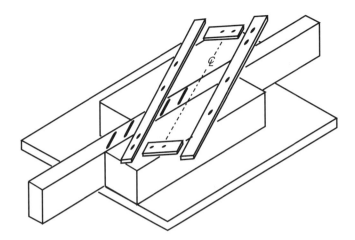

Figure 9-12.
Before you cut the real thing, set up your jigs and make a few test cuts with a piece of scrap trimmed to the exact dimensions of the stock for your stiles.

and overlap enough so light doesn't show through when the louvers are viewed straight on. The rails need to be beveled to accommodate the top and bottom lou-

Figure 9-13.
Four corner joints.

ver, and the spacing between the rails and the louvers should be the same as it is between louvers. Most important, the louvers should look "right." If they don't, make slight changes in the angle and the spacing until they do.

Assembling the Frames

When assembling the frames you have a bit of flexibility. There are a number of traditional joints you can use. Not long ago, no serious woodworker would have considered anything other than a *mortise-and-tenon joint* for making doors, and there are still some who get emotional when any alternative is suggested. But realistically, modern epoxies are so strong that almost any craftsman-like joint will do the job. Use whatever corner joint you prefer: *half-lap, mitered,* and *doweled joints* will all work fine.

Occasionally I still use mortise-and-tenon joints on cabinet doors, but making them takes quite a bit of time, and they waste a significant amount of wood. So I frequently resort to a device called a *biscuit joiner*—a small circular saw with a spring-actuated blade that cuts matching grooves in the stiles and rails of the door. After the grooves are cut, the two pieces are held together by a foot-ball-shaped spline soaked in epoxy. With the bis-

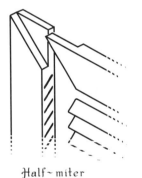

Half~miter

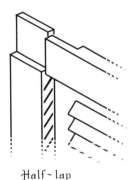

Half~lap

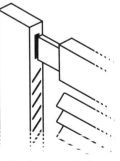

Mortise~and~tenon

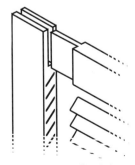

Finger or Bridal

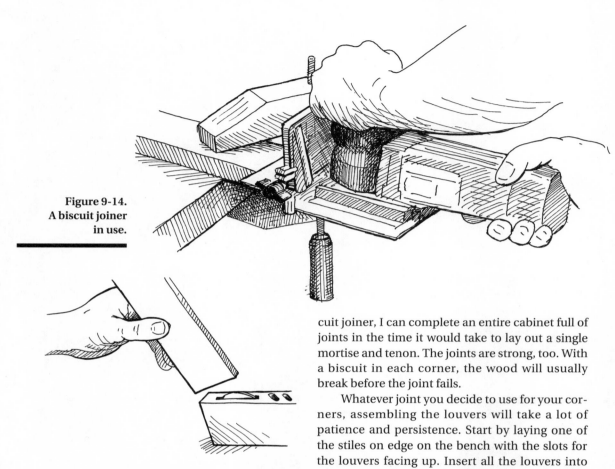

**Figure 9-14.
A biscuit joiner
in use.**

cuit joiner, I can complete an entire cabinet full of
joints in the time it would take to lay out a single
mortise and tenon. The joints are strong, too. With
a biscuit in each corner, the wood will usually
break before the joint fails.

Whatever joint you decide to use for your corners, assembling the louvers will take a lot of
patience and persistence. Start by laying one of
the stiles on edge on the bench with the slots for
the louvers facing up. Insert all the louvers into
the slots. If you cut everything right, you won't need glue for the louvers. Now take
the other stile and insert the louvers into the slots one at a time, working from one
end toward the other. Typically, about halfway through the entire thing will fall
apart and you'll have to start over. But keep at it: It gets easier after you get the hang
of it. Glue and clamp the corners, making sure they're perfectly square, and you're
ready for a final trim and finish.

Hardware

Now that your doors are built, we need to mount them on your new cabinets.
To do that, we need to reach out once more to embrace modern European kitchen
technology.

The doors we've just finished building are called *overlay* doors in the cabinet
trade because they overlay the front of the cabinet rather than setting into it (*inset*
doors) or fitting flush with it (*flush* doors). It seems like a logical enough way to
make doors, but overlay doors weren't used much in the past because the only
available hinges that allowed doors to open properly—knife hinges—didn't work

all that well. Knife hinges, which were mounted on the door's top and the bottom in the manner of a modern refrigerator door hinge, were flimsy and weak and totally inadequate for all but the smallest doors.

The hinges we want for our new doors are given different names by different people—invisible hinges, 32mm-system hinges, technical hinges, and European-style hinges are just four of the designations I've heard. They were invented in Europe, like the frameless cabinet system itself, and they are truly an engineering marvel. Using a system of levers and springs, they hold the door as securely as any hinge, but as the door is opened, it pops out away from the adjacent door before it swings open. This allows two doors to be used right next to each other—or next to a bulkhead or a drawer front that would interfere with a normal hinge. Manufactured with a confusing array of options, some of these hinges are made to open as little as 95 degrees for doors in close quarters, while others will open as much as 176 degrees. And once installed, they're adjustable on three axes. The brands I'm familiar with are Mepla and Blum, and they're available through any cabinet-supply store or from The Woodworker's Store listed in Appendix B.

The only trick to installing technical hinges is drilling a hole for each hinge in the door stiles exactly 1⅜ inches in diameter, ½ inch deep, and 3/16 inch away from the inside edge of the door. These holes are drilled with a special bit that drills a flat-bottomed hole. Cabinet supply outlets sell an industrial carbide version at about $35 each, which is worth the price if you intend to drill a lot of holes. But for the 10 or 12 hinges that will go on an average boat, a 1⅜-inch steel Forstner bit will work just fine and save you about $25.

If these hinges have a drawback, it's that they're not made specifically for marine use. However, they are built to be used in kitchens, which is perhaps the

Figure 9-15. European-style hinges and the special drill bit necessary for mounting.

second most hostile environment for metal, and both the Mepla and Blum versions are heavily nickel plated. Install them carefully according to the instructions that come with them, give them an occasional shot of WD-40, and they'll give you years and years of trouble-free service.

SINKS AND COUNTERTOPS

Well, that finishes up the cabinet itself. All that's left is to decide what kind of top you want on it. And this is another area where I've formed some unorthodox opinions.

The typical working countertop in the majority of boats built over the past 30 years was made of plywood surfaced with plastic laminate—usually Formica or one of the many similar products such as Pionite or Wilsonart. If your boat is more than 30 years old, the countertops were probably originally covered with linoleum.

Linoleum tends to peel, crack, and break, and while it may have been the best choice at the time, it is totally unsatisfactory for use today. Plastic laminate, on the other hand, still makes a durable and serviceable countertop. In fact most new boats have plastic laminate countertops. If you're looking for a quick and easy way to build a countertop, using a material that's easy to work with, inexpensive, and will look great when you're done, plastic laminate is hard to beat.

Plastic Laminate

To make a plastic laminate countertop, make a tick-stick pattern of the top and transfer it to a piece of ¾-inch AC plywood. AC plywood has one surface free of voids, a critical necessity for use under laminate. Cut the plywood to size, allowing for a 2½-inch overhang (including the fiddles) along the front edge. Check that the top looks right and fits properly. If it's the galley cabinet you're working on, make any required cutouts for the sink and stove now, before you glue on the laminate.

When you buy the laminate, get a piece that will hang over all of the edges by about 6 inches. There will be a lot of waste, but laminate is cheap, and an oversize piece will make installation much easier. Stay away from the thin material called vertical grade; it costs a little less, but it's difficult to work with, and it will telegraph every flaw in the plywood. Also, buy a fresh piece of laminate for each job; plastic laminate has a shelf life of about six months, after which it becomes brittle and significantly harder to work with.

To install the laminate, coat the underside and the plywood top—using a brush or roller—with a *thin* layer of contact cement (I like Weldwood, but you can use any good contact cement) and set them aside just long enough to dry tack-free. If you let the cement dry too long, it won't stick at all. Now cover the entire countertop with slipsheets (newspaper works fine) to prevent any contact between the glue-coated surfaces. Place the laminate on top of the paper and position it to overhang all sides of the plywood. When you get the laminate right where you want it, carefully slide the slipsheets out from between the laminate and the countertop; the glue will bond permanently the instant contact is made. Make sure the bond is complete by rolling with a heavy roller, or go over the entire surface with a block of wood and a heavy rubber mallet.

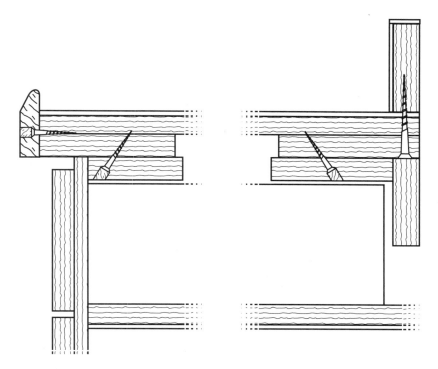

Figure 9-16.
Cutaway view of
cabinet construction
with plastic laminate
top and backsplash.

Test for a tight bond by trying to peel the laminate back from a corner. If you've done it right, the plastic will break before the glue releases, so be careful; you don't want to break the laminate—just make sure the corners are secure. Now simply run a router with a flush-trim bit around all the edges and dress them lightly with a fine file. The best bits for trimming laminate are cheap carbide bits that use a bushing, instead of the type with a ball bearing, but you must lubricate the edges with petroleum jelly. (Cut the scrap laminate into squares of different sizes and save them; they have dozens of uses around a shop as shims, trowels for smoothing epoxy, scrapers, filleting and fairing tools, and the light-colored ones make handy note pads.)

If you want a backsplash for your countertop, cut a piece of ¾-inch by 3½-inch wood to length, cover its face with laminate and trim the edges, then add laminate to the top. When you trim the edges, you'll get a better finish on the face side by using a 10-degree laminate-trimming bit. Mount the finished backsplash on the countertop with polyurethane sealant and drive several #8 X 3-inch screws up from below. If you used a color other than white for your countertop, ask your dealer to order the polyurethane color to match. Almost all colors are available, but most places will have to order it for you. Very few dealers will mention that the sealant is available to match plastic laminate colors because it's a nuisance for them, but it will make your new countertop sparkle.

Install the countertop by driving #8 X 2-inch screws up from underneath, through the mounting bracket and the front cleat. A warning to be careful not to

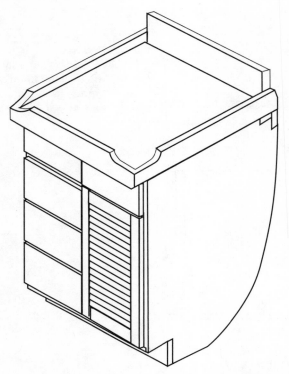

drive the screws up through the top might sound silly and obvious, but I'd hate to have to admit how many tops I've ruined doing just that. Always double-check the length of the screws you plan to use. You can bet there's one that's ¼ inch longer than the rest, mixed in among the others, just waiting to assassinate your new countertop.

Once the top is screwed down, trim the front edge with a decorative fiddle of natural wood. The best wood for fiddles is white oak (not red oak) because it won't absorb moisture and stain, but of course teak works well and is used much more frequently. Cut them and mount them as shown on all exposed edges of your countertop. Use the same sealant under the fiddles as you used for the backsplash and make sure that there's a good seal between the fiddle and the laminate.

Solid-Surface Material

Yes, I did say that plastic laminates are hard to beat. But I didn't say that they're impossible to beat. The new solid-surface countertop material made by DuPont under the trade name Corian, and by several other manufacturers under different names (Fountainhead by Nevamar and Surell by Formica are just two), is neither inexpensive nor easy to work with, but it is truly wonderful stuff. It was developed for your kitchen counters at home, of course, where its extremely high cost has made it a bit of a status symbol in the modern suburban environment. Corian and the others are impermeable plastics that won't stain or scratch easily and superficially resemble marble. All these materials are available in a number of colors and in thicknesses from ¼ to ¾ inch. Their biggest asset as a countertop is that they can be cold welded to form intricate shapes without even a hint of a seam or joint, or if you don't mind a slight trace of a joint, they can be assembled with conventional epoxy.

All manufacturers of solid-surface materials discourage amateur use of their products, and one (Nevamar) refuses to sell to anyone who has not completed one of their fabrication seminars. This would seem to indicate that these materials aren't as easy to work with as wood, which is true, but they can be worked with in any *advanced* home workshop equipped with *heavy-duty* hand tools and carbide blades. The concern over amateur use seems to be one of product liability more than anything else.

To build a Corian countertop for your galley, you'll need a sheet of ½-inch Corian, a preformed Corian sink bowl, and a number of seam kits, depending on the size of your job. The seam kits contain two tubes of chemicals that, when combined, form the substance that makes the solid and invisible joints. The most important joints in your countertop are where the backsplash joins the countertop and where the sink attaches. Usually the front edge of the counter is doubled or tripled in thickness for appearance, but a traditional wooden fiddle can also be used. The fiddles and other wooden parts are attached to the top with a special polyurethane adhesive the manufacturers sell for this purpose. The countertop is glued to the cabinet with this same adhesive.

If you don't feel comfortable building a Corian countertop yourself, don't feel bad. I can't stand working with the stuff. The chemicals used with these products are toxic and dangerous, and working with the material itself is a lot like working with fiberglass. A fine white powder settles over you and everything in your shop and forces the use of respirators and protective clothing. And then, as mentioned earlier, there is the expense: Corian currently sells for $22 a square foot for the ½-inch material, and the smallest piece you can buy is 30 X 98 inches—a little over 20 square feet—which comes to about $450. Add to this the price of the sink—about $300 for the smallest one—and you have a significant investment before you make your first cut. Cut it wrong, and that's a lot of money to be putting out with the trash.

Unless you have time and money to invest in one of the manufacturers' fabrication seminars and you have other uses for all that left-over material, your best bet may be to contact a certified solid-surface fabricator. These are independent craftsmen who have attended a series of training seminars and have passed a rigorous test of their fabricating skills. These seminars are given by companies like DuPont and their local distributors. One of the best fabricators around is Bill Holton of Essex, Massachusetts (see Appendix B). Bill understands old wooden boats because he has one himself, and he has done all my Corian work for years—he's a whiz at the dry sink described below. If you send Bill a paper or cardboard pattern or a detailed drawing of your countertop, he'll have your finished countertop back to you in less time than it would take to figure out how to mix those two tubes of noxious chemicals together. And telling him that you read this book automatically qualifies you for the 10 percent Jim Trefethen I-love-old-boats-but-I-hate-those-smelly-chemicals discount.

The Dry Sink

Before I close this chapter, I just want to get my two cents' worth in about sinks. The very best sink in a cruising boat is no sink at all. The problem with sinks on any boat that isn't 50 or 60 feet on the waterline is that they're entirely too small to be useful, yet they're invariably large enough to be a nuisance when you need to use the counter space in your galley—which is just about all the time. Not only that, but when you install a sink with the required plumbing in a convenient spot in your countertop, it will render the space under the sink useless for storage. Take a look under any sink in any boat—the entire thing is surrounded by unusable dead space.

Obviously you can't just eliminate the galley sink. You still need a place to wash dishes and clean the veggies. The answer is to build a dry sink similar to the one your great-great-granny used back before the average home had the luxury of

Figure 9-18.
The modified dry
sink shown in Figure
9-19 can be made of
¾-inch plywood and
covered with fiber-
glass and epoxy, but
the best choice is a
solid-surface coun-
tertop material such
as Corian, Nevermar,
or Fountainhead, to
name just a few.

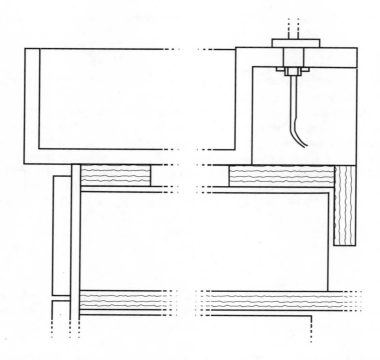

indoor plumbing. A dry sink is nothing more than a countertop that has a 4- or 5-inch lip fabricated all around the outside edge to keep whatever it is you're working on from slopping out onto the floor. Your dry sink will be a bit of an improvement over Granny's in that it won't really be dry. It will have a conventional faucet or pump, as you like, and it will also have a hose with a spray nozzle, just like at home. It will need a drain, of course, but since there's no sink bowl to dictate where the drain must be it can be located at the extreme rear of the dry sink—or off in one corner—where the required plumbing won't interfere with your precious storage space. When you need a sink to do the dishes or whatever, an ordinary plastic dish pan is 10 times more convenient anyway than that silly little stainless bowl you used to have.

One of the reasons you haven't seen many of this type of wet/dry sink is that until the solid countertop material came along, they were difficult to make for use in a galley. I did make several out of plywood covered with fiberglass and epoxy, but the amount of work required to get a fair surface just isn't worth it for a sink, and building a mold would be even more effort. The answer is to build your dry sink out of Corian (or one of the others) solid-surface material. A simple slab with four sides about 4 inches high is utilitarian, will last forever, and it looks terrific. The advantages of the dry sink outweigh the pain in the . . . well, you know, of working with Corian.

If you are a conservative sort of person when it comes to matters of consequence like old wooden boats, I may have tested your credulity with these some-

what unorthodox suggestions on interior cabinetry. If so, I can only suggest that you give them a
chance. They all combine to make difficult procedures easier and result in a product that is handier
to use and will give better service than those produced the old way. I've lived long enough to be
considered ancient and cantankerous by my kids,
and I've come to detest changes effected for the
sake of fashion or expediency or to take advantage
of an increasingly gullible and uninformed public
(molded hull liners and lime-green shag carpeting
come immediately to mind). But when change
results in genuine improvements that make our
old wooden boats less of a burden to own and
more of a joy to use, not to recognize it as such
and not to embrace it would be foolish.

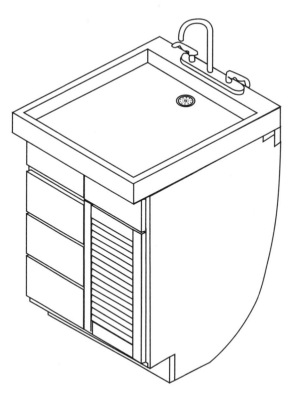

**Figure 9-19.
Great-Great-
Granny's dry sink.**

CHAPTER TEN

Little Boats—
Big Memories

Have you heard about the nostalgia craze? How could you miss it?

The mechanic who works on my truck (such as it is) owns a '55 Chevy—a pristine example of 1950s Americana replete with teardrop spots, fuzzy dice, full-moon hubs, and slightly anachronistic fox tails (*we* wouldn't have been caught dead with fox tails) flying from the twin radio antennas. The last time I had my oil changed, he complained that he couldn't drive his treasured Chevy anymore because so many people stop him in traffic wanting to buy it.

The other day I stopped for a quick lunch at the local pizza place just down the street from the high school. Big mistake. School was out early, and the place was jumping with exuberant teenagers listening to a jukebox playing Buddy Holly, Elvis, and the Everly Brothers. And right around the corner was an antique shop with a big red Coke machine out front—the old-fashioned kind that once sat in front of every gas station in the land. It still had the "Have-a-Coke-5¢" sticker on the front. The price? Only $1,200.

Sometime later, over at Pickering Wharf—down at the end by the old bridge where the lobsterboats tie up—I ran into a small-boat enthusiast I knew who proudly announced he'd just purchased an 18-foot 1953 Chris-Craft Riviera runabout in "pretty good" condition, but without an engine. After listening to a detailed description, I concluded that the boat was actually in pretty bad condition but certainly salvable, and I tactfully asked what he had paid for it.

"Only $6,500, but the guy needed cash, and he didn't know what he had."

Only $6,500, I mused, for a worn-out old 18-footer with no engine and requir-

**Figure 10-1.
A Chris-Craft
Riviera.**

ing at least a year's worth of weekends to get back in the water—not bad, not bad at all. My friend figured he could easily double his money by putting the old runabout back in shape and reselling her.

Old runabouts, like old Coke machines and old rock-and-roll singers, are selling for premium prices, and they represent one of the most popular fix-it-up projects around. If you're lucky enough to own one of these wonderful old boats, or if you can get your hands on one, you can have a lot of fun with it. Small boats, like runabouts and small motorboats, make the life of the renovator a lot easier than do bigger boats, just because of their size. The problems of finding a place to work, moving the boat around, and buying materials are vastly reduced. You won't need a truck to haul lumber home, and many supplies can be bought in quarts rather than 5-gallon buckets. And, unlike almost every other type of boat you're likely to encounter, an old runabout stands a good chance of earning you a profit if you decide to sell when you're done.

Chris-Craft was the most prolific builder of small wooden runabouts—a dozen models from 16 to 23 feet were listed in their 1950 catalog—but they were by no means the only builder. HackerCraft was a household word a few decades ago, and The Century Boat Company of Manistee, Michigan, advertised "the most expensively made runabout in the country." Familiar names like Thompson, Penn Yan, and Trojan got started by offering quality outboards, canoes, and runabouts. A few manufacturers used some imagination when advertising their products, and small speedsters with names like the Plycraft Rocket and the Fairliner Torpedo lit up the boat shows, promising performance by association with their dramatic namesakes.

Many of us who were born during or right after World War II (baby-boomers— although most of us don't boom as much as we used to, and we sure ain't babies) have fond if somewhat clouded memories of growing up in the peace and prosperity of the 1950s. We had defeated Hitler and conquered polio; the GI Bill was educating the masses; and with our feet planted firmly on the ground, we were headed for the stars. Nothing seemed impossible.

Today, as we smile at the reruns of "I Love Lucy" and try to deal with the realities of middle age, many of us attempt to reach back in time to recapture a piece of the magic of an era when "streetwise" meant you knew your way around town and graffiti was something you found on the wall in the men's room.

So there's a lot more to fixing up an old Chevy coupe or a mahogany runabout than meets the eye of the casual observer. The reward transcends merely having an old car or a boat the kids call awesome, bodacious, or wicked neat. If you know what it is, I don't have to explain it, and if you don't know what it is, I can't explain it. I can't help you with that old Chevy either, but let's take a look at that chrome-and-mahogany beauty you just dragged home from the flea market.

WORKS IN PROGRESS

The other day I loaded the whole family into the car and took a drive into the midreaches of New Hampshire—to Franklin and the Onion River Boatworks, Inc. An ex-Marbleheader named Ken Bassett is president, CEO, and occasionally the sole employee of Onion River, and he's a boatbuilder with a solid reputation for meticulous craftsmanship and authentic period restorations. I'd gotten word that Ken was putting the finishing touches on a 16-foot 1929 Hickman Sea Sled, and I wanted to get some pictures before he turned it over to the owner. A Hickman Sea Sled is a real rarity (see *WoodenBoat* No. 100, June 1991, for David Seidman's fasci-

Figure 10-2.
The Hickman Sea
Sled.

nating article about Albert Hickman and his Sea Sled), and any work on one must be in the realm of restoration rather than renovation—they are too valuable and rare to be merely renovated. I'd never even seen one, and it would probably be a while before I would get another chance.

The Hickman was in the finishing room when we walked into the shop, and I knew right away it had been worth the trip. She was truly a thing of beauty. Multiple coats of varnish gleamed on new mahogany decking, and an authentic 1932 Johnson V70 outboard hung in all its polished-aluminum splendor from the transom. The detail work was as good as it ever gets, and even the decals with the maker's name had been faithfully reproduced.

A little later, as I chatted about old wooden boats with Ken, I was able to check out some of his other projects. Ken's shop is as neat and clean as an operating room and so well lighted I was able to take photographs without a flash—even with the slow film I favor. At one end of the shop was the shell of an Old Town canoe with the gunwales and canvas removed. It was a smaller version of the one I'd renovated and used extensively as a teenager.

Needless to say, at the sight of the Old Town the ghosts of memories past plucked a few nostalgia strings, but what was next got them playing chords, stomping their feet, and singing along with the music. A practically original 1956 Lyman outboard in excellent condition and with a shiny Mercury outboard sat on a trailer, patiently awaiting some detail work and the spring thaw to get back in the water. Even the tacky little anchor-shaped vent in the bulkhead door was the same as on the Lyman I had as a kid.

The next and last project in the shop was a boat I didn't recognize. In fact it was so far gone that it was barely recognizable as a boat. Ken identified it as an 18-foot triple-cockpit mahogany outboard runabout built by the Brill Trolley Car Company in 1929 and rescued by Ken from oblivion. He patiently showed me where a well-intentioned previous owner had made inept repairs and had removed the center decking to enlarge the cockpit. He also pointed out that many small runabouts like the Brill were made by companies in the 1920s that had previously built milk wagons, oak ice boxes, or other wooden products that no longer had a market due to changing technology. Brill had been a major manufacturer of wooden trolley cars and began to build runabouts in a desperate attempt to find a new product they could make and sell using their existing tools and skills. Consequently, some of the original construction on the Brill was more appropriate for a horse-drawn wagon than a fine motorboat. It's possible that the dilapidated Brill is the only one of its kind; even if it isn't, it's still a fascinating example of boatbuilding from a turbulent era in our industrial history and well worth preserving in spite of its poor condition.

About the only things worth saving on the old three-holer were the framework and the concept. The poor condition of the original boat meant that a true restoration was impractical, so the finished product would be a renovation in the true sense of the word—it would look like a boat from the 1920s, and it would be powered by an old Johnson outboard from the same period, but it would be rebuilt using current methods and materials. Most important, it would be used on the water as a boat and not end up under a tarp in a collector's shed only to be taken out for boat shows and 4th of July parades. This was my kind of project, so I picked Ken's brain for clues as to how he planned to proceed, and he happily obliged my curiosity.

RENOVATING RUNABOUTS

The first thing Ken pointed out was that in renovating a small boat like the Brill, it's foolish to try to save money by cutting back on the quality of the materials. Many amateur renovators try to save a few bucks by using a cheaper vinyl rather than the original style of tufted leather, by using a lower grade of mahogany for the planking, or even by trying to save deteriorated components that should be replaced. But there just isn't a large enough volume of materials in a small boat to effect any real economy, and the quality of the finished product will suffer way out of proportion to the amount of money saved. If you plan to renovate a small boat and don't have the money, the time, and the commitment to use the finest materials and do the job right the first time, you and the boat will be a lot better off if you put her in the garage and wait until you do.

That said, Ken went over his plans for getting the little Brill back in the water. First he had brought it into the shop, cleaned it up, and given it a thorough inspection for structural damage and rot. The transom was beyond repair, and since all the stringers that gave the hull its shape tied into the transom, he'd had to replace it before removing the planking. Ken already had the new transom in place and was making the final attachment of the stringers.

Once the new transom is squared away, he'll remove all the planking and decking, saving it only for patterning, then discard it. It's too far gone to salvage, and since this is a varnished boat, new planking wouldn't match any of the old planking anyway. Once the skin is off, he'll inspect and repair the stringers, deck beams, carlins, frames, and clamp rail as appropriate. He'll fill all the old screw holes then inspect and repair the structural bulkheads. At this point, he'll replace the framing for the center decking removed by a previous owner. Fortunately the location of the decking can be determined by marks and fastening holes remaining in the original framing. The frames on this boat are the built-up type originally assembled with bolts—a feature that will make replacement easy.

Once the frame is complete, Ken will replace the skin, but first he'll give the entire frame several coats of sealer and paint to stabilize the old wood and seal the new wood. Many builders would install wiring and control cables at this point, especially on larger boats, because the interior of the boat is accessible from the outside. On your project, you should at least install the control devices temporarily to make sure you have all the necessary holes in all the right places in the bulkheads and everything is working properly. It's much easier to change things now than it will be after you've replaced the skin.

Figure 10-3. Ken Bassett working on the Brill.

As the next step, Ken will invite a couple of muscular friends over to help him invert the hull—it doesn't really weigh that much, at this point anyway—and will start reinstalling the skin. Although the original boat was single-planked in mahogany, as most boats of this type were, the first layer of the new skin will be 4-millimeter marine Okoume plywood from Harbor Sales in Baltimore. Not a cost-cutting move—the plywood will add substantially to the strength of the skin and to the stiffness of the finished hull. It will also provide a uniform surface onto which the outside planking will be epoxy bonded. Fortunately the Brill has a chine, so attaching the plywood will be fairly easy. Ken will give the interior surface of the plywood two coats of epoxy, then fasten and bond the skin to the frames. This, of course, contradicts what I said earlier about not using epoxy to bond planking to the frames. Fasteners are used without epoxy on most large, heavy boats because their hulls need some flexibility to allow for normal movement. That same flexibility in a lightweight, high-speed powerboat hull that will undoubtedly be hauled around on a trailer could quickly destroy the boat, so bonding the skin to the frames is an excellent way to increase the stiffness and strength of the hull.

The second layer of planking will be ¼-inch-thick Honduras mahogany epoxied to the plywood skin and flush-fastened to the frames. Flush fastening involves driving a countersunk flathead screw into the frame until the surface of the head is flush with the surface of the planking. This fastening method is favored in runabouts where the planking is too thin to hold a bung. Besides, it's quick and easy, and the exposed brass screw heads contrast with the varnished mahogany and give the whole thing a classy look. On the Brill, Ken won't bother to line up the slots on the screw heads simply because they weren't done that way on the original. A flush-fastened hull with all the screw heads absolutely flush and aligned is a project reserved only for those overly fastidious craftsmen immune to tedium.

The planking will progress from the garboard upward (which is really downward since the boat is upside down) to the sheer. Ken book-matches his planking, something you don't see every day, but it has an important advantage. To bookmatch, each plank is first cut to length and planed to ¾-inch thick. The plank is then resawn on the bandsaw, and each half is run through the planer once more to clean up the bandsaw marks. The resulting two ¼-inch-thick planks are nearly identical in size, shape, and color, and a mirror image of each other in grain pattern. They are applied on opposite sides of the centerline so that when the job is done, the planking on each side matches the other side perfectly. Planking progresses in an even and orderly manner, and when a varnished boat with a bookmatched hull is viewed bow on, the effect can be striking. On the deck the effect is spectacular.

Before attaching the planking, Ken will carefully mark the location of each frame and batten (reinforcing the seams) with a pencil line and then give the plywood skin two sealer coats of epoxy. Each plank will be spiled to the plank next to it and trimmed to a perfect fit, coated with thickened epoxy, and securely fastened to each frame with brass flathead screws. (Like many other things, brass screws aren't what they used to be. New ones are made using a powdered-metal technology that makes them useless in salt water. Bronze screws are always preferred, but if you must use brass screws for authenticity, imbed them in epoxy or try to reuse the old ones.) Any squeezed-out epoxy will be carefully cleaned off before it has a chance to set. When the planking on the hull is complete, the boat will be turned right side up, and the process will continue on the decking.

Ken pointed out that on the Brill the location of the third cockpit forward of the main cockpit was unusual for such a small hull, and many rebuilders would be tempted to deck over it. That would save the time and trouble of dealing with the detail, upholstery, and trim of the third opening, and it would make the finished product look more conventional. Fortunately Ken is determined to maintain the spirit of the original boat, so the finished Brill will include the original forward cockpit.

After the decking is in place, Ken will replace the cockpit coamings, and here he plans to exercise some artistic license. The original cockpits were trimmed with small pieces of mahogany screwed flat to the deck so they would lap over and cover the ragged ends of the original planking that didn't fit well at all. Since the new planking will be spiled to a perfect fit, he'll use a more conventional and attractive coaming. At this early stage, Ken hasn't quite decided just what the finished trim will look like, but a frame of steam-bent mahogany is a possibility.

Ken does all his own upholstery, and there's no reason you can't do the same. The original seats were most likely button-tufted with kapok. Both leather and certain vinyls would be appropriate for the time period, and there's no way of knowing what was on the original. Surprisingly, quality vinyl costs nearly as much as leather, so once again the decision will be based on aesthetics and not on economics.

Once the seats, floorboards, and engine and steering controls are in place, Ken will polish and restore the hardware. Luckily all the original brass trim was still on the boat when Ken bought it. Had there been anything important missing, such as a throttle lever or flagstaff socket, Ken simply would have found something from a similar boat from the period; or, if he couldn't find anything appropriate, he would have resorted to new hardware as similar to the original as possible. While it's important to preserve the spirit of the original boat in a renovation project, the details aren't critical, and many may not even be known. When restoring a boat such as the Sea Sled, however, it's common practice to have missing hardware faithfully reproduced at a machine shop or foundry.

Before the polished and restored hardware is reinstalled and before the upholstery goes in, Ken will give the entire boat a careful sanding with 120-grit aluminum-oxide sandpaper. He'll stain the new mahogany to match other runabouts of the same period, and complete the finish with up to a dozen coats of high-gloss Epifanes varnish. After the fourth or fifth coat, Ken will allow the boat to "rest" for several days before he continues the finishing process. This will allow the new wood to stabilize in relation to the old wood, and any microscopic movement affecting the finish will be over before the final coats go on.

About this time Ken got an urgent call from home. The household water pump wasn't working properly, and in February in New Hampshire this is a potential crisis that demands immediate attention. Besides, my kids had finished exploring the abandoned box cars that surround Ken's shop, and the sun was getting low over the western hills. It was time to round up the gang and head home. Before I left, Ken told me the Brill would take about a year to complete, and I resolved to make periodic trips to Franklin to check on his progress. As I said, it's my kind of project, and I'm always looking for an excuse to take a drive in the country.

RENOVATING CANVAS-COVERED BOATS

On the trip back from Onion River Boatworks, I had time to reflect on my good fortune in having visited Ken when I did. I drove to New Hampshire to see the Sea Sled, and that was certainly worth the trip, but the three other boats had been icing on the cake. It was strictly by luck that my visit had coincided with writing this chapter, and it was an even bigger coincidence that the Brill, the Old Town, and the Lyman represent a perfect cross section of small boats within the realm of the amateur renovator.

Finding Ken in the beginning stages of renovating the Brill was another piece of luck because, although I've always admired beautifully varnished runabouts, I haven't worked on them that much. And even though most of the procedures we've discussed so far apply to boats in general, it would be hypocritical to advise you on how to do something I haven't done myself. By imposing on Ken's hospitality and patience and listening to his plans for the runabout, I was able to learn a great deal, and you and I both benefit from Ken's vast experience and expertise in a specialized area where my own experience is limited.

I can speak with a little more authority on the next topic, canvas-covered boats, which include classic canoes, such as those built by the Old Town Canoe Company and White Canoe Company, both of Old Town, Maine, and the Chestnut Canoe Company of Fredericton, New Brunswick; the larger canoe-type boats with transoms, such as the Grand Lakes Guide Boats; a few larger outboard motorboats made by Thompson in Peshtigo, Wisconsin, and others; and dinghies and skiffs in a great many shapes and sizes.

(Traditionalists will argue that the Grand Lakes Guide Boat is a specific type of canoe, and indeed they're right. But there is a tendency to attach this label to any transomed canoe. Most canoe manufacturers built versions with a transom for a small outboard, and some, like Thompson and Old Town, built boats with canoe-type construction and transoms that were large enough for these craft to be called outboard motorboats. These are not Grand Lakes Guide Boats.)

All the boats listed above were originally built in essentially the same way. Closely spaced ribs—usually white cedar but sometimes ash or oak—were steamed and bent over a mold fitted with steel bands then covered with a layer of thin red-cedar planking. The inwales (on a small boat, the clamp is called an *inwale*) were installed with screws through the ribs. Then the planks were fastened with copper or brass tacks long enough to be driven through the ribs, so that when they hit the steel band on the mold, they were turned back into the wood and clinched. The hull was lifted from the mold, and the last few planks were attached by hand to give the hull some tumblehome. The canvas was applied and fastened around the edges and at the stem and stern with more tacks. Next the outwales (or rubrails), fore-and-aft breasthooks (called decks by canoeists), thwarts, seats, and sometimes a keel were installed. If the boat had a transom, it was supported by quarter knees. Semi-round strips of brass called bang plates were attached to the stem and stern with brass screws to cover the tacks. The inside of the new canoe was varnished and the canvas sealed with filler and painted.

The wales, decks, quarter knees, and thwarts of the Maine and Canadian boats were usually spruce or larch, but occasionally white oak, ash, and even mahogany were used. Sometimes spruce was used on the inside trim, and oak or ash was used on the outer wales and keel where the most wear occurred. All but the double-ended canoes and a few double-ended dinghies had hardwood transoms and a deck in the bow. Some of the larger motorboats had canvas-covered foredecks and longitudinal stringers for stiffness and to carry the seats. Canoes had thwart seats, suspended from the inwales, that were frequently caned, although some are found with rawhide seats woven like a snowshoe lacing. All emphasized sturdy, light-weight construction, and when they are properly renovated, they are a joy to own and use.

I've already related how I found my first canoe in a farmer's barn, but that was in the 1950s, and there aren't as many old canvas canoes lying around now as there used to be. Come to think of it, there aren't as many barns as there used to be either. If you want to do a canvas-covered boat project and you don't already own the boat, you'll have to buy one, and you'll be astounded at what you'll have to pay for it. Any rebuildable shell of an Old Town or a White, for example, will cost more than a brand-new boat made of fiberglass or aluminum.

There's a good reason for this seeming disparity: The old boats are worth more than the new ones because they're better boats. Anyone who has paddled a wood-and-canvas canoe or rowed a guideboat or peapod will tell you the same thing—there's simply no comparison between the old wood-and-canvas boats and the new plastic and aluminum ones. The experience isn't even similar. The delight of wood and canvas is no longer a secret, and many people are willing to pay extra for the old boats.

What To Look For

When you're looking for a rebuildable canvas-covered boat, be especially leery of extensive rot or of any structural damage that has caused the boat to lose its shape. Both are difficult, and often impossible, to correct. It isn't uncommon to find a nice old canoe in good condition except for the peaks of the bow and stern and one gunnel consumed by rot. Old canoes frequently ended up leaning against the backs of garages, upside down, and rotting away where they rested on the ground. If you find a boat with a lot of the rib ends rotted away, or if there is exten-sive rot in the peaks, you should probably keep looking, or at least consult with a professional before committing yourself.

Rot or damage in the outwales, thwarts, and keel will be easy to fix as long as the shape of the hull has not been affected. Replacing the inwales and decks is tricky. And if the boat has a transom that needs to be replaced, proceed with cau-tion. Although the transom isn't difficult to replace, in many cases the boat will have lost its shape. You could easily end up with a lot of very expensive kindling wood.

If you're lucky enough to find a canvas-covered boat made by a brand-name builder like Chestnut, Old Town, or White that's in very good condition with the original varnish and canvas intact, proceed with extra caution and consult an expert. If you have a restorable antique, it could be worth a significant amount of money, and *its value can be substantially reduced by a fiberglass and epoxy renova-tion such as I'm about to describe.* This process should be used only on boats that are "beat" but still serviceable. To use it on a restorable boat would be a travesty, not to mention financially imprudent.

Stripping the Canvas

Once you find your boat and get it secured on horses in a suitable work area, begin by removing the keel, bang plates, and outwales—usually secured by brass screws. This will expose the copper tacks that hold the canvas in place. Pry these out with a tack puller and strip away the old canvas, being careful of any patched areas where the canvas might be bonded to the planking by glue.

Sometimes you'll find an earlier renovator has re-covered a canvas-covered boat with polyester and fiberglass. Several companies sold "anyone-can-do-it" kits for fiberglassing wooden canoes through ads in sporting magazines. Sometimes the victims of these kits can be real bargains because the work was often ineptly done, and the boats look awful. In a few boats I've seen, the stuff was applied over the original wales, decks, and keel; apparently, the person who did the work didn't know how to remove the trim pieces. If you have one of these disasters, with a sound hull, remove the old fiberglass with a heat gun and a stiff putty knife or paint scraper. It's a lot of work, but keep at it. It'll be worth it.

Once you've exposed the planking, flip the boat over and work on the inside. Remove the screws that attach the ribs to the inwales and you can lift out the inside wales, decks, thwarts, and seats as one unit; don't disassemble them unless you must. Now strip the finish from the interior. Sometimes this can be done with a little sandpaper and a lot of work, but usually the old finish is so built up it's a lot quicker to use chemical paint remover. Any way you approach it, getting the inside clean is a lot more work than cleaning up the outside.

Once you've removed all the old finish, wash all the wood with denatured alcohol to neutralize any residual paint remover. Carefully inspect the entire hull and remove any ribs that need to be replaced. Don't worry about small areas of dry rot or small cracks or splits running with the grain around fasteners. And if a rib is broken but otherwise intact, you can leave it as long as the adjacent ribs are sound; the epoxy will add enough strength to carry the broken rib. You'll have to replace any ribs that are rotted through.

Rib and Stem Replacement

To remove a rib, carefully pry up the point of each clinched nail in the rib and drive the nail back through the hull until you can pull it out from the other side. When you've removed all the nails, the rib will slide right out. If the rib is from midships, it might be possible to use the old rib as a pattern to set up a duck board and make a new rib as explained in Chapter Seven. But because the hull tapers toward the ends, new ribs are easier to make and will fit better if you use the hull as a mold.

Build up the new rib from several layers of ⅛-inch cedar laid over a sheet of polyethylene plastic to protect the hull. Let the ends run long by several inches, and make it about ¼ inch wider than you want it to be when complete. Use thickened epoxy between the laminates and hold the rib in place with shores until the epoxy sets. The plastic sheet will allow you to remove the rib so you can trim and finish it to match the others.

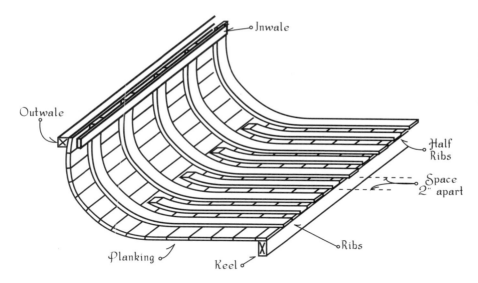

Figure 10-4. Removing and replacing the ribs in a canoe.

Install the new rib and fasten the planking to it with copper nails—just like the original. Drive the nail through the original hole in the planking until the point just comes through the rib, then back the point of the nail with the head of a sledge hammer or a 6-inch piece of railroad track while you finish driving it, so that the point of the nail clinches back into the wood, just like the nails you removed. There's a bit of a trick to this, so practice a few times on a piece of scrap. If you have a helper, two people can do the job more easily than one. Don't put nails back in any planks that need to be replaced. And while you're at it, re-nail any loose planking you plan to save.

If your boat needs a new stem or transom, carefully remove the fasteners from the ends of the planking. Usually these are brass screws, but sometimes nails are used, and sometimes you'll find both. Don't force anything; if the piece doesn't come right out, you've probably missed a fastener somewhere. Forcing it will only damage the ends of the planking. If the old piece was bonded with epoxy or polyester by a previous renovator, use a heat gun to soften the bond after you've removed all the fasteners.

When replacing a stem, use the old piece to set up your duck board, and make the new stem just as you would make a laminated frame. Make it slightly oversize so you can plane it to final shape and a perfect fit. Reinstall the stem using bronze screws and epoxy.

Hull Reassembly

Once the framing is squared away, replace any broken or rotted planks with new ones spiled to fit. Check the thickness of the old planking with a caliper and make sure the new planking is exactly the same thickness; if it isn't, the new plank will telegraph through the fiberglass skin. Once again, don't worry about small cracks and checks, but fill any seams that have opened up between the planks with thin strips of wood and epoxy. The strips will show on the inside of the hull, so don't use putty. Let the strips stand proud until the epoxy sets, then plane them fair with the hull. The secret to getting a perfectly smooth skin on your hull is to have a perfectly smooth hull to begin with.

Sand the entire hull inside and out with 100-grit aluminum-oxide paper on a padded sanding block. Get the entire surface down to bare wood, but don't remove any more wood than you must. If you insist on using your power pad sander, be aware that the sandpaper will cut the thin cedar very rapidly, and there's a real danger of sanding through the planking if you're not careful. Use a hard pad on the outside of the hull so the nail heads don't stand proud of the wood when you're finished, and a soft pad on the inside so the sandpaper can follow the contours of the wood. Clean up the areas between the ribs with a sharp scraper and hand-sanding, making sure to remove every trace of old finish. Since the inside will be varnished, you want it to look perfect, so take your time and get it right. Resist the temptation to scrape the planking between the ribs across the grain: The scraper will tear into the soft planks, and you'll never get the gouges out.

At this point you can strip the assembled wales, decks, and thwarts and other trim pieces with a scraper and sandpaper. Unless the outwales and the keel are in exceptional condition, it's frequently easier to make new ones. Use the old pieces as a pattern. If you can't match the wood used for the old ones, make the new pieces from white oak. Be particularly careful if you need to fit new decks. A poorly fitting deck can drastically alter the symmetry of the hull and throw the entire thing out of balance.

Sometimes accidents are fortuitous. A friend in Dunbarton, New Hampshire, once replaced the decks and recovered his worn-out wood-and-canvas canoe with fiberglass in a rather ham-handed manner. When he was finished, the boat had a noticeable twist to the port side. Since he was a lefty, he found the twist compensated for his paddling, and he no longer needed to use a J-stroke. I owned a plastic Mad River Voyager at the time, and my friend promptly challenged me to a race. Because of the advantage of straight-line paddling, he won by several hundred yards over a two-mile course. If the twisted hull didn't do anything else, it gave me a good excuse for losing the race.

Once you've stripped, repaired, or duplicated all the components, you're ready to reassemble the hull. Apply two coats of epoxy sealer to the entire hull. Do the inside first so drips that run out between the planks can be cleaned off from the outside. Turn the boat bottomside up and fill any cracks that remain with epoxy thickened with WEST System Microlight to peanut-butter consistency. If any cracks are large enough to allow the Microlight to show through from the inside, fill them with slivers of wood epoxied in place. Sand the Microlight and wood slivers flush with the hull, and give the exterior two sealer coats of epoxy. After a light sanding to remove the bumps and bubbles from the epoxy, your hull should be flawless. If it isn't, continue filling and sanding until it is.

Reinstall the assembly of the inwales, decks, and thwarts (and sometimes the seats) using thickened epoxy and lots of clamps. Use a clamp wherever the wale contacts a rib. You don't need screws here, even though they were used in the original construction, but if it makes you feel better or if you don't have enough clamps, go ahead and put some in, using the old screw holes as a guide. If the old holes no longer exist, install the screws in the ribs so they're slightly off-center. This way they won't interfere with screws for the outwales, which will be placed in the center of the ribs.

Covering with Fiberglass

Your hull is now ready for fiberglass, and here you need to make an important decision. I covered my first canoe, an 18-foot Old Town guide model, with two layers of heavy cloth, probably 8- or 10-ounce, and a lot of polyester resin. The result was a rugged hull that laughed at rocks in the rapids and could be driven into a minor gale by a single paddler. It could be ruthlessly dragged over rocks on portages, which was fortunate because the damn thing was too heavy to lift. And it went to windward well because it rode about 1½ inches below its design waterline, so there was hardly any freeboard left to offer wind resistance. Since then I've favored a single layer of light cloth (4- or 6-ounce, max) that will not exceed the weight of the original canvas. But with this light fabric you'll need to stay away from rocks and carry your boat over portages.

The weight of the fabric is based on the type of boat you have and how you plan to use it. Lake boats and outboards that will be carried on a trailer will benefit from a heavier fabric while canoes, car-toppers, and dinghies will be a lot handier with lighter-weight fabrics.

Whatever weight cloth you select, the application will be the same. Many canvas-covered canoes are small enough to be covered with a single piece of 60-inch-wide cloth. If you have a larger boat that will require two pieces of cloth, purchase the cloth wide enough so that the seam will lap the keel line by about 2 inches. With a single piece of cloth, drape the entire thing over the boat so that the excess hangs evenly on all sides. With two pieces of cloth, you must do each side separately; drape one side and hold the cloth in place temporarily with masking tape, tacks, or ice picks.

Mix about a pint of epoxy at a time and use a slow hardener unless it's unusually cool where you're working. Apply the resin with a foam roller, working from midships toward the ends. A helper or two will be appreciated for this operation because you need to get the entire piece of fiberglass wet out and smooth before the resin starts to set. A three-person team with two rolling and one mixing resin is just about ideal. One person, wearing heavy rubber gloves, should stretch and smooth the fabric as the resin is applied. Use enough resin so that there are no bubbles and the fabric is completely wetted out, but don't use so much that it drips or runs off the sides. Spread any excess with the roller or a plastic squeegee as you go. Don't worry about filling the weave of the cloth at this point; in fact, the cloth should show through the resin with an even texture and no shiny spots.

The most difficult area to get looking right is where the glass will be trimmed at the stems. Wet the cloth first, then trim it with a pair of scissors so that it overlaps no more than a half inch or so. You want the seam narrow enough to be covered by the bang plate. Once the cloth is wet and smooth, let the epoxy set until it's tack-free, then trim the excess cloth flush with the top of the inwales. Roll on a second coat of epoxy, and tip it off with a foam brush. On 4- or 6-ounce cloth this coat should leave a glass-smooth surface with none of the weave showing. If it doesn't, or if you're using heavier cloth, wait until the second coat is tack-free and give the glass another coat. Repeat the process until the surface is just the way you want it. Now go away and let the epoxy cure overnight.

When the epoxy has cured, block-sand the entire hull with 80-grit silicon-carbide paper until you've removed all surface imperfections. If you start to sand into the fabric, stop and roll on another coat of epoxy, and let it cure. After the 80-grit sanding, wet-sand the entire hull with 120-grit silicon-carbide, and when you finish that, do it again with 180-grit. Keep going right up through 600-grit—until she's as smooth as a boat-show sales pitch.

Finishing Touches

Now your hull is ready for paint. If you're considering a clear finish, think it over carefully. Strip-planked canoes, skiffs, and dinghies look splendid with a natural finish. But the old cedar-planked boats were built for a canvas covering, and to me, they don't look right if they're finished clear. Two-part polyurethane paint is the best choice for small boats. It costs a lot more than one-part poly, but here again we're not talking about a lot of paint, and the extra toughness and hardness will pay off in the long run.

If you're going to have a keel on your boat (whitewater canoes don't like keels), make a new one out of white oak. Install it with silicon-bronze screws and bed it well with polyurethane sealant. Don't bother to finish the keel—a finish wouldn't last past the first beaching anyway.

Clamp the outwales in place and drive a countersunk brass flat-head screw into the center of every other rib. Brass screws look better than bronze in the gunnels, and they will be protected by epoxy and varnish. Work from midships toward the end. If you've made new wales out of white oak, they'll usually bend into place without steaming. If the bend is really radical, you can help things along by wrapping the ends with rags and pouring boiling water over them until they soften a bit.

There are at least a dozen books in your local library that will tell you how to recane the seats, so I won't repeat that here. Apply a half-dozen coats of good varnish—no polyurethane, please—on the interior and outwales as detailed in Chapter Eleven, and you're done.

Oh, just one other thing. Select a good bottle of vintage champagne, collect your favorite other person—and the kids, if you have any—and drive to a secluded spot on any lake or stream. As your new old wooden boat slides gently into the water for the first time, grasp the champagne firmly by the neck and swing the bottle in a wide arc so that it connects with the bow—gently, now, and on the inside—where it will be wedged safely and snugly and won't be damaged. Toss in a cooler with a few sausages and some cheese from the local deli, some Cokes for the kids, a blanket, and anything else that seems appropriate. Now paddle or row (never motor) out to a little island or scrap of beach where you can sit and sip and enjoy and tell each other that this, indeed, is what it's all about.

RENOVATING LAPSTRAKE BOATS

Small lapstrake boats were produced by several major companies and a number of small builders into the early 1960s when the fiberglass revolution finally made mass-produced wooden boats impractical. Lyman was probably the most prolific of the corporate builders, but Old Town, Thompson, and Penn Yan were also well known for sturdy lapstrake hulls. Less well known were boats like the Zobel Sea Fox made in Sea Bright, New Jersey, and the Jersey Sea Skiff made by the Red Bank Marine Works of Red Bank, New Jersey. Of course there were many others.

In a previous chapter, I pointed out that lapstrake hulls are lighter and stronger for their weight than other types of boats because in lapstrake construction every fiber of the wood is put to work. Frames can be made extra light because the strakes are attached to each other and don't depend on the frames for all their strength. I said this already in Chapter Six, of course, but it bears repeating because this very efficiency of design and construction is the downfall of many lapstrake boats. The parts work so well together that the failure of any major component can be cataclysmic and lead rapidly to the destruction of the boat. Consequently, while a carvel-planked boat that has spent a few seasons sitting beside someone's driveway may make a good project boat, a lapstrake boat subjected to the same conditions will often be beyond repair.

Not too long ago I got a call from a very pleasant lady who said she needed some repair work done on an 18-foot Thompson outboard she had stored on a trailer beside her garage. Her husband had been ill, and they hadn't been able to use the boat for the past few seasons. I agreed to stop by and take a look at it the next day. When I arrived, the owner had already removed the cover. From 20 feet away the boat looked like a typical classy Thompson with the high transom and extra freeboard that made them a seaworthy and popular utility boat for the choppy waters around Marblehead. From 10 feet away I could see that the varnish was gone and rot was well established in the mahogany around the windshield. From 2 feet away it was obvious that the boat was a goner. The mahogany trim around the windshield was, as I suspected, beyond repair, but that was the least of the problems. The drains in the transom had become plugged with leaves, allowing rainwater to puddle in the bilge. After two seasons, a large number of the plywood bottom planks and about half the frames from midships to the stern were rotted through, and the bottom 20 percent of the transom was soft and oozed water when you pressed on it. Even though from across the yard the Thompson seemed to be in fine shape, I had to tell the lady that the cost of fixing the hull would far exceed the value of the boat when it was finished.

Selection

While the case of the old Thompson isn't typical, it's unfortunately very common. A skilled amateur boatbuilder could save the boat with a lot of time and hard work, but when you look at what is available on the used-boat market for just a few thousand dollars, it doesn't make sense to bother with it. While worn-out old mahogany runabouts are being accumulated like baseball cards by collectors and eager speculators willing to pay prices that would have bought a fleet of similar boats a few years ago, fine old lapstrake boats languish on the market. Here is just a sample of ads from a local classified advertiser: WOODEN GRADY WHITE: 16' wht w/35hp motor, $600 BO; 23' LYMAN: w/50hp Mercury Great fish boat. Turn key & go, $500; 18' THOMPSON: wooden lapstrake w/controls 2-axle trailer, $950; 19' PENN YAN CABIN CRUISER: lapstrake wood construction sleeps 2 etc. Inc. trailer, $800; 19' LAPSTRAKE: fishing boat w/85hp Evinrude & Cox trailer, $800; ATTN WOODEN BOAT LOVERS: 16' Lyman lapstrake. 1950s, Good Cond. Full Canvas 40 hp Merc runs exc, w/ trailer, $2,600.

There you have a half-dozen ads from one publication for wooden lapstrake boats, all within a radius of about 15 miles, and all but the last are under $1,000, and that last one is probably a beauty. At these prices, you don't need to spend a lot of time fixing a boat that's not already in pretty good shape to begin with.

If you would like a small wooden lapstrake boat, look for one with a sound hull, tight fasteners with no corrosion or electrolysis, no rot, and all original trim and hardware. Check the seams carefully from the outside. If the paint is cracked, the hull is working, and it will probably start leaking soon. Avoid boats with obviously amateurish repairs, and look for a boat that is essentially original in structure with no owner-inspired additions, such as a new pilothouse or changes in decking. Dragging a small boat around on a trailer can cause a great deal of damage, so check the condition of planking and frames where they bear on the trailer rollers. If the boat needs new canvas and upholstery and a paint job, so much the better. Since you're going to renew these three anyway, the worse condition they're in, the lower the price and the better for you. Peeling and flaking paint will mask the fact that the hull is in top condition and will chase away a lot of prospective buyers who can't see past the surface. You'll end up with a beautifully serviceable boat at a bargain price and leave behind a delighted seller who just wanted to get the thing out of his yard.

**Figure 10-5.
A Lyman Islander.**

Face-lifting

Once you select your boat and get it home, renovating it should be a matter of cleaning it up and putting on a really first-class finish. Take the time and trouble to do an epoxy-based finish topped with two-part polyurethane paint, and you'll be the owner of a true classic requiring no more maintenance than the most modern of plastic boats and all for less than a tenth of the cost. Plus I'll go on record as predicting that the same crowd that has driven the price of the classic mahogany runabouts into the stratosphere is about to discover these small lapstrake boats; the price of a good one is bound to rise precipitously in the near future.

Start your renovation by removing the motor, the control cables, and all the hardware. Carefully note the location of each component as you remove it so you can reinstall each one properly. The more fixtures and trim you remove from the hull, the easier the refinishing job will be.

A natural finish looks spectacular on many of the smaller, open lapstrake hulls, but if you want that, you must remove every trace of the old paint and varnish, which is a lot of work. The best approach is to work in a small area of several square feet and get it completely stripped with chemical paint remover and scrapers before moving on to the next small area. This way you won't get discouraged by trying to do the whole thing at once, and you'll be able to see what the end result will look like. This little preview will either encourage you to continue or lead you to decide that the condition of the wood doesn't warrant a clear finish. Either way, progressing a patch at a time will make the job easier to manage.

Bleaching Wood

If you're putting a clear finish on the interior, you may find that the wood is unacceptably dark once the paint has been removed. If so, bleaching the wood is a fairly straightforward process. Household bleach is the easiest to use. Dilute plain old Clorox about half and half with water; slop it on and hose it off; repeat the process until the wood is the desired color. Oxalic acid is another option you can find in many professional paint-supply houses. It comes in a crystalline form that you dissolve in water—about two ounces to a gallon—and apply just like Clorox. Both bleaches tend to turn the wood a whitish color some people find objectionable.

A third option that avoids this whiteness problem is to apply one of the two-part teak cleaners the unfinished teak masochists are so fond of using every two or three months. The only products I've used to bleach planking are made by Amazon, so I can't comment on any of the others, but they all work about the same. The first step is to apply a cleaner that must be scrubbed into the wood with a bronze-wool pad. This is hosed off and the second step, called teak prep, is applied, leaving the bleached wood with a pleasant yellow color. The third step is an oil I never use because the interior of the boat will be varnished. Always try a test patch before you commit yourself—some of the two-part cleaners are caustic and can damage the soft fibers of woods such as cedar and spruce.

If the color of your wood is beyond repair there's still hope. Behlen makes a *color dissolvent* that virtually removes all color from many woods. Oak, ash, mahogany, and white cedar will be rendered virtually pure white, while red cedar and a few other naturally dark woods will retain some color. This is the strongest bleach available and must be used with extreme caution. It is reactive with metals, so there's some concern about the effect it will have on fasteners. Even more than with other bleaches, it's imperative that you try this stuff on a test patch first.

Behlen's color dissolvent is applied with a brush from a glass or plastic container and allowed to work until the desired degree of bleaching is reached; then the neutralizer is washed on to stop the process. After the wood dries, water-soluble aniline dyes are applied that penetrate into the fibers to give the bleached wood a rich color that closely matches the natural color. Both the color dissolvent and the aniline dyes are available from Garrett Wade (see Appendix B).

Sealing the Interior

If you're going to paint the interior with epoxy, you must remove the old finish regardless of whether the final finish will be paint or varnish. Putting epoxy over old paint doesn't work because the paint prevents the epoxy from saturating the wood and the ultimate finish-to-wood bond will be no better than the original paint bond. For a natural finish, every trace of the old paint must be removed, but if you plan to paint the interior, you don't have to be so fussy about bits of paint that remain here and there. Of course, if the interior paint is in really good condition, you might save yourself a lot of trouble and forget the epoxy; a light sanding and a fresh coat of paint may be all that's required.

Figure 10-6. Cleaning lapstrake joints with a hacksaw blade.

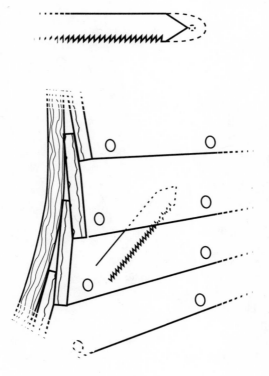

Get some friends to help you turn the boat over, then strip the paint and varnish from the outside just the way you did the inside. If the rivets, screws, nails, or whatever attaches the planks to each other at the laps are tight and the seams show no signs of looseness or leaking, you can proceed with the epoxy sealer. If there's any sign of looseness between the laps, your best bet is to refasten the hull or bond the planks with epoxy.

Epoxy-bonding Planks

Refastening is covered in Chapter Seven, but if you want to epoxy-bond your planks, the process involves cleaning the lap joint between planks of all the old dried paint, sealant, and caulking, and filling the joint with epoxy. The result is an exceptionally stiff and strong hull.

It's usually not necessary to epoxy-bond any but the bottom planks. If the entire hull is loose enough to warrant this drastic treatment, you may be better off looking for another boat. While it's OK to bond large sections of a hull, such as the bottom, never use this treatment on individual planks or patches in a random manner. Small areas should be repaired using conventional repair techniques discussed in Chapter Seven.

Start by grinding a sharp point on the end of an 8- or 10-point hacksaw blade. Heavily wrap the other end with tape so it won't tear up your hand. Force this tool through the lap between the planks with a sawing motion so that the teeth of the hacksaw blade rasp away the mating surfaces of the planks. Don't let the point of the saw blade penetrate the joint any more than it has to; you don't want the blade to damage the inside of the planking. Saw right up to the fastener, but don't let the blade cut into it. Reverse the blade in the slot you've made and saw in the other direction to the other fastener. This is tedious work, but it goes more quickly than you might think.

To bond the planks, first paint a saturation coat on the planking, inside and out, making sure the epoxy runs through the slot you made with the saw blade and coats the mating surfaces. Before the first saturation coat sets, force epoxy thickened to the consistency of peanut butter into the slot so that it oozes out the other side. The best tool for this is a stiff-bladed putty knife. Clean the excess epoxy off the inside and outside laps with a sharpened stick or a tongue depressor, leaving a fillet over the joint. Below the waterline on the outside you can leave a fairly heavy fillet, but above the waterline and on the inside a smaller fillet will look better.

The gains at the stem and stern where the strakes make the transition to flat planking can present problems. If the gains are matching progressive bevels, the saw blade will usually follow the contours of the wood with no trouble. But if the gains are matching rabbets, you'll need to grind a hook into the end of your saw blade and rake out the old paint and compound. In this case you won't be able to clean the entire seam, but if you epoxy the inside and outside seams, the center won't matter.

Once you're satisfied all the seams are tight, give the entire hull another coat of epoxy sealer and finish as described in Chapter Eleven. Reinstall the hardware, hang the outboard back on the transom, and you're off.

But first, stand back and take a look at what you've got for your efforts. In the same issue of the classified advertiser where I found the six wooden boats listed

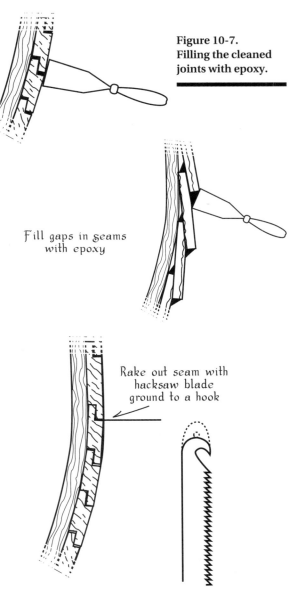

Figure 10-7.
Filling the cleaned joints with epoxy.

Fill gaps in seams with epoxy

Rake out seam with hacksaw blade ground to a hook

Figure 10-8.
Filling the joints in the gains.

above, these four ads also appeared: 16' STARCRAFT: Super Fisherman Model, 28hp Evinrude w/trailer. Must be seen, $5,500; 15' SEA NYMPH: Bass Boat, 28hp Johnson, galvanized trailer, $5,595; 1987 AQUASPORT: center console, 90hp Yamaha, water skis used once, $8,000; 1990 17' WELLCRAFT: Low hours w/extras very clean, $10,500.

These are all fine examples of modern fiberglass or aluminum outboards, of course, but the boats in the two sets of ads are practically identical except in age, style, and hull material; yet the asking prices of the plastic boats are almost uniformly 10 times greater than those of the wooden ones. Furthermore, you and I both know that if you were to buy one of these plastic boats, it would depreciate substantially over the next few years; the value of your wooden lapstrake can go nowhere but up.

But don't just gloat over the money you saved. Think of the aesthetics. Here you have a boat that sets you apart as a person of refinement, taste, culture, and class—a connoisseur of boats of distinction and quality. I don't know about you, but I have a hard time telling any of those noisy little plastic boats from any other noisy little plastic boat. Not only that, they all seem to have noisy little plastic owners, and I can't tell them apart either.

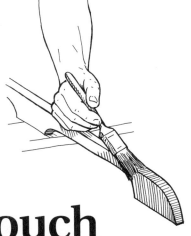

CHAPTER ELEVEN

The Finishing Touch

One of the important factors leading up to *attemptus futilitus*, that dread tendency prevalent among those who would fix and build wooden boats to drastically underestimate the time and resources required for a project, is the lack of appreciation and understanding of the finishing steps. Were you to contemplate building a new hatch cover, for example, you would carefully consider the kinds of woods you would need, where you would get the stock, how it would be milled, how the rabbets and dadoes would be cut, how you planned to glue and clamp the joints, what kind of fasteners you would use and how many, and even how you would bung the holes. Then you'd sand her down, add a couple of quick coats of varnish, mount the hardware, and you'd be done, right? *Wrong!* There's no such thing as a couple of quick coats of varnish—unless you want your carefully constructed hatch cover to look as though it were built by a rank amateur.

When planning any boat job, no matter how small or how large, you should estimate between 25 and 50 percent of the total effort, expense, and time for finish work. I know this sounds like an exaggeration, and it's very hard to explain to anyone who hasn't already screwed up a lot of nice work by taking shortcuts, but except for structural integrity, the finish is the most important part of the entire job. In fact, to an outside observer it *is* the entire job because the finish is the only thing they'll see.

Nonsense, you say. The finish is only the superficial surface, the function of which is to keep out the weather. As long as something is built right, it doesn't matter what you put on it—house paint is fine.

You make a good point, I answer charitably. You'll know it's built right, and you might even convince me it's built right. But everyone else who sees a slapdash finish is going to think it was slapdash work, that it was done on a slapdash boat, and that it was done by a slapdash person. They will form their impressions based on what they see, not on what you did or how you did it.

Who cares? you say; as long as you know the work was done right, it doesn't matter what others think about it. That's fine, I say; what really matters is what you think of the work you do. But if it doesn't look good when you're finished, you won't like it either. You won't be proud of work that looks awful, no matter how much effort you put into the actual structure. If it looks terrible, you'll feel terrible about it; you won't want anyone to see it; you'll feel self-conscious at the fuel dock; your friends will laugh at you and call you names behind your back; your spouse will lock you out of your house; your kids will start to deny you're their parent; and your dog will pee on your foot—all this because you were too lazy to put a proper finish on your work.

Howard Chapelle, in *The American Fishing Schooners*, points out there was no practical reason to make a fishing schooner look good. These boats were built to work the fishing grounds and to make a profit for their owners—nothing else. Although sturdy, they weren't necessarily expected to last a long time. In fact, the average life span of a working schooner was well under 10 years. In spite of this, the builders of these boats, their owners, and their captains took great pride in the grace and beauty of the boats. The paint job was as important then as it is now.

The importance the appearance of a boat has for how we feel about ourselves was driven home this past cruising season as we took our second vacation Down East in the *Duchess*. On the first trip we had concentrated all our effort into making the old girl seaworthy and had no time for cosmetics. She looked terrible, with primer splattered everywhere and all her brightwork and hardware covered with white paint. We had a great time as we traveled from place to place, but we couldn't help but feel a bit sensitive about the appearance of our boat. No one asked any questions about the *Duchess*, and even our friends would look at their feet and talk about the weather when we mentioned her. I'm still not sure if the contemptuous sneers of the dock boys were real or manifestations of my own self-conscious imagination.

Our second cruise on the *Duchess* was a study in contrast. By then we had replaced some planking, painted the hull and deck, cleaned the deck hardware, and cleaned or replaced and freshly varnished the mahogany trim. We still had a lot of work to do, but from a distance she looked pretty good. Everywhere we went we got compliments. "Nice lines," people would shout in passing, or "Who's the designer?" they would ask. In Rockland Harbor some guy rowed over in his dinghy just to take our picture. The effect a positive reception has on the self-esteem of the skipper and crew is enormous. The *Duchess* was the same boat we had sailed into the same harbors the year before. She had the same lines and the same designer—the only real change was a little varnish and a coat of paint.

OK, back to that hatch cover we were discussing earlier . . . let's say you've built the thing, what next? Well, since it's an expert piece of work, you want it to look that way, so let's do a first-class varnish job on it. The first step will be the preparation of the surface.

SURFACE PREPARATION

One objection I have about many of the do-it-yourself boat books is that even the excellent ones make statements like ". . . next sand the surface with 400-grit sandpaper and then . . . ," and that's all they say about surface preparation. This is a shame because no finish, varnish, or paint is ever going to be any better than the surface it's applied to. Surface preparation is the most important step in the finishing process, so let's take our time and discuss it in detail.

SANDPAPER

The first step to a professional-looking finish is selecting the sandpaper. Sandpaper is graded by the type and amount of stuff glued to the backing paper or cloth. Thus, 400-grit garnet paper has the equivalent of 400 grains of garnet silicate on every square inch of the cutting surface. This number is printed on the back of the paper followed by an A-through-D letter code that indicates the weight of the paper. A is the lightest and D the heaviest paper that's practical for our use, although industrial sandpaper is available in weights up to J.

Sandpaper is divided into categories by type—cabinet, production, premium, and industrial grades—roughly according to function. Open and closed coatings are another indication of the density of the grit. No-load (called No-Fil by Norton) paper is open-coat paper containing a white zinc stearate surface treatment that helps keep the paper from clogging in power sanders. So the complete designation for a single sheet of sandpaper might be "100D Silicon Carbide Open Coat No-Load Production Paper." And you thought sandpaper was just sandpaper.

One interesting development of the past few years is the widespread marketing of peel-and-stick papers, notably Stikit papers made by Porter Cable. Using these papers greatly facilitates power sanding when the sander is fitted with a special pad. Changing paper when it gets dull or when you need to change grades is faster and easier with this stuff, and it's great for making sanding blocks for hand sanding. Because the paper is glued to the pad or block, it's more rigid and actually cuts much more efficiently. The big drawback is its cost, which can be about double that of regular paper—and the regular stuff isn't cheap. The answer is to buy special Stikit pads for your sanders (from Woodworker's Supply or any good tool supply), then get some spray adhesive from the art-supply store. Using spray adhesive to mount regular sandpaper to your sander and sanding blocks can be done quickly, and it will minimize your inventory of paper while giving you a wider selection. It will also save you a ton of money.

Speaking of saving money, always buy sandpaper in sleeves from a supply house, never by the sheet from the local hardware store, and never, never, never from a marine hardware store. A sleeve contains either 50 or 100 sheets of 9 X 11-inch paper, depending on the grade. Buying it this way will get you the best price, and you'll always have plenty on hand. And having a lot around is important because effective sanding technique demands that you throw away paper as soon as it starts to get dull and stops cutting. If you spend a buck or more for a sheet of sandpaper down at the marina, you'll be understandably reluctant to buy it in sufficient quantities and even more reluctant to pitch it until every last piece of grit is gone. The first secret of a professional-looking finish on your old wooden boat is to buy a lot of high-quality sandpaper and use it freely.

Flint Paper

Flint paper is as close as you'll ever get to actual *sand*paper because the stuff glued to the paper is essentially sand; it is also essentially useless. This is the cheap stuff you find in the local hardware store—light gray, white, or beige in color. The grit falls right off the paper as soon as it comes in contact with wood, sand gets all over your work, and it just makes a mess. Don't buy flint paper, and if you already have some, throw it away so you won't be tempted to use it.

Garnet Paper

Easily identified by its red color, garnet paper is wonderful stuff, and a lot of really finicky woodworkers refuse to use anything else on their fine joinery. It cuts like a dream when it's fresh, but it dulls very quickly, it won't stand up to power sanding, and it's expensive. For me, these three drawbacks far outweigh its advantages, so I don't use garnet paper anymore. You should give it a try, though—you might end up swearing by it.

Aluminum-Oxide Paper

Aluminum-oxide paper is a good, dependable all-around paper for power and hand sanding in the rough grades. Tan or beige in color, it's tough, inexpensive, reasonably durable, and cuts well. In grits from 40D to 150C it will handle about 80 percent of all your sanding needs.

Silicon-Carbide Paper

Where aluminum-oxide paper in the coarser grits leaves off, silicon-carbide paper takes over. You should get the white no-load paper in grits from 180A to 400A. For my money, silicon-carbide paper cuts just as well as garnet paper, and although it costs a little more, it lasts much longer. In effect, it's more economical.

Silicon-carbide paper also comes in a black, resin-bonded, closed-coat waterproof type that is essential for wet sanding. If you want a really fine finish you can see your face in, you'll need a good assortment in grits from 100C to 1200A; I find the grits above 400 to be the most useful.

Emery Cloth

As the name implies, this isn't sandpaper at all but emery powder bonded to a heavy cloth backing. It's handy stuff for polishing metal and cleaning up old rusty tools you buy in junk stores. Some even swear by it in the very fine grades for sharpening chisels and plane irons. Because it's black, it is easy to confuse emery cloth with silicon carbide, and you might try to use it for wet sanding. You'll only make this mistake once, however—the mess it creates is incredible.

SANDING NEW WORK

OK, now that you've figured out what you're going to need for your surface preparation, let's take that hypothetical hatch cover you built and secure it on your workbench or on saw horses with clamps, making sure all surfaces are protected from the clamp jaws with softwood blocks, strips of carpeting, or other suitable padding. With a heavy scraper, strip away any squeezed-out epoxy and any other surface imperfections. The best scraper for removing epoxy is a hook-type paint scraper. I like the ones that Sears sells, but most good paint stores have them. Don't try to do too much with the scraper; they tend to gouge new wood easily, and they can do a lot of damage. If any wood remains that needs to be removed around corners or between joints, clean it up with a sharp hand plane.

Begin sanding the hatch with 60D aluminum-oxide paper in your half-sheet pad sander. Take a soft-lead pencil (No. 2 is fine) and make light scribble marks all over the surface of the hatch. Be careful that the pencil point does not dent the wood. Don a fresh dust mask and hearing protectors, and simply sand away all the pencil marks. Repeat this process at least two more times with the 60-grit paper. This coarse grit cuts quickly, so after the third pencil mark has been sanded away, all the tool marks and other major surface defects should have been sanded out. If any remain, continue with the pencil marks and the 60-grit paper until they're gone.

At this point the surface will have no visible defects, but it will be uniformly rough and may have "whiskers" from the coarse paper. Switch to 80- or 100-grit paper, and do the pencil-mark and sanding ritual three more times until the whiskers are gone—then three more times with 120 or 140 grit. The pencil marks help you keep track of where you've sanded and ensure an even job. By now the surface of the hatch cover should be smooth and free from any visible surface defects, even small scratches.

Were this a piece of hardwood (especially a dense wood like cherry or maple) destined for interior use and you planned to use an oil finish, you would continue with the pencil-mark/sanding routine right up through 400 or even 600 grit, until the surface of the wood became like a piece of glass. However, for varnish we need a little tooth—a very slight texture left on the surface that will help the finish penetrate and adhere to the wood.

SANDING OLD WORK

Let's back up for a moment and suppose the hatch cover you've been working on was a part of your boat when you bought her, and you've decided to refinish it. Your approach will vary, depending on what type of finish you decide to use, but the first step in all cases is to secure the hatch to horses and remove all the hardware.

In the unlikely event that the old varnish is in good shape with no cracks, checks, blisters, or peeling and is just chalky or faded, with a few superficial scratches on the surface, all you need do is sand away the surface film with 180- or 200-grit paper and proceed with the varnishing. This sanding must be done by hand with a sanding block—never with a power sander. Be extra careful around corners and edges; you don't want to sand through the old finish if you can help it.

If the old finish is deeply scratched, blistered, or peeling, every trace of the old varnish (or paint) must be removed. This is best done with heavy two-handed pull-type scrapers or with chemical strippers like Strip-EZE or 5F5, but 40-grit open-coat sandpaper in your pad sander will also work very well on varnish. Never use your disc sander or belt sander for removing varnish or paint from a piece of trim or a fixture; you will surely ruin your work. And wear a good dust mask; old varnish and paint can be loaded with lead.

Once you've removed the old finish, inspect the surface of the wood and decide whether to proceed with varnish or paint. Frequently an old hatch cover in perfectly good condition structurally has been badly stained by rust and other oxides that have deeply penetrated the wood; hardware has been relocated during a rerigging, leaving unsightly screw holes; or Dutchman repairs have been made with ugly, contrasting wood. You might call this distress patina and character, and on certain boats you might be right. On other boats, that hatch cover is going to look like an old piece of driftwood no matter how much work you put in it or how much varnish you put on it. We'll talk more about when to paint over brightwork, but right now you must make the decision based on your preferences. Any thought that you must use varnish because that particular piece of wood has always been varnished is pure emotionalism and utter bilge water—if you think it will look better painted, then paint it.

VARNISH

There is an awful lot you don't need to know about varnish. In fact volumes have been written that are chock-full of stuff you don't need to know about the subject. Doctoral dissertations have been given on the socioeconomic implications of the polymerization process (there are none), and studies on the deleterious effects of ultraviolet radiation on the molecular linking of petrochemical resins have been published that are guaranteed to cure the most chronic insomniac.

What you do need to know about varnish, and its first cousin polyurethane, is what it is, when to use it, and how to use it. With that in mind, we'll skip the tediously tiresome technical terminology and plunge headlong into the carefully researched and always welcome nitty-gritty.

What It Is

Traditional varnish has been around since the Middle Ages, and in a form roughly equivalent to what we use today. It's essentially a resin dissolved in a solvent and suspended in oil, with some heavy-metal oxides added as dryers. In Charlemagne's day, pine pitch was the resin, turpentine was used as the solvent, and linseed was the most-often-used oil. Today we're more likely to use a petro-chemical resin, such as phenolic, dissolved in a combination of solvents that is essentially paint thinner. Tung or China Wood oil with numerous additives is the most popular oil. For hundreds of years, the dryer of choice was white lead oxide. We now know lead is highly toxic and have outlawed most domestic use. Other metallic compounds, such as cobalt, have replaced lead.

There are hundreds of formulations of varnish, using different resins, solvents, and oils. Varnishes vary in hardness, in drying time, and in price. The term "solids content" refers to the percentage of stuff that stays on the wood after the solvents evaporate and the oil cures and is also reflected in the amount you pay for the varnish. While you might think you can save money by buying a cheap brand of varnish, what you usually get is a reduced solids content and a lot more solvent.

Polyurethane differs from varnish primarily in the molecular characteristics of the film formed when the solvent flashes off and the oil dries. Linear polymerization is the term used (and that's as technical as I want to get) for the formation of long chains of molecules that raft up, fore-and-aft and beam-to, to form an extremely tough surface. One-part polyurethanes harden, or cure, by the evaporation of a solvent in the manner of ordinary varnish. Two-part polyurethanes harden by catalysis—a chemical reaction caused by mixing chemical compounds.

Marine-grade varnishes and polyurethanes differ from the ordinary paint-store stuff in that they need additional ingredients to deal with the considerable adverse effects of ultraviolet radiation from the sun, increased oxidation caused by freely circulating air, and contaminants such as crystalline salt, dirt, and atmospheric pollutants. Ultraviolet absorbers (UVAs) act to reflect, absorb, or dissipate ultraviolet radiation, and anti-oxidation agents purge residual oxygen from the varnish during the curing process. The effectiveness of these additives is demonstrated with a simple experiment. Leave a piece of wood painted with several coats of regular varnish or polyurethane out in the elements for a while. In a matter of months every trace of the varnish will have disappeared, and you'll be left with bare wood. Properly applied and maintained, marine varnishes will last for years and years in the harshest environment.

When To Use It

There's no question that varnish makes a beautiful and functional finish for woodwork on a boat. There is also no question that varnish does not protect wood quite as well as paint, or that it's more work to apply and to maintain than paint. Varnish is necessarily transparent and admits light. Light is, of course, energy, which converts to heat when it's absorbed by dark-colored wood. The darker the color, the more heat is generated, and heat eventually works to destroy the finish. This light-to-heat conversion is the reason your black Sun Shower works so well in the summer and why people foolish enough to paint their cabintops with dark colors can't go below decks until after dark.

Many old wooden boats with an abundance of brightwork that are to be used as boats and not show pieces can be immeasurably improved by liberal applications of white paint. This is heresy, of course, but it's true. On many boats, expanses of varnished wood aren't really that attractive to begin with. And a neat paint job will outshine shabby varnish any day of the week. Varnish is more difficult to maintain than paint, not because modern varnishes are not as strong as paint, but because varnishes show scratches and scrapes and normal wear more readily than paint. The worst effect of varnish, however, is the way boats with a lot of it make paranoid neurotics out of their owners.

The next time you notice a boat with a lot of fancy brightwork, tied to a nearby dock, take a few moments and perform this harmless little exercise in the study of human nature. First make sure the owner is in sight of his boat (they almost always are); the farther away he is the better, but he must be able to see you and the boat. Next walk slowly toward the boat, affecting an air of casual interest. At this point the owner will stop what he's doing and affix you with an intense stare of suspicious hostility. Pause amidships and casually look up and down the deck, admiring the woodwork. About 8 chances in 10 the owner will bound down the dock to fling his body between you and his prized varnish—his arms and legs spread wide like a man shielding his family from the onslaught of a pack of rabid dogs. Next walk slowly toward the bow while maintaining your air of interest and note the sideways, crab-like shuffle of the owner as he attempts to stay between you and his boat.

If you were a sadistic sort of person, you could, at this point, say something like, "Say, a couple'a coats'a paint, and this here'd be a real pretty boat." But since we have no desire to see the fellow reduced to the consistency of a stranded jellyfish, and since the risk of heart failure, high blood pressure, and an unprovoked attack by a berserk boatowner are all quite high, you should break off the experiment with a pleasant complement and your sincere assurance that you wouldn't even think of touching anything. We've proven our point, to wit: People who have a lot of varnish on their boats don't have a lot of fun on their boats.

No, I don't advocate painting over all the varnish on all boats. The varnished mahogany deckhouse of a fine old Bunker & Ellis cruiser is as much a part of the design as the sheerline; painted spars on a Concordia Yawl just don't look right; and a Chris-Craft from the 1950s doesn't look like a Chris-Craft without a varnished transom. But most old wooden boats will be a lot more fun, a lot easier on their owners, and a lot better-looking if brightwork is minimized and used as an accent to white woodwork, not as a way of life.

So go ahead and varnish away on your coaming caps, deck rails, hatch covers, grab bars, and Dorade boxes. But paint the transom and the deckhouse and maybe even the deck and spars. With careful planning and proper technique, you'll have a nice-looking boat, and you won't have to stand guard duty every time you're tied to a public dock.

THE EPOXY UNDERCOAT

The use of epoxy as an undercoat, primer, or filler prior to varnishing or painting has become the standard practice I use in all finish work except for recoating existing finishes. It works because of two basic facts: One, epoxy sticks to wood better than either paint or varnish does; and two, varnish and paint stick to epoxy better than they stick to wood. Epoxy is also reasonably clear, so it can be used under varnish to fill small defects that will match the finish and won't be obvious. And it has build characteristics that are much better than those of paint or varnish.

Most people who object to the use of epoxy under paint or varnish voice the same argument that was discussed in Chapter Seven: It won't let the wood breathe. And the answer is the same: There's no requirement for the wood to breathe. All you need to do is ensure that moisture can't enter the wood unevenly and thereby cause differential expansion of the wood fibers; or you can strengthen the wood to the extent that it can resist that expansion. The first is accomplished by coating all surfaces of the wood with epoxy, not just the surface to be painted or varnished. The second is accomplished by reinforcing the resin, usually with fiberglass.

A more valid objection to the use of epoxy under varnish, but one you don't hear very often, is that epoxy under varnish can change the color of the finish. This color shift is hardly noticeable on dark woods like teak and mahogany, but it can be a problem on lighter woods like oak and Sitka spruce. Some epoxies have a reddish cast, and others have a noticeable greenish tint. Also, when epoxy is applied in very humid conditions, it can absorb enough moisture to cloud the surface noticeably in a process called "blooming" by the experts. WEST System has a catalyst (#207) for epoxy used under varnish that corrects most of these color shifts and moisture problems, but if you suspect you might have difficulties, it's always best to try a test patch first.

When one piece of woodwork requires both paint and varnish, like the traditional white tiptop on a varnished catboat mast or the varnished trim around a painted hatchway, always do the varnish work first. Then any varnish that slops over onto areas to be painted will be hidden by the paint. If you do it the other way around, cleaning the paint off the wood that will be varnished can be quite tedious.

Now that you have your new hatch cover nicely sanded, support it on 10d finish nails driven into the horses, and you're ready to apply the first coat of sealer. Mix the epoxy, using a slow catalyst any time the temperature is above 70 degrees. For clear finishes use WEST System #105 resin with #207 hardener to avoid color and moisture problems. Many boatbuilders will thin the mixture for the first coat of epoxy by about 10 percent with lacquer thinner or epoxy thinner (acetone flashes off too fast) to get better penetration of the epoxy into the wood, even though some manufacturers (notably WEST) don't recommend this practice. Jim Derck at Gougeon Brothers says they don't recommend thinning because even though it does allow greater penetration of the epoxy into the wood, the thinner may have a deleterious effect on the resin that weakens it enough to more than offset any advantage gained. I've done it both ways without trouble, but in situations where a good bond is critical, it would be foolish to go against the manufacturer's instructions.

Before applying the epoxy, thoroughly wipe down the wood with acetone and clean paper towels to remove any trace of surface contaminants, resins, and oils. Don't use rags because even freshly laundered ones can contain impurities, particularly silicone, that can cause difficulties with your finish. This solvent wash is particularly important on oily woods like teak, but resinous woods like spruce also need a careful cleaning. To be on the safe side, clean everything thoroughly just before you apply the epoxy.

Paint the epoxy on the hatch cover with a disposable bristle brush (called a chip brush) or a foam roller. The brush works better with the viscous epoxy if you make the brush much stiffer by cutting about half the bristles away. You can keep these brushes for a day or two in a coffee can of solvent, but don't bother to clean them; at about 50¢ apiece, it's just not worth the trouble. (Chip brushes are available at quantity prices from Jamestown Distributors, listed in Appendix B.)

Paint epoxy onto the bottom of the hatch cover first, then turn it over so it's supported on the nails and do the top. This way you won't have to wait for one side to cure before you can do the other side, and the small indentations in the underside can easily be sanded out. If you notice that the epoxy disappears in some areas of the wood you've coated, just apply more as it is needed. This drying is caused by the epoxy seeping into the wood, which is just what you want to happen.

Allow the first coat to cure overnight. The next day you'll notice the surface of your hatch cover is covered with tiny bubbles of hardened epoxy. The epoxy may also have raised the grain of the wood so that it's as rough as coarse sandpaper. It looks terrible, but don't despair. The bubbles are caused by air from inside the wood that is displaced as the epoxy penetrates the surface, so the more the better. Porous woods like red oak and mahogany will bubble much more than denser woods like spruce. Some hardwoods, like cherry or birch, will bubble hardly at all.

You may also notice a waxy film on the surface of the epoxy. This is amine blush, a greasy by-product of the catalytic curing process that's easily removed with clean water and a green Scotchbrite scouring pad. A vigorous scrubbing with the pad will also remove most of the bubbles. Continue the sanding with 120-grit no-load paper on a felt-lined sanding block. Try not to break through the surface film of epoxy, but this is admittedly difficult at this stage, and a break-through here and there is no big deal. The important thing is to remove all the whiskers and bubbles and to get a smooth surface, even if it means sanding away all the surface epoxy. If your sandpaper clogs up quickly, you've either not de-waxed properly, the epoxy hasn't cured properly, or you need to switch to a coarser-grit paper.

After the first coat of epoxy has been sanded smooth, the hatch cover may still look awful—sort of splotchy and uneven. Don't worry; apply a second coat just as you did the first, only this time you can switch to a faster catalyst if you like. If you thinned the first coat, don't thin this one, and be a little more careful about drips and sags because sanding them out is going to be a lot tougher. You shouldn't get any bubbles or whiskers in the second and subsequent coats.

Let the epoxy cure, then de-wax and sand the second coat just as you did the first. Apply a third coat, but this time when you sand it is imperative that you not cut through the surface film into the bare wood. If you do sand through, paint the entire hatch cover with a fourth coat of epoxy. Above all, resist the temptation to varnish over any sanded-through spots. Although you can hardly see them now, they will show up quite noticeably as ugly blotches under the varnish.

As you progress, the problem of dust becomes more and more important. Make sure you thoroughly clean your hatch cover after each coat. Beware of tack rags that may contain silicone; I prefer a clean cloth or paper towel just barely moistened with acetone. Some boatbuilders will hose down the entire shop floor to control dust while finishing. This is fine, but it can raise the humidity in the shop to the extent that it affects the epoxy. Whatever you do, don't try to work on another project in the same area where epoxy (or paint or varnish for that matter) is curing: Do some paperwork or listen to music or, better yet, just go away until tomorrow.

If your hatch cover has a lot of flat areas where you want a perfectly smooth "piano" finish, you must get the epoxy coat uniformly flat and level. Make a sand-

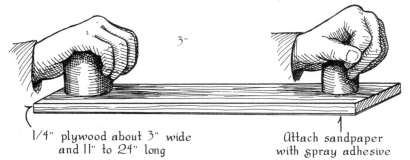

3"

1/4" plywood about 3" wide
and 11" to 24" long

Attach sandpaper
with spray adhesive

Figure 11-1.
A homemade
sanding board will
help you achieve a
uniformly flat and
level coat of epoxy.

ing board out of a ¼-inch piece of ash, oak, or other flexible wood (quality plywood will work fine) 3 inches wide and 11 inches long—just the right size for a third of a sheet of sandpaper. Attach small handles at each end of the board, making sure they don't interfere with the board's flexibility, and glue on a piece of 140-grit aluminum-oxide paper.

With your sanding board, lightly sand the entire surface of the hatch cover just enough to knock down the high spots in the freshly cured epoxy. Low areas will show up as shiny spots. If there's a lot of epoxy, you can continue sanding until these shiny spots are gone, but if there's any danger of sanding through, give the low areas another coat of epoxy to bring them level with the rest of the surface, then sand out as before.

Small defects in the wood, up to about ⅛ inch deep, can be filled with epoxy at this point. A good trick is to mix the epoxy and wait for about 20 minutes for it to start to set, then use this thickened mixture to fill knotholes and other flaws in the wood. If it still wants to flow out, covering it with a scrap of plastic wrap will usually add enough surface tension to keep it in place until it sets. Don't use thickening agents in epoxy under varnish because they'll show through quite dramatically. Make Dutchman repairs in any major defects—but you should've done this before you started sanding.

Thoroughly sand the last coat of epoxy and you're ready to start varnishing.

BRUSHES FOR VARNISH

The best brushes for varnish work are expensive, but if you take good care of them, they will last a lifetime. Any top-quality natural-bristle brush, such as China bristle, will work fine, but I prefer badger-hair brushes. They load better and flow better than anything else I've ever used. No matter what kind of brushes you choose, they must never be used for anything but varnish. Once a brush is used for paint, the residue that gets under the ferrule is nearly impossible to remove by cleaning or soaking. No matter how clean the brush looks, if you varnish with it, the paint residue will leach out and ruin your job . . . I guarantee it.

I've talked to several good craftsmen lately who swear by disposable foam brushes for varnishing, but the ones I've tried don't hold enough varnish to keep them from dragging, and they're impossible to keep free of air bubbles. I can recommend them only for your crudest work.

For years and years I agonized over the tedious ritual of cleaning brushes—sloshing the things around in progressively cleaner baths of foul-smelling solvent, then a final bath in hot soapy water; and still they wouldn't be clean. Frequently, on a small job, I would spend more time cleaning the brush than applying varnish. I finally found the answer to always having clean brushes: Don't clean them at all.

The terrible burden of brush-cleaning drudgery has been lifted from my shoulders by two clever products of Yankee ingenuity: the Sureline Professional Brush

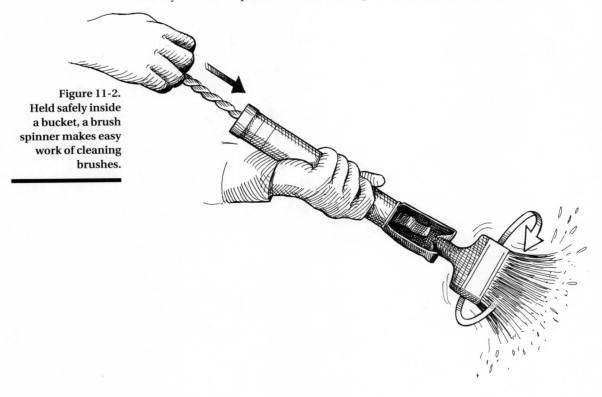

**Figure 11-2.
Held safely inside
a bucket, a brush
spinner makes easy
work of cleaning
brushes.**

Spinner and the #10 Advanced Heavy Duty Brush Keeper, both of which are available at your local professional paint store. To use the spinner, simply insert the handle of the brush in the spring-clamp jaws and give the handle a vigorous pull: The brush spins rapidly around its longitudinal axis and flings the residual varnish out into the environment where it splatters everything and everybody within about a hundred yards. If you want to avoid a pointillist paint job on everything in the neighborhood, carry out this spinning operation inside a barrel or large bucket.

The #10 Brush Keeper is nothing more than a sheet-metal box with a tight-fitting lid and clips to hold the brushes inside. The box is filled half-full of a suitable solvent (I use clean diesel fuel, but kerosene, turpentine, or paint thinner are also fine), and the brushes are hung from the clips so that the bristles and the ferrule are suspended in the solvent. To use a brush, simply remove it from the box and give it a spin in the brush spinner, and you're all set to go. The entire operation takes only a few seconds. You will, of course, need separate brush keepers for your paint and varnish brushes. And there's no reason you couldn't make perfectly good ones out of large coffee cans.

APPLYING VARNISH

Selecting the kind of varnish to go over epoxy is very important because while some work fine, others that normally are perfectly good products don't work at all. Captain's Varnish by Z-Spar is one of the best, and Epifanes works very well, although it takes a bit longer to dry. For some reason neither Schooner by Interlux nor Helmsman by Minwax seem to work worth a damn over epoxy, although they're fine over bare wood. If you have a favorite varnish you'd like to use over epoxy, it's imperative that you try it on a test piece before you apply it to an expensive piece of woodwork.

Properly applied, varnish is more laid down than brushed on. If everything is just right—the temperature is moderate, humidity is low, viscosity is just so, your attitude is upbeat, the moon is not in phase with Saturn, and the sun spots are at a minimum—varnish goes on like a dream. At other times it will drag and sag and make your life miserable.

The first coat of varnish should be thinned about 10 percent whether it's applied over epoxy or bare wood. Always thin in accordance with the manufacturer's spec sheet and application guide, which you should get when you buy the varnish. If the sales clerk tells you it's on the back of the can, walk right out of the store and find another place to do business; all manufacturers have separately printed spec sheets, and all good dealers make these available to their customers.

Many manufacturers will give thinning specifications in seconds from a specific viscosity cup, usually Ford or Zann. A viscosity cup is nothing more than a small plastic cup with a small hole in the bottom. To use one, you simply fill the cup with varnish or paint and, with a stop watch, time how long it takes to drain out. The use of a viscosity cup is critical for most applications from a spray gun but much less so if you're using a brush. Just thin until the brush stops dragging, and be careful not to exceed the specified maximum thinner-to-paint ratio.

Always apply varnish from a one-quart paper paint pot—never straight from the can. Stir completely but very carefully to avoid incorporating air bubbles into the material. Thoroughly load your brush and apply the varnish with long, full strokes. If there's a noticeable resistance to the forward motion of the brush, you're either trying to use a cheap brush, you haven't loaded the brush properly, or the material is still too thick. If this is your first varnish job, the chances are about 10 to 1 that you're trying to get by with an inadequate brush.

As the varnish flows onto the work, keep your brush loaded and try to keep a definite wet edge. Stroke from the edge outward into the dry areas. You need to get the varnish as thin as possible without breaking the flow, and this will take a little practice.

Tip the surface with light passes of the loaded brush to remove surface bubbles—another maneuver that requires some practice to master: You'll know when you're doing it right. Wear surgical gloves, brush with one hand, and pick stray bristles and dust with the other. Don't worry about a few brush marks; good varnish will level and flatten small surface irregularities as it dries. You must resist the strong temptation to repeatedly brush over the same area. This will only starve your brush and cause air bubbles and drags.

After your wood has its first coat of varnish over the epoxy base, it will start to look pretty good, and you'll feel quite proud of yourself. That's fine, but don't rest on your laurels just yet. Most varnishes need 24 hours between coats, and since you'll need a minimum of 6 and as many as 12 coats, you still have a long row to windward. Don't get discouraged, though; all the hard work is done, and the amount of time spent varnishing and sanding is really quite small. It's the drying that takes forever.

Sanding between coats of varnish is important and can determine the success or failure of your varnish job. Always block-sand flat areas, or use your sanding board where appropriate, but leave your power sanders in the tool box. Curved areas can be hand-sanded, being extra careful not to sand through on the edges and corners. I like to wet-sand with 400-grit silicon-carbide paper, but this is messy and takes a little longer than dry sanding. Dry sanding is fine too, but the paper tends to clog fairly fast. Those little green Scotchbrite pads work well for contoured areas, and some people even use them with sanding blocks and on power sanders. Try it different ways until you determine what works for you. The important things are to sand the surface absolutely flat; to remove all the dust, drips, and drags; and not to sand through the film.

The second coat of varnish goes on just like the first, except you'll probably need to thin it only about 5 percent—just enough to keep the brush from dragging.

Repeat the process 4 to 10 times and you're done. Just like Wonder bread—nothing to it.

MAINTAINING VARNISH

Once properly applied, varnish is fairly easy to maintain—as long as you don't have too much of it. The most important thing in renewing varnish is to do it before it obviously needs to be done. Once a year is usually often enough in most areas of the world, but in the Tropics, because of the intense ultraviolet radiation, twice a year is more like it. Once the finish starts to peel or blister or to show bare wood, the entire job must be done over.

Start by masking off the varnish areas using Scotch (3M) #218 Fine Line Tape, a polypropylene tape that resists solvents and won't damage adjacent paint areas. Do not use paper masking tape for varnish work. Next, sand lightly with 400-grit silicon-carbide paper, wipe with alcohol, and apply a fresh coat of varnish thinned 5 to 10 percent—just enough to keep the brush from dragging. This fresh coat will renew the surface film and repair light scratches and abrasions that are the natural result of using a boat as a boat. Deeper scratches and gouges need to be sanded out to bare wood, then built back up with repetitive coats of epoxy and varnish until the result matches the original.

It's perfectly OK to switch brands of varnish when recoating the entire job. And the problems that develop with some varnishes over epoxy seem to occur only on the first coat—subsequent coats are fine. But because of color differences between different products, you should stick with the original brand if you're repairing small areas. It's also perfectly all right to apply paint over varnish that has been thoroughly sanded and cleaned. The paint will adhere with no problems; the only drawback is that even small scratches in the paint will show the varnish underneath and look like large scratches.

One of the best places to do varnish work is out in the middle of the harbor (on a mooring or at anchor) where you're safe from dust and wind-blown grit. Pick a dry, overcast day when the breezes are light; varnish in the morning so the surface will dry before the evening dew; and never varnish in direct sun. The worst place to varnish is where most people end up doing it—at the boatyard in the spring with newly hatched insects flying about and all the activity kicking up clouds of dust.

POLYURETHANE

My best advice on applying clear one-part polyurethane to brightwork is simple: Don't do it. Sure, I know polyurethane has a lot tougher surface film than varnish, and that it's easier to apply, provided you're not real fussy about the end product. But polyurethane varnish has one big drawback that makes it unusable for most boat work.

Remember my explanation from a few paragraphs back about how polyurethanes work by a polymerization process that forms a molecular film on the surface of the work by linking molecules? Well, polymerization only works while the material is curing—thus the imperative instructions on most manufacturers' spec sheets that subsequent coats of polyurethane be applied within a certain time period, usually 8 to 24 hours. Once the polyurethane has cured, the bond with subsequent coats is no longer chemical; it's solely mechanical and not nearly as strong. Conventional varnish adheres to previous coats by a process called "biting," which means the solvents in the fresh varnish soften and dissolve the resins in the old surface, so when the new coat dries it has become a part of the old coat. When a new coat of polyurethane is applied over an old coat, it's much like covering it with a sheet of Saran Wrap. The coats build up in distinct layers, and when the mechanical bond fails, the stuff comes off in sheets—just like peeling off a sheet of plastic. Consequently, polyurethane surfaces are difficult to repair, and the only correct way to do it is to strip off all the old finish and start from scratch. It's much easier just to use varnish to begin with.

Two-part polyurethane varnishes are another thing entirely; they make one of the hardest, toughest, and most durable finishes ever developed, and there's never any problem applying them over epoxy. They don't give the same depth of finish as the "real" stuff, but it will take a real nitpicker to tell the difference. They're a bit harder to apply, but they dry faster, and they won't require as many coats. The big drawback to two-part finishes is that they're dangerous to use because they all contain isocyanate, one of the most toxic substances known to man. One sniff of this stuff will blow your brains right out through your ears, so while a regular carbon-filter organic-compound mask is adequate for applying it with a brush, if you're using any kind of spray equipment, a positive-supply air respirator, such as an Air Hat, should always be used with any two-part formulation.

The reservations I have about polyurethane apply only to clear finishes. Polyurethane paint is wonderful stuff, so why not talk about that next?

PAINT

Once you learn to varnish, painting will be a breeze. It's not that painting is easier than varnishing, it's just that it's largely the same thing. In fact most marine paints are formulated from the same assortment of stuff as varnishes and polyurethanes, with appropriate pigments added for color. The surface preparation for paint is different than for varnish, and you don't need nearly as many coats to get a first-class job.

Colors

"There's only two colors to paint a boat—white and black—and only a fool would paint a boat black."

There is a lot of truth to this bit of ancient Down East wisdom, and there's a very practical reason for it. White gloss paint on the hull of a boat reflects about 90 percent of the light that hits it. Flat black paint reflects less than 5 percent. For comparison, varnished mahogany reflects 30 to 40 percent of the light that hits it. If you doubt these figures, borrow a hand-held light meter from a friendly photographer (they're much friendlier than plumbers) and check yourself. First take a light reading directly from the sun, then take another directly off the paint and compare the two as a ratio—amazing, isn't it?

Light absorbed by dark-colored paint is converted to heat and goes to work immediately bubbling your paint job, cooking your interior, burning your feet, and generally making your life miserable. Reflected light bounces off into the stratosphere or somewhere else where it won't do any harm, taking much of the ultraviolet with it. So if you absolutely must paint your boat with some color other than white, make it a lime green or perhaps a light shade of robin's-egg blue. Save the dark colors for boottops, sheer stripes, and other accents—just like brightwork.

The argument that favors white paint over colors also favors gloss over flat or semigloss paints. Most marine paints are formulated with a high-gloss surface because the gloss is more resistant to the elements and will last longer than flat paints. Also, many gloss paints, especially the polyurethanes, contain UVAs (just like varnish) that migrate to the surface as the paint dries, forming a protective film. The addition of a flattening agent in semigloss paints destroys or degrades this UVA barrier.

There is one case where flat white paint is justified. When the exterior surfaces of a boat are rough and uneven—such as where a previous owner has tried to strip the topsides paint with a belt sander—and the hull is gouged beyond practical repair, the defects will show up loud and clear through a gloss paint job. Fairing these gouges is a long and tedious job requiring skills achievable only through practice. A coat of flat paint will hide them very nicely until you can get around to repairing them.

Here's a neat trick you can use while fairing a badly gouged hull: Apply a coat of high-gloss white paint first and apply your fairing compound over it. You'll be able to see every little blemish. Don't try this with epoxy, though; use trowel cement.

One-Part or Two-Part?

There are three popular types of marine paints from which to choose—alkyds, one-part polyurethanes, and two-part polyurethanes. Unlike varnishes, where I can recommend one to the exclusion of the others, each of these types of paint is quite useful under specific circumstances.

If the painted surfaces of your old wooden boat are in good shape, with no blisters or peeling, and you suspect the existing paint is an alkyd, there's little to be gained by stripping to the bare wood. Go ahead, after a careful sanding, filling, and cleaning, and apply another coat of alkyd. Since the bond of the new paint won't be any better than the bond of the old paint, there's nothing to be gained by using a polyurethane, and you'll save some money by staying with the alkyd.

If, on the other hand, you have a lot of new wood, or you've completely stripped the old paint so that you can proceed as if it were new wood, and if the hull is very tight with dry bilges and no working seams, you should definitely consider a one-part or a two-part polyurethane over an epoxy base and an epoxy primer. The surface gloss will be superior, and it will last longer than an alkyd.

The decision to use a one- or a two-part system involves both practical and economic factors. I favor Interlux paints simply because I've had good luck with them. This is not a plug for Interlux; I'm sure others on the market are as good, and some are probably better, but I haven't had any experience with them. Interlux's one-part Brightside polyurethane has been quite satisfactory. Their two-part Interthane Plus polyurethane is also great; it covers better, it gives a marginally finer finish than Brightside, and it's substantially harder and tougher, but it costs more than twice as much. That can be a pretty big "but" if you have a large boat.

As a general rule I always use an epoxy base wherever I can, and I always use the two-part Interthane over the epoxy. If, however, I don't use the epoxy base, I use the Brightside polyurethane or an alkyd.

SURFACE PREPARATION FOR PAINTING

Start your surface preparation for paint the same as you would for varnish. If the existing paint is in good shape, a diligent sanding and a solvent wipe are all that's required. If the old paint is blistered and peeling, it must be stripped to the bare wood. However, whereas varnish must be stripped in its entirety to avoid an unhealthy mottled appearance in the finished product, it's OK to strip the bad areas of paint but leave the old paint where it's still sound—as long as you plan to repaint with the same type of paint you're removing.

If you're painting over old varnish, go ahead and leave any that is sound, as long as you plan on using alkyd paint. If you're going to use polyurethane, wood the entire job. Carefully sand all surfaces with 80-grit, no-load aluminum-oxide paper.

EPOXY BASE COAT

On above-the-waterline wood that has been completely stripped or is new, you should consider using an epoxy undercoat. If done properly, the epoxy will give you a base for a two-part polyurethane surface that will rival fiberglass in durability. However, the caveats mentioned before are worth repeating. You should always coat all surfaces of solid wood that are going to be epoxied, or at least be able to ensure they can be kept reasonably dry. If you intend to epoxy the outside of a hull, it's best to epoxy the inside too, or at least those areas you have access to. Coating the interior is not as important on plywood hulls because of the inherent stability of the material, but it's still best to coat everything you can get at when it's practical.

When you make a new part, say a new deck beam, or when you've removed an old one, you can apply a few coats of epoxy, and primer if appropriate, before you install it in the boat. This way all bearing surfaces, which would otherwise be inaccessible, will be coated, and you can do the work in the shop were you can get at it.

Only tightly caulked hulls with no working seams should be epoxied, and then only above the waterline. Epoxy will drastically limit the swelling of the planking. If you have any doubt that your hull is appropriate for epoxy, it's best to avoid it, or at least consult with a professional boatbuilder or a competent marine surveyor before you proceed.

THE PRIME COAT

When you apply paint over an epoxy base coat, the primer is optional. Most paints, including bottom paints, will adhere to epoxy quite well without a primer, but sanding a smooth surface may be easier when it's been primed. Many paints also cover better over primer than over bare epoxy. Apply primer according to the manufacturer's specs—to the letter. With alkyds the recommended primer is frequently a coat of the paint thinned about 10 percent. For polyurethane over epoxy, either skip the primer entirely or, if the spec sheet doesn't recommend a primer for epoxy, use the primer recommended for fiberglass.

Many times it's easier to repair small surface defects after a prime coat has been applied because it's easier to see them. I use epoxy thickened with WEST System Microlight for filling, light fairing, and leveling over a primer because it's extremely tough, it trowels well, and it's easy to sand. Interlux makes a trowel cement that's OK once you get the hang of applying it, but it's an oil-based product that takes forever to dry. A lot of boatbuilders use autobody filler (Bondo) at this stage, but I've had bad luck with it popping out at inopportune times. Bondo has the one big advantage that it sets in minutes while epoxy may require an hour or more before it can be worked, so I must admit I do use Bondo for small repairs when I'm in a hurry.

Whatever you use, make sure the entire surface is filled and faired and sanded as smooth as it will be when it's painted. Most paints do not sand well, and repairing surface faults at the primer stage is much easier than trying to do it later on.

BRUSHES FOR PAINT

The brushes you select for paint will be less critical than those for varnish, but you'll still need good ones. And since you've no doubt taken my advice and restricted the amount of varnish work to trim pieces, there will be a lot more of

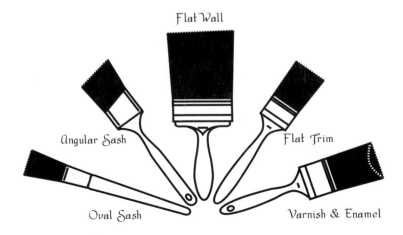

Flat Wall

Angular Sash

Flat Trim

Oval Sash

Varnish & Enamel

your boat to paint than there was to varnish, which means you'll need a wider selection of brushes. Both natural bristles and synthetics work fine with most paints. Just make sure to keep them clean and stored in a brush keeper. Always match your brush to the job you're asking it to do. You wouldn't try to paint a hull with a 1-inch brush, so don't try to paint the toerail with a 4-incher.

APPLYING PAINT

I prefer to apply paint with a good brush instead of a roller or a spray gun whenever it's practical and I have the time. It's a mindless task, and standing on the scaffolding on a quiet day in the boatyard I can let my mind wander a million miles while I think away all the accumulated thoughts I've been saving for just such a moment. Once the rhythm is established—dip, tap, brush, brush, brush; dip, tap, brush, brush, brush—it becomes a self-perpetuating exercise in hypnotic repetition, a pleasant reverie that would go on forever if not interrupted by the need to move the ladder, the end of the job, or the bothersome requirement to periodically refresh the paint bucket.

Paint should always be applied from a paint pail—never straight from the can. Thinning requirements vary with the different manufacturers, but most paints will benefit from being cut 5 to 10 percent. Some manufacturers have a liquid additive that helps the paint flow. This is usually nothing more than paint thinner with a high oil content, which won't flash off quite as quickly as the regular stuff. It's particularly helpful on warm, dry days or when there's a breeze.

Always paint from high spots to low spots, keep a wet edge, and since we don't have to be paranoid about air bubbles as with varnish, brush out the surface. Proper brushing will ensure complete coverage with the thinnest film possible and prevent drags, sags, drips, runs, and curtains, all of which somehow remind me of my favorite niece's teenage boyfriends.

All the foregoing is fine except when using two-part paint. What would be a pleasant afternoon of leisurely slapping away the hours with a paintbrush turns into a race against the clock. Once you mix those two cans together, you have only a specified length of time before the whole thing turns into a very expensive glop resembling chicken soup that has been left in the refrigerator too long.

Painting large areas with two-part paint calls for a different technique and involves two people. The first, usually the less skilled of the two, applies the paint with a short-nap roller while his partner follows along behind with a loaded tipping brush, leveling the surface and doing the detail work. It is amazing how quickly two diligent workers can paint a 40-foot hull using this method, and it's equally amazing how good a job results. If the surface has been properly prepared, temperature and humidity cooperate, and there's not a lot of dust in the air, the result will be as flawless as any professional spray job.

This roll-and-tip method only works with two people because the paint must be tipped as soon as it's applied or it will start to set. Working on a cool day will retard the curing process, but low temperature also affects the viscosity and makes the paint harder to brush out. If you try to skip the tipping step and just use the roller, the texture of the roller will not flow out, and your entire boat will look like it's covered with badly applied nonskid.

Most two-part paints spray very well, so if you must work alone, it might be best to rent spray equipment. The exposure to harmful, even deadly, chemicals present in all two-part formulations is greatly increased by spraying, so a complete "moon suit" with every inch of your skin covered and a positive-supply air respirator are essential. Spray painting is tricky, and it will take more than a little practice before you get the hang of it. So if you want to spray paint, learn to use the equipment before you spray your boat. Try it out on something less important first—like your car.

Most quality marine paints will cover primed wood in two coats, but three will make a more durable job. Two-part paints cover better than one-part paints, which helps recoup some of the extra cost. The majority of marine paints require 24 hours to set and, of course, should be sanded lightly between coats.

I hope this chapter has convinced you that the finishing of your old-wooden-boat project is a complex and time-consuming process. Painting and varnishing are two of the most demanding tasks you'll perform, and they take a lot of practice and experience before you get them just right; it's not something you can learn to do by reading about it. But when the last piece of brightwork is varnished, the last drop of paint has finally dried, and you step back and view the results of months of toil and effort, you'll know it was worth it. She finally looks like what you envisioned when you started this project those many chapters ago.

Suggested Reading

My old pal Spencer Paul never liked to read much; he was always worried that his brain would fill up and rupture if he tried to pack in too much information. A pity. Old Spencer died with plenty of room left in his brain, and had he considered more the capacity of his liver and less the capacity of his brain, he would be with us yet.

There are literally thousands of good books, in and out of print, dealing with boats and boatbuilding, and a great many of them will be helpful to you in your wooden-boat renovation project. The best advice is to read every one of them; the more information you pack into your brain cells, the better you'll deal with decisions as the need arises. And you needn't worry about your head exploding: The average brain has plenty of room for everything ever written about boats; getting it in there is the tricky part. As you wade through the boatbuilding literature available at bookstores and your local library, you'll find a few gems that stand out. And since it really isn't possible to read everything ever written, I'll share with you a short list of my old favorites as well as a few newer ones that everyone interested in fixing up old boats should have in their library. Some are included because they contain helpful and useful information; others are just plain fun to read. A rare few are both. I have listed them by author in no particular order except as they came to mind.

BOOKS

Chapelle, Howard I. *Boatbuilding.* W. W. Norton & Company, 1941 and 1973.
 Howard Chapelle fancied himself a boat designer and a builder, and the degree to which he achieved these ambitions is the subject of profound debate. His designs are mostly superbly drawn renditions of antique craft, and it's doubtful if he ever built more than one or two boats in his life. Where Howard Chapelle excelled was as a marine historian, and it is largely because of his tireless research, detailed writing, and meticulous drawings that we know as much about our nautical past as we do. *Boatbuilding* tells us how boats should be built and how they were built, but very little about how they are built; however, it is a must-have item in every wooden-boat library.
 Everything written by Chapelle is worth reading, but three other books of his are among my favorites: *The American Fishing Schooners*, W. W. Norton & Company, 1973; the classic *American Small Sailing Craft*, W. W. Norton & Company, 1951; and *The History of American Sailing Ships*, Bonanza Books, 1935.

Steward, Robert M. *Boatbuilding Manual*, 3d ed. International Marine, 1987.
 This most useful book differs from Chapelle's work in that it tells us in unadorned prose and with straightforward, meat-and-potatoes instructions how to build a boat. Where Chapelle wrote about boats then built a few, Steward built boats, lots of them, then wrote about it; and the differences in the two works are both subtle and profound. Read both and you will understand how a traditionally built wooden boat goes together; this understanding will be a tremendous help in any renovation project, be it small or large, skiff or schooner.

Gardner, John. *Building Classic Small Craft*, Vol. 1. International Marine, 1977, 1991.
 John Gardner probably knows more about the origins and development of small American watercraft than any man alive today. What Howard Chapelle did for the traditional American sailing craft, John Gardner has done for the skiffs and dories and peapods and dinghies that are as much a part of our heritage as larger craft. Each craft is drawn to the tiniest detail and described in such a way that a replica of each could be built without the builder ever having seen an original.

Payson, Harold "Dynamite." *Build the New Instant Boats.* International Marine, 1984.
 Although Harold Payson has become the modern guru of quick-and-easy boatbuilding, some who are not familiar with his techniques and his books might assume that quick and easy means slipshod. Nothing is farther from the truth; Mr. Payson is a meticulous craftsman and a highly

skilled woodworker, and the boats he builds (mostly from Phil Bolger designs) are as seaworthy and as sturdy as any small boat built by more traditional means; in fact many of them are a lot more durable. If you are new to boatbuilding or to general woodworking, building one of these little boats is a great way to get your feet wet (figuratively speaking, of course).

Alvord, Douglas. *On the Water*. Yankee Books, 1988.

Douglas Alvord is emerging as an important chronicler of marine history, and this meticulously researched little book is a wonderful record of the development of American small boats since colonial times. It's also a good read anytime. However, it's not so much the words but the pictures that make this book a worthy addition to your library. The illustrations are simply superb as they manage to capture the very essence of the watercraft they depict and the spirit of the people who build and sail them. To look at Alvord's artwork is to understand the bond that can exist between the nebulous human soul and those specific assemblages of wood and wire and rag and sweat that we call boats.

Bingham, Fred P. *Practical Yacht Joinery*. International Marine, 1983.

This rather pricey book ($35 for a paperback is a lot, but read on) was the best book on the market for the novice or intermediate woodworker, whether they were building a full-size replica of the *Golden Hind* or a bookcase for the den. Almost every conceivable way of putting two or more pieces of wood together is discussed in clear text and illustrated with simple, understandable drawings. The publisher is offering a revised edition, *Boat Joinery and Cabinetmaking Simplified* (available Spring 1993) for $21.95. Apparently, no one told them that prices only rise.

Story, Dana. *Frame Up*. Ten Pound Island Book Company, 1986.

Dana Story is unique among marine historians in that he gained his vast knowledge of the boatbuilding trades, particularly those that apply to Essex schooners, through actual experience rather than from reading the accounts of others. He was raised in the oldest continuously operating boatyard in the country, and to read his account of the launch of a new fishing schooner is like being there. Story writes with the articulate sophistication of a college professor who can, at times, be wistful, but without a trace of nostalgic emotionalism. Another book by Dana Story well worth reading is *Building the* Blackfish (International Marine, 1988).

Casey, Don. *This Old Boat*. International Marine, 1991.

Of all the books on boat maintenance and refurbishing published in recent years, this is the most useful to the owner of a small cruising sailboat. And although it was written specifically for the owners of small fiberglass sailboats, it contains a wealth of information and advice on engines, rigging, electrical wiring, steering systems, and even refrigeration—all of which applies to boats built of any material. The last chapter of the book contains enough information on sewing such things as sail covers, awnings, and cushion covers to easily save you the price of the book with one project. Also unique among how-to books, *This Old Boat* is fun to read. See the section on electricity for a crystal-clear explanation of the mysteries of electrons as portrayed by hormonally addled teenagers.

Calder, Nigel. *Boatowner's Mechanical and Electrical Manual.* International Marine, 1990.

This book is one of those rarities of modern publishing: a highly technical book that is both informative and easily understood by the layman. While it covers some of the same subjects as Casey's book listed above, it covers them much more extensively and in greater detail. Read, for example, the page or so of text that Casey devotes to alternators, and you will understand how these nefarious devices of the devil work. After reading Calder's 10 pages on the same subject, you will not only understand how they work, but the next time you are offshore at night in the fog motoring across a shipping lane into a 10-foot sea with a half gale blowing right on the nose and your alternator decides to take the night off, you won't have the slightest compunction about diving below decks and convincing that sucker to get back to work.

Wittman, Rebecca J. *Brightwork.* International Marine, 1990.

This lovely book graced the shelves of the Spirit of '76 bookstore in beautiful downtown Marblehead for more than a year before I paid it more than a passing glance. It's not that I wasn't interested in the subject; it's just that the book is loaded with gorgeous, glossy, four-color photography, and I have come to mistrust books that emphasize photography as fluff pieces appealing to people with large wallets who don't read much: coffee-table books in the vernacular of the trade. How wrong I was; once I bothered to read the text, it became obvious that this was *the* definitive work on finishing brightwork. The author is obviously completely familiar with the subject and writes with an enthusiasm that betrays a love for the very act of slathering freshly sanded wood with all sorts of clear finishes. If you have a boat with a lot of brightwork and intend to resist my advice to paint over the majority of it, get this book—you'll love it.

Vaitses, Allan H. *Covering Wooden Boats with Fiberglass*, rev. ed. International Marine, 1981, 1989.

This book details the procedures Vaitses developed over the years for resurrecting old hulls by completely encasing them in polyester and fiberglass. If your boat is in really bad shape, this may be the only way to save her.

Vaitses, Allan H. *What Shape Is She In?* International Marine, 1985.

If you are even thinking about buying a used boat, made from what-ever sort of material, buy this book first and read it from cover to cover. It won't replace a good survey once you find a boat you are interested in, but it will give you the background you need to reject on first inspection 95 percent of all the boats you look at. It also contains excellent advice on how to find a good surveyor and what a surveyor can and can't do for you.

Fine WoodWorking on Boxes, Carcases, and Drawers. Fine WoodWorking. Taunton Press, 1985.

This is a collection of essays and articles from *Fine WoodWorking* magazine and contains many valuable tips on general woodworking. The entire *Fine WoodWorking* series includes a dozen or more volumes; all are well worth having, but this one is one of the best.

Kushner, Harold. *Who Needs God.* Simon & Schuster, 1989.

This book doesn't have anything at all to do with boats, of course, but if you allow yourself to get involved with a boat-renovation project of any magnitude, sooner or later you're going to encounter things that don't go just the way you thought they should. This book enjoyed a long run on the *New York Times* best-seller list because of Kushner's unique ability to make people feel good about themselves when things go wrong. And besides, when you work on old wooden boats, you need someone you can talk to who is available 24 hours a day, who is always sympathetic, and who will never talk back or load you up with hindsight-generated advice on how you should have done something—guess who?

Gould, Stephen Jay. *Bully for Brontosaurus.* W. W. Norton & Company, 1991.

This is another *New York Times* best-seller that doesn't have the slightest thing to do with boats, and that is precisely the reason it is included here. When you become involved with old wooden boats, it is easy to become obsessed with them. How many people do you know who seem to know everything there is to know about boats and nothing about anything else? I know a lot, and they tend to get a little boring at times. It's like listening to a fiddler who only knows one tune. Of course, you needn't read Gould's books unless you are interested in his subject; but please, for the sake of humanity, read something besides boat books. My favorite subjects after boats just happen to be natural history and popular anthropology, and I devour the mass-market books written by Gould and the likes of Carl Sagan and Stephen W. Hawking. So if I can't bore you with talk about the relative merits of bulwarks and taffrail logs, I can bore your socks off talking about Donald Johanson's theories on the evolution-ary development of sub-Saharan protohumans. It's really nice to be flexible.

PERIODICALS

Unfortunately, in recent years many of the grand old yachting magazines with long traditions of service to the boating community have become the property of lubber conglomerates, and the editors of many of them seem reluctant to print anything that would be even mildly offensive to advertisers or potential advertisers. The result is that there are very few boating magazines that print anything of substance, and even fewer that will print anything negative about any product regardless of how ill conceived it might be: reviews of products such as the so-called lightweight anchors (an oxymoron of mindbending magnitude) that are frequently printed next to a full-page ad for these same products are just one example.

Fortunately there are a few magazines that have not completely become shills to their advertisers, and these are still worth their cover price. My favorites are:

WoodenBoat (P.O. Box 78, Brooklin, ME 04616)

When Jon Wilson brought out the first issue of *WoodenBoat* in September 1974 (80 pages; $3), the few remaining oddballs who enjoyed wooden boats, like me and my friends, thought it was pretty funny. Sure it was a terrific magazine right from the start, but anybody could have told him that most of us wooden-boat freaks couldn't read; a lot who could, didn't; and the rest of us didn't have enough money for magazines anyway. Today, that attitude has changed drastically, and everyone who owns a boat, regardless of what it's made of, should have a subscription to *WoodenBoat*. Virtually every issue has one or more articles that make it worth keeping, and as a result, it's the only magazine I save rather than clip articles from on a selective basis. In fact, I don't know anyone who reads *WoodenBoat* who doesn't save each issue.

Practical Sailor (Box 819, Newport, RI 02840)

The reason *Practical Sailor* doesn't have to shill for its advertisers is simple: It doesn't have any. Therefore the magazine can and does say exactly what's on its mind, and the result is the only publication on the market that can be relied on for a candid assessment of the plethora of boats and merchandise foisted upon the public by the boating industries. *Practical Sailor* was the publication that blew the whistle on Rule Industries when they "improved" the venerable Danforth anchor. The new model is cheaper and easier to manufacture, but its holding power is demonstrably less than that of the old ones, and to my knowledge, not one other major publication has even mentioned this; you'd think it wasn't important. No advertising means a rather thin (32 pages average) and pricey magazine, but word for word it's the best deal around, and if I had to get by with only one marine periodical, this would be it.

Cruising World (5 John Clark Road, Newport, RI 02840)

Whether you are a cruising sailor with dreams of sailing off to the far horizons or are planning just an overnight cruise to the little island across the harbor, *Cruising World* will be of interest to you despite an increasingly precipitous slant toward the bareboat charter businesses that seem to make up its largest body of advertisers. Of course there is nothing inherently wrong with bareboat charter; it's a fine way to enjoy sailing for those who are unable or disinclined to own a boat. Anyway, *Cruising World* is still a great magazine for those of us who like to cruise. Every issue contains a balance of exotic stories of sailing away to faraway lands, written by real sailors who have really done it, and good practical advice on everything from kedging off a sandbar and coastal navigation to cooking brown-rice goulash while heeled 20 degrees.

National Fisherman (P.O. Box 908, Rockland, ME 04841)

Even though *National Fisherman* has, in recent years, dropped its coverage of pleasure boats in order to concentrate its efforts in support of the beleaguered commercial fisherman (although rumor has it this is changing), it remains one of my favorite magazines. There are still a lot of articles on boats and equipment of interest to anyone who ventures onto the water. And they still have John Gardner on the masthead, and his writings along with those of Roger Taylor, Greg Rössel, and Dynamite Payson more than justify the cover price—even if you don't catch fish for a living.

Sources of Supply

B efore I launch into a list of recommended places where you can purchase some of the tons of stuff you'll need to renovate even a small wooden boat, let me say that inclusion on this list doesn't constitute an endorsement of any particular company past the fact that I have had satisfactory dealings with them. And likewise, just because a company doesn't appear here shouldn't reflect adversely on that company in any way. It simply means that I have never had any personal dealings with them.

When buying supplies, always buy in commercial quantities as close to the source of supply as you can. Never *ever* buy supplies from the local hardware store. Purchase sandpaper by the sleeve and screws in boxes of 100 from a wholesale or discount mail-order house or in case lots directly from the distributor. Electrical wire and terminals should always be purchased from an electrical supply house. If you need one terminal or screw, buy the whole box anyway; you will eventually use them up and you'll save a small fortune. If you're rewiring a boat, buy wire by the spool, which may contain from 100 to 500 feet or more depending on the size of the wire, and ignore the American Boat and Yacht Council (ABYC) color-code charts that are listed in almost every book on the subject ever printed. (Calder lists 21 different colors of wire that you would need to buy in order to comply with the ABYC code. It's a great reference, but you would go crazy trying to follow it to rewire a single boat.) Buy one spool each of 8-gauge, 12-gauge, and 16-gauge two-conductor tinned wire in any color you like, and it will take care of 90 percent of all your wiring needs. If you don't have the size wire called for in the charts, just use the next largest size that you happen to have. If the charts call for 10-gauge wire, use 8; and if it calls for 18, use 16 and so on—you'll save a lot of money and aggravation and you will end up with a better electrical system. If the lack of color coding bothers you, put matching colored tape on the opposite ends of each run of wire.

To purchase supplies from a wholesaler or other commercial outlet, you need only two things: you need a company name or something that sounds like a company name (The Duchess Boatworks, Inc. works every time), and you need to know what you are talking about. Wholesalers and manufacturers are in business to make money, and they really don't give a damn who they sell their products to as long as they make a buck in the process. Most wholesalers and manufacturers refuse to deal directly with the public because retailing is a time-consuming, frustrating, and labor-intensive process that can easily double the cost of the products sold. Wholesalers and manufacturers operate on narrow profit margins of 5 to 20 percent and simply can't absorb the expense. Retailers, however, use a typical markup on most marine products of 100 percent, so the retailer can afford to hire someone to stand around and answer silly questions from a customer intent on buying a handful of screws. (The degree to which the average sales person is qualified to answer those questions is another problem beyond the scope of this book.) However, if you know exactly what you want, and you want a large enough quantity to meet minimum-order requirements, most wholesalers and some manufacturers will be happy to sell to anyone. They ask for a company name and in some cases a tax number (use the first letter of your last name and your social security number with no spacing) simply because it is an effective means of weeding out nuisance calls. If you don't have a company name, you'll probably be given the name of a local retailer or, in worse cases, hung up on. In other cases, your order will be gladly taken, but because wholesalers want to avoid being in the awkward position of competing with their customers who are retailers, you will be charged the manufacturer's suggested retail price—usually 20 percent or so higher than that charged by the discount mail-order houses—regardless of the size of your order.

When you give the receptionist or the sales person a company name, he can fill in the appropriate block on the sales sheet; this makes everyone, including the boss, happy, and the savings to you can be dramatic. For example, a gallon of acetone from my local marine discount house (a national chain with very good prices) costs $8.85. My local solvent distributor, Houghton Chemical Corporation, will sell me a 5-gallon pail of acetone for $28.13 ($5.63 per gal.). For $167.79 ($3.05 per gal.) they will deliver a 55-gallon drum of the stuff. That's a net savings of nearly 60 percent over the best retail price around.

Purchasing materials in large quantities close to the source works particularly well with items such as lumber (go straight to the mill if you can), fasteners, hardware, and solvents, but less so with things such as paint and epoxies because of the large minimum orders most wholesalers of these products require. As with everything else we have discussed, the best advice is to do your homework, shop around, and use common sense when purchasing anything.

The following is a list of suppliers and companies I have dealt with over the years, most of which issue catalogs that are worth sending for. Once again they are listed as they came to mind and are grouped in general categories.

The best source of fasteners and other hardware items that I have found is:

Jamestown Distributors
28 Narragansett Avenue
P.O. Box 348
Jamestown, RI 02835
Free catalog
(800) 423-0030
Jamestown Distributors also carries a good selection of hand tools at reasonable prices.

For another good source of fasteners call Rick Sadler at:

Chesapeake Marine Fasteners
10 Willow Street
Box 6521
Annapolis, MD 21401
Free catalog
(800) 526-0656

If you need a lot of screws—say 5,000 #14 X 2-inch flatheads for a refastening job—call:

Pan American Screw
1651 1st Avenue
Hickory, NC 28603
No catalog, commercial accounts only
(704) 328-2457

For deck hardware, rope, line, and chain contact:

Hamilton Marine, Inc.
Searsport, ME 04974
Free catalog
(800) 969-6352

For caulking supplies and tools and esoteric items such as mast hoops and rudder gudgeons contact:

The WoodenBoat Store
Brooklin, ME 04616
Free catalog
(800) 225-5205
or

The Wooden Boat Shop
1007 NE Boat Street
Seattle, WA 98145
Free catalog
(800) 933-3600

For epoxy and fiberglass supplies call:

Gougeon Brothers, Inc.
P.O. Box 908
Bay City, MI 48707
Free price list, catalog, and technical manual
(517) 684-1374

and

System Three Resins
P.O. Box 70436
Settle, WA 98107
Application Guide $5; free catalog
(206) 782-7976

and

LBI, Inc.
973 North Road
Groton, CT 06340
Catalog $3.50 (free with order)
(800) 231-6537

The undisputedly best sources for used hand and power tools are the yard sales and flea markets that take place on every weekend in and around every community in the land. If you are cruising the Maine coast and plan to motor up the Saint George River to Thomaston (The croissant sandwiches at the Thomaston Cafe Bakery make this trip worthwhile all by themselves), tie up at the town landing next to Lyman Yacht Services and hike up the hill to:

The Thomaston Tool Works
8 Knox Street
Thomaston, ME 04861
No catalog, no price list, no nothin'
(207) 354-8706

This incredible store is likely to have just about any used tool you can imagine, from industrial stitching machines for sailmaking to antique caulking irons, and always at fair-to-bargain prices. The last time I was there I bought a perfectly serviceable bit brace for $5 Canadian (we had just returned from the Bay of Fundy), which sells at the discount stores for about $65; that's a significant savings. A word of warning, however: The hours tend to be a bit erratic, especially in the off-season, so it's a good idea to call first.

If the idea of buying old rusty tools is abhorrent to you and you insist on buying new tools and want the very best obtainable, just down the road from The Thomaston Tool Works is:

Lie-Nielsen Tool Works, Inc.
Route 1
Warren, ME 04864
Free catalog
(207) 273-2520

The product list from this company is rather short—mostly hand planes and chisels and only about a dozen of those. But everything is handmade, and the quality and workmanship is such that you might wonder if you are buying tools or art objects—in truth they are both.

Two good sources for new hand tools of a more ordinary nature are:

Woodcraft
313 Montvale Avenue
Woburn, MA 01801
Free catalog
(800) 535-4482

and

Garrett Wade
161 Avenue of the Americas
New York, NY 10013
Catalog $5 (and worth it)
(800) 221-2942

For new power tools, the best prices are through the discount mail-order companies, just two of which are:

Trendlines
375 Beacham Street
Chelsea, MA 02150
Catalog $2
(800) 767-9999

and

Woodworkers Supply, Inc.
1108 North Glenn Road
Casper, WY 82601
Catalog $2
(800) 645-9292

For carbide router bits contact:

MLCS, Ltd.
P.O. Box 4053
Rydal, PA 19046
Free catalog
(800) 533-9298

The best source for lumber and plywood in large quantities—say 500 board-feet of lumber or 12 sheets of plywood—is your local lumber wholesaler, who should be listed in the Yellow Pages under (of all things) Lumber, Wholesale. For marine plywood, smaller quantities of hardwoods, or for specialty woods such as Sitka spruce or Brazilian purpleheart call:

Boulter Plywood
24 Broadway
Somerville, MA 02145
Free catalog
(617) 666-1340

or, for plywood only

Harbor Sales Company, Inc.
1401 Russell Street
Baltimore, MD 21230
Free catalog
(800) 345-1712

For sandpaper, grinding discs, and other abrasives call Jim Carter at:

The Widden Company, Inc.
15 Spring Street
Peabody, MA 01960
Free catalog
(508) 531-0300

or

Red Hill Corporation
P.O. Box 4234
Gettysburg, PA 17325
Free catalog
(800) 822-4003

For Great-Great-Granny's dry sink or for solid-surface countertop materials and supplies call Bill Holton at:

Corifab
2 Maple Street
Essex, MA 01929
(508) 768-6636

For plastic laminate for countertops, go to your local lumberyard (the cost of shipping the stuff is prohibitive), and for the hinges and other European-style hardware call:

Frederick Shohet, Inc.
51 Concord Street
North Reading, MA 01864
Price list on request, commercial accounts only, no minimum order
(800) 356-0073

For the Teflon tape mentioned in Chapter 9 and as another source for European-style hinges call:

The Woodworker's Store
21801 Industrial Boulevard
Rogers, MN 55374
(612) 428-2899

Although I have no personal experience with these suppliers, friends on the West Coast highly recommend:

Doc Freeman's
999 N. Northlake Way
Seattle, WA 98103
Free catalog
800-423-8641
800-247-2149, WA state

Fisheries Supply
1900 N. Northlake Way
Seattle, WA 98103
712 (!) page catalog, $10
800-426-6930

206-632-4462

Flounder Bay Boat Lumber
1019 3rd Street
Anacortes, WA 98221
206-293-2369
Olson Lumber Co.
9300 Aurora N.
Seattle, WA 98103
800-533-4381

Seattle Ship Supply
Fishermen's Terminal
Seattle, WA 98119
206-283-0830

The Wooden Boat Shop
1007 N.E. Boat Street
Seattle, WA 98105
Catalog $3
800-933-3600

Glossary

There are literally thousands of terms and words that refer to parts of boats, and there are a lot of regional discrepancies in just what a particular part is called. This glossary will give the generally accepted definitions as I have learned them over the years. But since most people who love old wooden boats also love to argue about the proper names for the various parts of them, this section will also offer considerable ammunition and opportunities for the more advanced readers to take verbal potshots at the author. That's OK—fire away; it's all part of the fun.

Most of the words and terms listed below appear in the preceding text, but some do not; I have included the latter only because they are fun to have as part of any nautical vocabulary.

Futtock, for example, is a word that I have known most of my adult life, and not once have I had a chance to use it in conversation—but I'm ready. Someday I just know I'll walk into somebody's shop while he's working on a futtock, and I'll be able to say, "Gosh, that's a nice-looking futtock ya got there." I can hardly wait.

It's practically impossible to define one part of a boat without using terms that describe other parts. One word always leads to another. It's like crossing a river by jumping from rock to rock, so don't be surprised if you need to refer to a definition other than the one that you came for. I'll try not to leave you in the middle of the river.

Afterdeck: The afterdeck is the weatherdeck abaft the foredeck.

Backbone: The backbone of a hull is the collective term for all the pieces that form the center structural support. It may include the stem, gripe piece, stem knee, keel, keelson, deadwood, skeg, sternpost, rudderpost, horntimber, transom, and sometimes the centerboard trunk.

Battens: Battens resemble stringers but are mounted on the outside of the frames and are usually let into them. They are used to reinforce the seams of plywood construction and on carvel planking where extra strength is required, such as on high-speed powerboat hulls. Where I grew up, not far from the Chesapeake Bay, many boats were built using splayed planking on the bottom (planking that is perpendicular to the keel rather than parallel to it), and this planking was fastened to battens.

Bilges: The bilges are the round areas of the hull between the topsides and the keel.

Boottop: The boottop is part of the paint scheme. It is a broad stripe of paint just above and parallel to the actual waterline.

Breasthook: The breasthook is a triangular block much like a knee that reinforces the bow where the clamps and shelfs (never say shelves) attach to the stem; breasthooks are also used at the sternpost on a double-ender. On small boats and canoes, the breasthook is called a *deck*, of all things.

Bridgedeck: A bridgedeck is a narrow deck between the cockpit and the entrance to the cabin on a sailboat. It is also boat-show talk for a flybridge.

Broken Sheer: Broken sheer is a sheerline that is interrupted or stepped to accommodate partial bulwarks or a raised deck.

Bulwarks: Bulwarks are the continuation of the hull planking above the deck of a boat providing a high (4 inches and up, depending on the size of the boat) protective rail. Bulwarks usually contain small openings just above the deckline, called *scuppers,* to allow water to drain out. When bulwarks are used only on the aft section of a hull and are a solid extension of the planking, they are called a *bulwark taffrail.* It's just a plain taffrail when the caprail is supported by spindles or stanchions.

Butt Blocks: Butt blocks are blocks of the same type of wood as the planking, cut slightly wider than the planking and short enough to fit between the frames, used for reinforcing butt joints.

Buttocks: Buttocks are just what they sound like they are—the fat area of the hull amidships. The buttock lines on a set of plans define the planes of the hull that would result if you sawed the boat into slabs that were parallel to the centerline of the hull.

Camber: The camber is the transverse arch of the deckbeams, designed to provide drainage of the weatherdeck and increase headroom below.

Caprail: The top trim of bulwarks or a taffrail is called a caprail.

Carlin (or Carling or Carline): Carlins (sometimes called *headers*) are fore-and-aft structural members that support the ends of halfbeams.

Centerboard: A centerboard is a retractable keel that is housed in a centerboard trunk, which is usually built on top of the keelson.

Chine: A boat that has an essentially flat bottom that joins the sides of the boat at a distinct angle is called a *chine boat*, and the line that the angle forms as viewed from the side is called the *chine*. The batten that is let into the frames and used to reinforce this seam is called, appropriately enough, the *chine batten*; and if the batten is on the outside where it can be seen on the finished boat, it's called a *batten chine*. The term "hard chine" is heard frequently but is often misused in referring to any boat with a chine. It should refer to a chine angle that is *less than 90 degrees*, as might be found on a runabout or a hydroplane.

Clamp: The clamps are attached to the inside of the frames and carry the deckbeams. On small boats the clamp is called an *inwale*.

Coaming: A coaming is a raised member perpendicular to a deck that surrounds an opening in the deck—such as a hatch or the cockpit—to prevent water from running below decks. Fore-and-aft coamings that are extensions of the cabin trunk are called *monkey boards*, and the transverse sections are called *headledges*.

Counter: Counter is used frequently as a synonym for *transom*, usually by salesmen at boat shows and others who are trying to sound nautical. The counter is actually the area of the hull above the DWL between the rudderpost and the transom. The term *reverse counter* was coined by boat-show hypesters to describe the wrong-way transoms that became faddish as a result of an anomaly that developed in the IOR (International Offshore Rule) measurement when the offshore racing crowd switched from the old CCA (Cruising Club of America) rule. Wrong-way transoms really look sharp and add to the sleek and powerful look of high-tech racing machines, but I used to think they were pretty dumb on a cruising boat. A few years ago, however, some slick designer came up with the idea of molding steps into them. At least now they have a function.

Covering Boards: Covering boards—more properly called *planksheer*—are the outermost planks on a deck—the ones that cover the ends of the frames and support the bulwarks or toerail.

Cuddy: A cuddy is a small cabin or compartment formed in the bow or stern of a boat by a halfdeck. In the stern a cuddy is most frequently called a *lazarette* (sometimes *lazaretto*).

Deadrise: Deadrise is the amount of upward slope of the bottom from the keel to the bilges amidships. A boat with no deadrise is said to be dead flat.

Deadwood: The deadwood is made up of timbers that are bolted together to form any part of the keel that does not add structural support to the actual hull; it acts as a filler between the rudderpost and the garboard rabbet.

Deck: For our purposes, deck refers to the parts of the boat that are intended to be walked on outside the cockpit and are exposed to weather. If a deck is not exposed to weather, it's called a *cabin sole*. This definition excludes the cabin-top.

Deckbeam: A deckbeam is a transverse structural member resting on the clamp or shelf (or sometimes both) that supports the deck and gives it its shape.

Deckhouse: A deckhouse was originally a structure built on top of the weatherdeck and usually (but not always) used as a pilothouse. Today a deckhouse is any cabin raised higher than a trunk cabin. A deckhouse usually provides a steering station.

Decking: Decking is the material from which the deck is made, which on an old wooden boat may be planking, plywood, fiberglass, and combinations of any or all three. (Question: If deck planking is decking, how come hull planking isn't hulling? I don't think I'll ever understand how the English language works.)

Deckline: The deckline on a set of architect's plans is the line that defines the deck on the deck plan (top view) and the body plan (bow-on or stern-on view). This line on the elevation, or profile, is called the *sheerline*.

Entrance: The entrance is the part of the hull below the DWL forward of midships.

Fairing Batten: A fairing batten is not a part of a boat, but a boatbuilder's tool. It is usually a long, supple strip of hardwood the builder uses to scribe a fair line. How do you tell if a line is fair? You look at it—if it looks fair, it is fair.

Flitch: A plank or board that has the natural shape of a tree and still has its bark.

Floors: Floors don't have anything to do with the cabin sole. They are the athwartship structural members that connect pairs of frames to each other and to the keel and ballast by means of keel bolts. Floors are perforated with limber holes to let the bilge drain into the sump.

Flush Deck: A flush deck is one that has no raised deck or cabin trunk protruding from it.

Foredeck: The foredeck is the weatherdeck forward of the mainmast.

Forefoot: The forefoot is the curved section of the bow between the stem and the keel. The forefoot and the gripe piece are not the same thing, and this can be confusing. Try to think of the forefoot as the line drawn by the designer on the plans and as seen by viewing the boat in profile. The gripe piece is the piece of wood that forms the forefoot. On many smaller boats, the stem is attached directly to the keel and reinforced with a stem knee, and the gripe piece is omitted. However, all boats have a forefoot.

Frames: The frames are the athwartship vertical members to which just about everything else attaches, and which give the hull its shape. Some types of construction will have frames every few inches, while others have only a few located at strategic spots. There are many ways of making frames, but they are usually either sawn or bent, although on newer boats laminated frames have become popular with the advent of epoxies.

Garboard: The garboard (sometimes called the *garboard plank* or the *garboard strake*—only slightly redundant) is the lowermost plank installed adjacent to and on each side of the keel.

Gripe (or Gripe Piece): In addition to being what a lot of you have to say about the price of this book, a gripe is the curved member of the hull that connects the stem to the keel and forms the forefoot. Frequently the gripe is reinforced internally with a knee. (Used as a verb, gripe means to lash a dinghy to the deck, and it describes the tendency of some boats to point up in response to weather helm.)

Halfbeams: Halfbeams are beams interrupted by a deck opening such as a hatch or cockpit and therefore don't extend across the width of the deck. They are supported on the inboard ends by carlins.

Halfdeck: A halfdeck is a partial deck (it need not be half of anything) over the bow or stern portion of a small boat, such as that on a daysailer, forming a cuddy.

Horntimber: The horntimber connects the rudderpost to the transom and supports the overhang. Some older boats with radical overhang and wide transoms may have several horntimbers.

Keel: Trying to define a keel is a good way to start an argument among any group of wooden-boat people. I call anything that's a part of the backbone and hangs down into the water to provide lateral resistance and directional stability (this excludes centerboards and leeboards) a keel. Thus, everything below the garboard rabbet, including the deadwood, the ballast, and the skeg on a powerboat, is a keel. Everything above the rabbet but still part of the backbone is a keelson, even though the keelson and the keel are often hewn from the same piece of wood.

Keelson: The keelson is the longitudinal member that sits on top of the keel and provides the attachment points for the frames and floors. It is often made from the same piece of wood as the keel.

Knee: A knee is a short, triangular block of wood used to connect and reinforce two other members of the hull. Knees are analogous to the shelf brackets you might have at home. Frequently, the knee is identified by the piece it supports (stem knee, transom knee, etc.), and when a knee is let into a piece to make the lines fair, it is sometimes called an *anchor stock* (not to be confused with the cross piece of a fisherman-style anchor, also called a stock.) The knees used to reinforce the clamp to the transom are called *quarter knees*; and the knees used to reinforce deckbeams are called *hanging knees* if they are mounted on the bottom of the deckbeam, and *lodging knees* if they are mounted on the sides of the deckbeam parallel to the deck.

Leeboards: A boat that has always fit my concept of what a boat should be is the Meadow Lark ketch designed by L. Francis Herreshoff and described by him in *Sensible Cruising Designs*. One of the things that makes this boat so attractive is its shallow draft, which is achieved by the use of leeboards—huge barn-door-looking affairs built like rudders and suspended from the lee rail to act as a centerboard, giving lateral resistance and preventing leeway. A few of Phil Bolger's sharpies have leeboards, as did the Dutch sailing barges that once plied the shallow waters of the Zuider Zee.

Longitudinal Members (or Wales): The longitudinal members of a hull are all the pieces that run fore and aft, except the parts that make up the backbone and the planking. They include the clamp, shelf, stringers, battens, inwales, and chines.

Mast Partners: The partners are the solid blocks on either side of the mast where it penetrates the deck.

Plank: A plank is a single piece of material that is fastened (pinned, riveted, bolted, nailed, screwed, glued, or—in days of yore—sewn on with sinews of beasts) to form the outer skin of the hull. Where the ends of the planks meet in a streak, the butt joints are reinforced with butt blocks, except in lapstrake construction where they are most often joined by scarfs. A plank that is edge set is sprung sideways to fit the adjacent plank. A plank that is edge fastened is attached to the adjacent planks, usually by nailing or gluing or both.

Poopdeck: The poopdeck is the weatherdeck aft of the mizzen or, on a single-masted vessel, the weatherdeck onto which a sea will break if you get pooped. The term poopdeck is hardly ever used in conversation except in a jocular fashion by drunken lubbers at cocktail parties.

Quarterdeck: The quarterdeck is the weatherdeck between the mainmast and the mizzen.

Rabbet: On a set of plans, the rabbet is the line that defines the lower and forward edge of the planking. On a boat, the rabbet is the collective term for the groove cut into the keel and stem (and sometimes the gripe) to receive the ends of the planking and the inboard edge of the garboard. The *garboard rabbet* (sometimes called the *keel rabbet*) is a longitudinal groove cut into the sides of the keel to receive the garboard, and the *stem rabbet* is cut into the stem to receive the spoon ends of the planking.

Raised Deck: A raised deck is a portion of the deck raised to accommodate a cabin forward or aft or both without resorting to a cabin trunk—usually used with broken sheer.

Ribband: At one time or another I have heard battens, stringers, clamps, and shelfs all referred to as ribbands, usually by somebody who is trying to impress somebody else with how much he knows about boats. Ribbands are longitudinal strips that builders use to hold the molds in position until the frames are set. They are removed as the planking progresses or after the battens are fastened to the frames and hardly ever become a part of the finished boat.

Rubrail: The trim that is mounted on the hull just under the toerail is called the rubrail. Rubrails can also be any longitudinal protective strip of wood mounted on the planking anywhere above the waterline. When mounted on or just above the waterline (usually on powerboats) they are called *spray rails*. On a small boat the rubrail is sometimes called an *outwale* when it is part of the gunwale.

Rudderpost: The rudderpost is the vertical member of the frame that defines the aft extreme of the keel and to which the rudderstock is attached. The rudderpost is also an important line of the plans that is extended up through the deck even though the actual rudderpost usually stops at the horntimber. On many boats, particularly double-enders with outboard rudders, the rudderpost is the same as the sternpost, and there is no horntimber.

Rudderstock: The rudderstock is the part of the rudder that attaches to the rudderpost or sternpost or transom and extends into the boat to receive the tiller or bellcrank (quadrant) or other steering apparatus. The rudderstock is frequently called the *rudderpost* by a lot of people who know a lot more about building boats than I do, but I don't think it's technically correct. But like my old pal Spencer Paul said just before an overindulgence of Jack Daniels sent him to that big boatyard in the sky: "When ya been building boats as long as I been building boats, ya gets ta call it any goddamn thing ya wants ta call it."

Run: The run of a hull is the section of the hull below the DWL and abaft amidships. You will frequently hear a boat described as having a long run aft or a flat run aft. Since aft is the only place run can be, this is an egregious redundancy, and you should in all cases make sure that the perpetrator of this travesty is immediately corrected.

Scarf: A scarf or scarf joint is a long, tapered joint designed to maximize the contact surface area of two pieces of wood being jointed together. Scarfs are designated by the ratio of the length of the taper to the thickness of the material being joined. Thus a 12-to-1 scarf would be 12 inches long for every inch of thickness in the stock.

Sections: The sections are the vertical planes that intersect the hull perpendicular to the plane of the centerline—as if you sliced up the hull like a salami. On a set of plans, sections are given numbers called *stations*. (If these architectural terms have peaked your curiosity about boat plans and you would like to learn more about lofting, laying down, half breadths, tables of offsets, diagonal planes—more about the design of boats in general—try to get a copy of *Skene's Elements of Yacht Design* by Francis Kinney.)

Sheerline: The sheerline is the profile of the top edge of the hull where it meets the deck or bulwarks. If the ends are higher than the middle, it's just plain sheer. If the middle is higher than the ends, it's called *negative sheer* or *reverse sheer*. And if it goes both ways, forming a shallow horizontal S-curve, it's called *dolphin sheer*.

Sheerstrake: The sheerstrake is the uppermost plank on a hull and usually what gives a hull its sheerline, although this can also be determined by the bulwarks.

Sheerstripe: The sheerstripe is part of the boat's paint scheme and is usually a broad stripe of contrasting paint that follows the sheerline.

Shelf: If a shelf is used, it is mounted on top of and perpendicular to the clamp to support the deckbeams.

Skeg: The skeg is an extension of the keel aft to give directional stability to a hull. Generally the term skeg is applied to small powerboats and skiffs, while *deadwood* is applied to sailboats and large powerboats.

Stealers (or Stealer Planks): Stealers are tapered planks that don't run the full length of the hull.

Stem (or Stempost): The stem is the forward-most vertical member of the hull and usually contains the stem rabbet. Practically all the major longitudinal members terminate at the stem in the bow, and at the transom, rudderpost, or sternpost at the stern.

Stem Rabbet: The stem rabbet is a continuation of the garboard rabbet into which the spoon ends of the planking are fitted and fastened.

Stopwater: A stopwater is a short piece of softwood dowel inserted transversely through the backbone anywhere a seam crosses the rabbet, such as where the stem joins the gripe and the gripe joins the keel. These seams are virtually impossible to caulk, and the idea is that the stopwater will swell when it gets wet, making the seam watertight.

Strake: A strake is a plank, plain and simple.

Streak: A streak is a line of planking all the way around a hull.

Stringers: Stringers are fastened to the inside of the frames and are used to stiffen the hull and to carry or distribute the weight of other parts of the hull. They are usually identified by where they're used or by what they do (bilge stringers, engine stringers, etc.).

Toerail: If the boat doesn't have bulwarks, the trim piece on the outer edge of the deck that corresponds to the caprail is called the toerail. A toerail on a boat that doesn't have lifelines and stanchions is called a *lubber tripper.*

Topsides: The area of the hull from the waterline to the sheerline.

Transom: The flat, more-or-less vertical stern of a boat.

Trunk Cabin: A trunk cabin or raised cabin is a section of the weatherdeck raised by a cabin trunk to accommodate a cabin below decks.

Tumblehome: This may be what you do after a night on the town (the British call it falling home), but in nautical terms it's the inward slope of the topsides. Tumblehome isn't used much on low-priced plastic production boats because it greatly complicates the molding process, but it's one of those things, along with sheer, that makes a boat look like a boat.

Waterline: The term waterline is more complicated than it would seem. When a designer talks about a waterline, he's referring to any plane that defines a section of the hull that is parallel to the baseline (the line from which all other horizontal lines and planes are measured—usually on the shop floor), to the LWL (load waterline), or the DWL (design waterline or datum waterline)—as if the boat were sawn into horizontal slabs. The DWL (or LWL) is a function of the design of the hull and is used as a reference by the builder. The actual waterline, especially in a renovation project, is a function of ballast and how well you caulked the seams and remembered to close the seacocks. I have been asked, several times, the best way to determine the actual waterline of a boat, and although I've heard of all sorts of crazy schemes, the only one I know of that really works is to launch that sucker on a calm day, put all your gear aboard, load up the fuel and water tanks, wade in, and mark the waterline off with ice picks. You must reestablish the actual waterline after a major renovation project because displacement often changes, and if you don't get your waterline right, your boottop will look funny.

Weatherdeck: The weatherdeck is the entire deck that must be made watertight, including the cabintop and the cockpit sole.

The list of words and terms that apply to your old wooden boat could go on forever, but this just about covers the most important ones. If you're fortunate enough to live near a boatshop that does work on wooden boats, you might want to go over the list one more time, then pay them a visit and try out some of the words you've learned on a few of the old-timers who work there. But if you find anyone working on a futtock, don't say a word; give me a call, and I'll be right over.

Index